❈ Godden's Guide to English Porcelain ❈

✺ Godden's Guide to ✺
ENGLISH PORCELAIN

by Geoffrey Godden F.R.S.A.

HART-DAVIS, MACGIBBON
GRANADA PUBLISHING
London Toronto Sydney New York

Published by Granada Publishing in
Hart-Davis, MacGibbon Ltd 1978

Granada Publishing Limited
Frogmore, St Albans, Herts AL2 2NF
and
3 Upper James Street, London W1R 4BP
1221 Avenue of the Americas, New York, NY 10020 USA
117 York Street, Sydney, NSW 2000, Australia
100 Skyway Avenue, Toronto, Ontario, Canada M9W 3A6
Trio City, Coventry Street, Johannesburg 2001, South Africa

ISBN 0 246 11002 3

Printed in Great Britain by William Clowes & Sons Limited
London, Beccles and Colchester

Contents

TO JONATHAN

Preface

This book sets out to provide a simple, straightforward and I trust reliable guide to English porcelains. It examines the essential but so often neglected points concerning the introduction of porcelain into the British Isles and its subsequent development. The methods of manufacture and the styles of decoration are explained without getting tied up in technicalities, and I analyse the reasons why we admire one pot and reject another. In other words the aim is to set some standards.

I hope to steer the reader clear of the many pitfalls that lie in the path of the collector, to cover many points not mentioned in other books on ceramics, and to open the reader's eyes to the pleasures that await an inquisitive new collector.

Acknowledgements

Many of the questions which I have tried to answer in this book were first posed to me by collectors, both new and established, when they visited my showrooms or attended my study weekends in Worthing and so I am greatly indebted to numerous collectors who have pointed out to me aspects of collecting which are not covered in the so-called standard reference books. I am regretfully unable to acknowledge each collector's assistance, indeed I do not know their names, but many readers may well recognise their own questions as they read this book and if this is the case, please accept my thanks.

To a great degree the many new illustrations in this book have been drawn from objects in the stock of Geoffrey Godden, Chinaman or from the stock of the parent firm Godden of Worthing Ltd. The sources of all illustrations are listed below. I am most grateful to all these individuals, firms or museums for their generous assistance in supplying photographs and to the many photographers who produced such excellent reproductions.

Messrs Christie, Manson & Woods Ltd, 44, 47, 75, 80, 82, 93.

Major G. N. Dawnay, 74.

Geoffrey Godden, Chinaman, 1, 8, 10–12, 14–16, 24–8, 30–35, 39, 40, 43, 46, 49, 51, 52, 54, 57–8, 61, 63–5, 69, 70, 72–3, 76–8, 81, 83–6, 88, 90–91, 97, 100, 102, 108.

Messrs Godden of Worthing Ltd, 7, 19–20, 22–3, 45, 53, 105–6.

Mr and Mrs G. Godden, 2–3, 6, 13, 21, 29, 62, 66, 68, 87, 92, 94, 96, 98–9, 101, 103–4, 107.

City of Liverpool Museums, 71, 79.

Messrs Phillips, 67.

Rous Lench Collection, 36.

Henry Sandon, Esq., 5.

Messrs Sotheby & Co., 9, 17–18, 37, 41, 50, 55.

Messrs Sotheby's Belgravia, 95.

Messrs Tilley & Co., 56.

Victoria and Albert Museum, 38, 42, 48.

Messrs Worcester Royal Porcelain Co. Ltd, 4.

On a personal note I must record my gratitude to Miss Rosemary Manley for translating my scribble and transcribing it into a presentable typescript. Also my sincere thanks are extended to Derek Gardiner, A.I.B.P., of Worthing for posing so advantageously the specimens from our showrooms and examples from my private collection. To my wife Jean my gratitude for bearing so well her solitude while I have been all but locked away preparing this work when I should have been helping her in so many ways and lastly to our son Jonathan for his real interest in my porcelains–an interest that prompted this book.

Geoffrey Godden
17–19 Crescent Road
Worthing, Sussex

CHAPTER ONE

Porcelain, the material

CHINESE PORCELAINS

The word 'porcelain' is used to describe a unique, quite beautiful material matured and made translucent by great heat. As well as being beautiful it is a workable and durable material. It was introduced in China somewhere about AD 700 (the exact date is not known), about a thousand years before a similar ware was produced in Europe. The earliest Chinese porcelains were not necessarily delicate, light and thin as are later examples but were often quite heavy and rather similar to stonewares. Nevertheless by the Ming dynasty, between 1368 and 1644, the Chinese porcelains had been refined, the manufacturing processes perfected and the resulting porcelains are similar to, or even surpass, our present-day conception of this exceptionally fine material.

The often superb Ming porcelains were frequently painted with a rich cobalt blue–a pigment painted on the raw unglazed and unfired body–and these wares are the prototype of a vast and interesting range of Oriental and European porcelain which we refer to as 'blue and white', but more of that later (Chapter 4). Although we tend to think of the Chinese as the originators of blue and white porcelain it is believed that this wonderful colour was imported into China from Persia, where the basic materials Erythrite and Cobaltite were found and used by the Persian potters on their glazed pottery. Later, in the middle of the fifteenth century the Chinese began to make use of their newly discovered native Cobalt–Asbolite, a mixture of the oxides of cobalt and manganese.

Just as the first cobalt used by the Chinese potters was imported, so too were some of the designs or shapes; there is evidence of the influence of Near-Eastern wares as well as Mongol designs. Nevertheless, from the fifteenth to the mid-eighteenth century these mainly blue painted Chinese porcelains represent the only true porcelains known to man. They were widely exported and everywhere held in high repute, objects worthy of royal gifts and articles deemed suitable for mounting in precious metals. Countless chemists and others sought to win untold riches by seeking to learn the mystery of porcelain manufacture and to introduce porcelain into Europe.

JAPANESE PORCELAINS

Before turning from the East to the Western efforts to produce porcelain, I must mention the Japanese porcelains. These wares are little understood in Great Britain but they had a very real influence on English manufacturers and when they started to produce porcelain in the mid-1740s and 1750s it would seem that they more often chose to copy Japanese designs than Chinese. It is often thought that the Dutch were the main importers of Japanese porcelains into Europe and some modern authorities have even stated that the Dutch East India Company held a monopoly in the trade. In practice this was clearly not so and tens of thousands of pieces were imported in the early eighteenth century by the English East India Company and sold in their London auction sales; in fact it would seem that some homecoming East Indiamen carried to London more Japanese porcelain than Chinese, and all this at a period some fifty years before porcelain was made in England. The standard book on these fine Japanese wares is Soame Jenyns's *Japanese Porcelain* (Faber, London, 1965), although my forthcoming book on Chinese export-market porcelains will contain much new information on the related Japanese pieces.

PORCELAIN

The English word 'porcelain', the French word 'porcelaine' and the German word 'Porzellan' are believed to have been derived from the Portuguese 'porcella' meaning cowrie shell, the suggestion being that the white shiny surface of this sea-shell is similar to the Chinese porcelains first imported into Europe by the Portuguese.

TRANSLUCENCY

The difference between porcelain and pottery lies in the fact that porcelain is (when correctly fired) translucent whereas pottery is opaque. This property is best shown if you pass your hand between the light and the porcelain. You will see the shadow of your hand like a cloud rolling across the sky. Many people place great importance on the degree of translucency in a given porcelain but at this early stage in the story it is best to remember that for any mix the degree of transmitted light is very variable. Much obviously depends on the thickness of the piece, a thin cup will for example show better translucency than a thickly-potted dish. Less obvious is the fact that slight differences in the firing temperature affect to a remarkable degree the translucency of the porcelain—over-fired pieces are more translucent, under-fired examples show less light.

WHITE-SURFACED EARTHENWARES

While the main attribute of porcelain is now believed to lie in its translucency, its initial impact on a world accustomed to clay-coloured pottery must have been the clean, smooth *white* body. The potters thought the easiest way to emulate this white porcelain was to coat a relatively coarse and clay-coloured earthenware body with a thin surface-coating of a whitened clay or more often with a glaze made opaque and white by the addition of tin-oxide. Such wares were widely made in the Near East, also in Southern Europe, where the term 'maiolica' was used; further north in France the description 'faience' was adopted; while in Holland the same general type of tin-glazed earthenware was called 'Delft', after the geographical centre of that trade. In the British Isles there was a tendency to use the term 'delft-ware' (with a small 'd'). All these basically similar white-coated earthenwares are discussed and featured in Alan Caiger-Smith's excellent book, *Tin Glaze Pottery in Europe and the Islamic World* (Faber, London, 1973).

The Italian maiolica wares of the sixteenth and seventeenth centuries were in their way far more decorative than the Chinese porcelains of the same period, for the lower firing temperature needed for pottery permitted the use of overglaze enamel colours and in objects like large circular dishes the Italian potters, or rather their painters, treated the tin-glazed pottery as a canvas and some wonderful decorative work was produced.

In Holland and Great Britain these delft-type tin-glazed earthenwares were more subdued and were very often decorated with cobalt blue. They usually show a distinct Chinese-air in the decoration. The potters were no doubt producing a poor-man's version of the fashionable Oriental porcelain; their products, however, had many defects in use. The underlying clay body was friable, weak and porous, also the covering white tin-glaze tended to crack and flake away from the body particularly at the edges, so exposing the porous clay-coloured body. The delft-wares now seem to have a great charm and indeed they are highly decorative and collectable, but to the housewife of the eighteenth century they must have caused much concern. In practice the wares could not be trimly potted, or rather the thick white glaze blunted the potting. The body and tin-glaze did not seem very suitable for the manufacture of teawares (the staple article of the porcelain trade) at least few delft examples have survived. One can almost hear the housewife craving for clean, trim porcelain on her table–not earthenware dressed up in a white coat!

THE EARLY EUROPEAN PORCELAINS

There were one or two isolated attempts to make a type of porcelain in Europe before 1700, but these were little more than trials, and while examples such as the extremely rare Italian Medici porcelain of approximately the period 1575–87 command very high prices on account of their rarity, they had no discernible influence on the introduction of porcelain into England. There were also some efforts to produce a type of porcelain in France in the seventeenth century but the first real success was achieved in Germany in *c.* 1707–10. The place was the famous castle of Albrechsburg near Meissen in Saxony and the persons were the alchemist Johann Friedrich Bottger and the famous physicist Ehrenfried Walther, Count von

Tschirnhaus. In about 1707 a very fine and hard stoneware was produced. This was cut and polished as one would precious stone. In about 1708 a fine white body was discovered very similar to Chinese porcelain and before long the Courts of Europe were striving to set up rival porcelain factories. In general terms, only the products of the German State Factory at Meissen, near Dresden, and the French National Factory at Sèvres were to influence the English manufacturers, and the dominant influence was to remain with the Eastern porcelains.

HARD AND SOFT PASTE

There are two basic types of porcelain. The Chinese and the Japanese were of the type which we now call true or hard-paste porcelain, and the Meissen and most European porcelains were also of this type. On the other hand the early Vincennes or Sèvres porcelains of the period 1745–72 is of the artificial or soft-paste type as was most eighteenth-century English porcelain. Visually the true porcelains, or rather their surfaces, appear white and glittery and they feel cold and unfriendly, at least to British hands. The hard-paste porcelains are rather brittle and they tend to chip at the edges; such a chip or body fracture should appear conchoidal or glass-like with flakes or facets. The body is indeed physically hard and in the old days collectors were encouraged to take a file to their porcelain. It is said that if hard-paste the metal file will not cut the body whereas a soft-paste body can be quite easily cut on the edge of a foot-rim or similar spot. One can often see a little nick cut into English porcelain where some unsure person has been ill-treating his treasures! Such a person will, however, still be unsure for a good quality file in reasonable condition will in fact cut most so-called hard-paste porcelain. The old test is at best unreliable and is an affront to one's porcelain. It should be possible for the novice with a little practice to be able to differentiate by eye and touch between hard-paste and soft-paste. For practice one needs to have available reference pieces to handle frequently–these pieces need not be expensive perfect examples; damaged objects or factory 'wasters' are all that are needed.

  The soft-paste porcelains, especially those of Bow, Chelsea and Derby, while not feeling exactly soft–except to the banished file–do have an almost warm and friendly feel, at least the related covering glaze does. While a hard-paste porcelain has a hard glittery glaze a soft-paste body has a relatively soft glaze. This glaze will on plates and dishes often show knife cuts or perhaps some slight staining. A soft-glaze seems more prone to breaking up into the network of fine hair cracks, whicn we call 'crazing', than hard-glazes. One has often been told that the enamel colours tend to sink into the soft-paste glazes and that they stand or lie on top of a hard-glaze. In practice, however, this is a dangerous rule to apply for much depends on the amount of flux added to the enamels and to the firing temperature, and with some English glazes, such as those used at Worcester and Caughley, the colours do in fact tend to remain on the surface because the glaze is *relatively* hard. If the underlying soft-paste body is exposed by a break or chip it should appear granular like a lump of sugar, not conchoidal like glass or flint. The soft-paste body when exposed by a chip will also appear slightly stained and coloured, not a pure white.

I have described hard and soft pastes as having these relative characteristics but there is a school of thought that suggests that these terms relate to the firing temperature, the hard-paste being fired at a high or 'hard' firing of some 1300 to 1400°C, the soft or artificial English wares being matured in a soft fire of about 1200°C. The results would in each case be much the same as those described in the two previous paragraphs.

The object of knowing if you are handling true hard-paste or the soft-paste variety is to narrow down the possible source or origin of the example and also to tell in some cases if a piece is a fake or reproduction. If the porcelain you are holding is hard-paste then it can be Oriental, Continental, or if English it could be from the Plymouth, Bristol or New Hall factories, for some factories made hard-paste and some soft. Continental fakes and reproductions of Chelsea, Bow, Derby and Worcester porcelains will be of hard-paste whereas the original would have been made of soft-paste or one of the several subdivisions to be discussed later.

THE CHEMICAL MAKE-UP

First, let us examine the chemical make-up of the two basic types of body. True or hard-paste porcelain comprises china-clay or 'Kaolin' (that is, Silicate of Alumina) and china stone or 'Petuntse' (Silicate of Alumina, Potash and Soda) fused at or above 1300°C; the related glaze comprises Petuntse, Lime and Potash. The normal method of firing European hard-paste porcelain is to set and dry the unglazed object with a low initial 'biscuit' firing, then to glaze the object and to fire again at a high temperature in the 1300°–1400°C range, so that the body and the glaze mature and bond together. The Chinese method was to glaze the raw unfired ware and then to have just the one high-temperature firing.

Although the Chinese method was known in Europe and in England through the writings of Father d'Entrecolles (a Jesuit missionary, at the Chinese ceramic centre of Ching-tê-Chên), as spread in various early-eighteenth-century books such as Du Halde's *Description de l'empire de Chine*, with English translations published in 1738 and 1741, the earliest English porcelains and the methods employed in its manufacture differed widely from Chinese hard-paste.

The great difficulty was that the essential raw materials, Kaolin and Petuntse, were not available in England–or at least they had not yet been discovered–and while the would-be porcelain manufacturers had presented before them in a tantalising manner the imported Chinese porcelain and they had no doubt heard of the riches to be earned from such porcelains or 'china ware' as it was then called, they had to discover new ways of making similar material.

I think it was fortunate that the British had not discovered the raw materials needed to make true porcelain, for if an abundant supply of Kaolin and Petuntse had been available in the 1740s ordinary, dull, straightforward copies of export-quality

Chinese wares or of Dresden porcelain might have been produced. As it was, objects were made which suited the available materials, pieces that may not be as technically slick as the Dresden porcelains but which possessed a friendly warm feeling and an air that is so English. I say that they are very English, which is correct, but we must not lose sight of the fact that Chelsea and other early English porcelains are remarkably similar in body to the early French soft-paste porcelains.

THE BASIC TYPES OF BRITISH PORCELAIN

In an effort to find a body having some translucency, glass was added to various mixes. This gave rise to the need to find a material to bond the body together, so that the glassy mix would not melt and distort out of shape at too low a temperature. What was needed were the bones to add strength to the glassy flesh, indeed at some factories notably at Bow and Lowestoft (pp. 77 & 120) calcined (burnt) bones were added to the mix for this purpose and very successful they proved. Many other materials were used; Silica in the form of ground, calcined flint or sand; chalk (lime) was also tried; various clays such as pipe-clay were helpful and clay was even imported at great cost from North America; but most important some experimenters added Steatite or soapstone (Silicate of Alumina and Magnesia) from Cornwall.

We therefore have some subdivisions of eighteenth-century soft-paste porcelain:

The glassy bodies, such as Chelsea, early Derby and Longton Hall

The bone-ash bodies, such as Bow, Lowestoft, Derby (after *c.* 1770) and some later Chelsea porcelains

The soapstone bodies, such as early Bristol, Worcester, Caughley and some Liverpool porcelains.

Some of these English soft-paste wares are referred to as 'frit-porcelains' because part of the glassy mix was first 'fritted', that is, baked or fused together then ground to a powder and added to the basic clays.

From about 1790 into the 1810s several factories produced a type of hybrid-hard-paste porcelain. These little-understood wares are discussed in Chapter 6, and from about 1800 there was the introduction of bone-china, a white workable body that was to become the standard British porcelain superseding all others. This 'English Bone China' is discussed separately, see Chapter 7.

ANALYSIS

The attribution of English porcelain by means of an analysis of the mix is not and never can be an exact science, although in many cases such analysis can be very helpful. For example, if on testing a white cup we find no bone-ash in the form of Phosphoric Acid then this cup will not have been made at Bow or at one of the other factories that are known to have used a significant amount of bone-ash (some

40 to 50 per cent) in its porcelain. Similarly, if we test a blue and white leaf-dish and find present some 30 to 45 per cent soapstone in the form of Magnesia then we can consider that such a piece was made at Bristol, Worcester, Caughley, or some of the Liverpool potteries. However, we must remember that any one factory was apt to change its recipe from time to time, either in an effort to improve the porcelain visually or more often in an endeavour to make it more workable and more stable in the kiln. Also, the supply of raw materials may have been unreliable, necessitating a change if the factory was to remain in operation during times of shortages. Remember also that the ingredients would not have been so pure as modern manufacturers would expect. One must also bear in mind that many, if not all, factories used some ground-up porcelains from other sources in their mix. Certainly the area of the Caughley grinding-mill contained a bewildering range of Chinese as well as English porcelain, fragments of which would or could have varied the Caughley 'standard' mix to some extent. There are contemporary accounts of mills around London grinding Oriental porcelain for re-use by the potters, and the closing 'lots' in each East India Company china-ware sale comprised cases of damaged porcelain, some of which seems to have found its way into English porcelain bodies. Any one factory during its working life used several differing bodies—there is no *one* Chelsea paste, no *one* Derby mix.

While explaining the chemical make-up of porcelains and while writing of analysis I should make it clear that no collector lacking chemical knowledge and equipment can carry out a complete analysis. There is a fairly simple standard method of testing for bone-ash or Phosphoric Acid (see *Burlington Magazine*, vol. 51, September 1927, pp. 142–4), but apart from this the porcelain has to be professionally tested and a small section of the example is required, or at least a hole has to be drilled to provide a 'specimen'. In recent times porcelains have been submitted to Spectrographic analysis. Normally the result is not complete, although in years to come when we have been able to build up a reference collection of master character-patterns for various makes of porcelain this system may well prove very helpful but again the necessary equipment is unlikely to be available to most collectors.

In the 1950s much importance was placed on the reaction of ultra-violet light on porcelains, for by the use of such special 'lamps' different fluorescence could be discerned. Personally, I find these lamps unhelpful for as I have already explained the mix could and often did vary from month to month within any given factory. Moreover, one has to be accustomed to using such a lamp to be able to discern the differences in fluorescence. It also seems that the rays react on the rather soft English lead glaze, rather than on the underlying body.

Be not dismayed, there are many other reasonably reliable ways of identifying English porcelains and it is often forgotten that we should collect the object for its own grace and beauty rather than because it was made at factory 'A' or at factory 'B'. It is regrettable that some collectors purchase a poor example because it was made at their favourite factory and pay no heed to a gem from another factory.

CHAPTER TWO

Manufacturing processes

Having found a workable mix that would produce a white translucent body when correctly fired, the would-be porcelain manufacturer had relatively few other difficulties to surmount–given that he had funds available to establish a factory, buy equipment and raw material, and pay his work-people–for the methods of manufacture differ little from those traditionally employed to produce pottery, stoneware or delft-type wares. The all-important manufacturing 'know-how' was largely available in the mid-1740s when the English porcelain story was unfolding. We here discuss these traditional methods of production.

THROWING

There are two basic methods of turning a shapeless lump or mass of clay into an object of beauty and use (two, apart from the primitive non-commercial method of forming by hand–as one can do with plasticine). A potter seeking to produce a set of identically shaped objects has to fall back on some form of mechanical aid. For objects having a circular plan such as cups and saucers, plates, bowls and simple vases or pots, one has the potter's wheel, a device aptly described as the only machine made by man that has done nothing but good! The old wheels were turned by hand-power or by the potter's foot, turning by various gears or pedals a heavy circular wheel on which the potter 'centres' his lump of clay. Once exactly centred the spinning clay can be pressed and coaxed upwards or outwards into the desired form. By means of fixed gauges or pointers a series of objects of similar size and shape can be produced by the skilled operator. It is fascinating to see a good 'thrower' at work deftly producing vase after vase or bowl after bowl from his lumps of clay.

Such thrown wares if intended for use and for subsequent decoration are normally dried to a leather or cheese hardness, to use apt descriptions, and are then trimmed on a wheel or lathe with the aid of a sharp chisel-like turning tool. The purpose is to pare away surplus clay, to reduce the walls of the object to a visual daintiness and a true shape as well as to obliterate the marks or ridges formed by the fingers during throwing. In some modern pottery produced by studio potters these throwing marks are left to give a robust lively appearance, but for the more delicate porcelain wares trimming is necessary. Also at this cheese-hard stage the foot of the object can be formed by gouging out surplus clay from the thick base. There are some exceptions but objects formed by hand on the potter's wheel will be of circular outline. To such a circular outline one can of course subsequently add a handle to form a cup, or a spout and a handle to form a teapot or jug. The potter's wheel was much used in the porcelain industry up to about 1800 but to a lesser extent after this, as the then fashionable oval or rococo forms did not lend themselves to being thrown on the wheel.

There is no great virtue in throwing porcelain objects on the traditional wheel; indeed for large-scale factory production other methods have advantages and impart less stress on the clay. There is, however, the point that hand-thrown wares can have a certain spontaneous fitness of purpose, a clay sense, not found in moulded wares. A good thrown bowl, for example, will have a natural line and 'life'.

MOULDING

Moulding is necessary for most non-circular objects and is often employed for convenience in the manufacture of wares which could be thrown. Moulding is ideal for long runs of objects which have to be identical in form and size or for intricate shapes, figures or groups. For some wares the important method known as 'jollying' is employed. Here we have the marriage of throwing and moulding. Thrown objects have a plain surface (unless it be separately embellished with added or 'sprigged' relief designs) so that objects with a recessed or embossed design such as fluting, ribbing or a floral pattern (see Plate 3) have to be jollied or moulded. First someone whom we would now call an art director or designer has to think up a basic shape or design. He, or a modeller, then prepares a positive master-model (larger than the finished article) and from this many working moulds can be prepared. These working moulds were sometimes of plaster of Paris but some factories such as that at Worcester favoured 'pitcher' moulds, i.e. fired-clay. Moulds could also have been made of wood or of metal but these were suitable only for the press moulding technique (p. 20).

The jolly-mould would be affixed to the wheel-head, the thrower would then prepare a 'liner' or bat of clay and press this into the low revolving mould. The clay takes up the recessed or embossed design from the mould to form the exterior design, while the potter with his hands or with a 'profile' forms and smooths the inside surface, turning the walls to the correct thickness and in so doing compressing the malleable clay well into the patterned mould. The charged mould is then set aside, the clay starts to dry and in so doing the body will slightly contract away from the mould and the object can be withdrawn when capable of being handled in the cheese- or leather-hard state. The foot is then formed by turning. This description relates to an object such as a bowl or cup having the moulded decoration on the exterior but a similar process can transfer a relief or impressed design to the inside of an object, to a saucer or plate for example. The process is reversed so that the

Plate 1 A plaster of Paris press-mould (*right*), with two unglazed 'wasters' from the Caughley factory site, shown with a completed leaf-dish of the 1785 period. *Geoffrey Godden, Chinaman*

patterned mould of the appropriate size and design has laid upon it a bat of clay; this is then pressed down upon the mould so taking up the design. The top of the clay-bat, the reverse of the plate or saucer, is then shaped with the help of a profile.

Apart from the jollying method, employing as it does a patterned mould and the turning wheel, there are two basic methods of moulding mainly employed for non-circular or intricate objects.

There is the traditional form of press-moulding, where thin bats of prepared clay or rather the porcelain body are pressed into and against a mould. The moulds are normally in two or more pieces or units which are linked or married together by means of male and female locating notches (see Plate 4). Articles made from such two-piece moulds will normally show a slight seam-mark where clay has pressed into the joint between the two parts of the mould, although these seam-marks should at least have been reduced and made less apparent by 'fettling': the piece once hard enough to handle safely should have been wiped over with a fettling tool, rag or brush to remove such blemishes before the 'biscuit' firing.

Some small objects such as leaf-dishes were formed from one-piece moulds such as that shown in Plate 1. This open mould from the Caughley factory site is shown with matching unglazed 'wasters', or spoilt and discarded pieces, and a finished example. One can picture how a thin bat of clay was formed and pressed into the mould, the clay being pressed against the mould and the top or inside smoothed relatively flat with a damp cloth. This is rather similar to the method employed when forming the pastry-case of a tart by pressing into the tart pan the thin 'bat' of rolled pastry. The clay image when semi-dried on contact with the plaster of Paris mould will shrink away from it so that the dish can be extracted and the mould re-used, after drying.

Units such as solid, but shaped and relief-patterned, handles, knobs, etc, would have been formed by pressing a roll or ball of clay into a two-piece mould, the two parts of which would be squeezed together to shape the whole. Such units would then be affixed to the main object–a vase for example–by means of a thin coat of 'slip', this being the same body diluted to the consistency of thick milk or cream. The little twig-handle on the Caughley leaf-shape dish just mentioned and shown in Plate 1 would have been so made and affixed to the main-piece by slip while each part was semi-dried.

Some, mainly small irregularly-shaped, objects, such as trays and teapot-stands were sometimes formed by a subdivision of press-moulding, by a process rather similar to jollying. Here one has a prepared shape mould or 'hump' which forms the inside of the tray or stand when a bat of clay is laid over it and pressed down to take its shape and the surplus material at the edge cut away, as one would trim off the pastry overflowing the edge of a pie-dish.

SLIP-CASTING

Some factories favoured the press-moulded technique while others practised the alternative method of 'slip-casting'. Here an absorbent mould normally of plaster of Paris has to be made from the permanent and hard 'block' or 'master-mould'. The two or more component pieces of the mould are then assembled and tied or otherwise fixed together but leaving an open top or bottom. Into this opening is poured 'slip' until the mould is full. The plaster of Paris mould will take up the surplus water from the slip nearest to it so forming a skin, the longer the slip is left in the mould the more water will be absorbed and the thicker the outside skin will become until it has formed a wall. After a period gauged by experience (depending on the size of the mould, its condition, etc) and by the degree that the slip has sunk down from the top of the mould, the surplus slip will be poured out and the mould left to dry and set the coating of hardening porcelain within. On drying, this porcelain-slip will slightly shrink away from the mould which can be taken apart to leave a perfect but slightly smaller and reversed replica of the mould shape. As I have previously explained, the slight projection or seam where the different parts of the mould joined are later trimmed away or 'fettled' and any other units such as handles can be added or the foot turned on the wheel or lathe before the piece receives its first firing.

Plate 2 A Lowestoft ribbed moulded tea-caddy and cover shown with part of the original plaster mould, *c.* 1780. *Author's Collection*

One side of a plaster mould for a Lowestoft porcelain tea-caddy is shown in Plate 2. You can see a male locking notch on the side and when the four sides were assembled the outline of the caddy would be complete. A glazed and decorated caddy from such a mould is also shown; it is smaller in size because on drying and firing ceramic bodies shrink to a surprising degree, from some ten to thirty per cent depending on the mix.

The cover to this caddy (a unit so often missing now) would have been moulded separately, as would have been the flower-knob and the leaves, these last two embellishments being formed in a simple press-mould used for sprigging, see p. 25.

A characteristic of slip-moulded ware is that the relief or indented design will appear in reverse on the inside of the object, for the walls are of equal thickness. If we look again at the Lowestoft caddy (Plate 2), a convex rib on the exterior will re-appear as a concave indentation inside. If the Caughley leaf-dish shown in Plate 1 had been slip-cast the leaf-like feet under the base would show a mirror image of them inside the dish, as would have been reflected the serrations present on the outside edge.

Plate 3 A finely moulded Worcester coffee cup, *c.* 1755. *Author's Collection*

PLASTER MOULDS

Plaster of Paris is a relatively soft material (powdered Calcined Gypsum mixed with water, a mixture which sets rapidly) and the moulds tend to wear in use. The relief or other pattern will lose its sharpness, the edges wear and the joints tend to open, resulting in more prominent seams appearing on the moulded object. Two sauceboats, for example, from the same mould but made at different times in the life of a mould would appear very different to the discriminating collector. One would have a sharp, clear moulded pattern, the other would be flat and dull in comparison. The manufacturers employed several methods of preserving the moulds and they were normally painted with soft-soap or a similar preparation before use but the fact remains that they had to be renewed or re-cut from time to time. They were also prone to handling, or rather mishandling, damage and they were troublesome and bulky to store. Yet moulds were essential to the running of any porcelain factory and some of the eighteenth-century porcelains that issued from these plaster cases are delightful; especially the thin Worcester pieces such as the odd cup shown in Plate 3. Most of the credit for such minor masterpieces must go to the designer

Plate 4 Parts of a plaster mould and various slip-cast component parts needed to produce the complete model. *Royal Worcester Porcelain Co.*

and/or the block-maker cum mould-maker but in most cases we now have no idea of the names of such important people. In modern times other materials have tended to replace plaster of Paris; the new pliable rubber-like moulds assist production and are less prone to damage.

FIGURE MOULDING

I have already explained that handles, knobs, spouts and similar appendages were formed separately and fixed to the main body with 'slip'. Ornate objects, such as figure or animal models or groups, were built up from many components, each moulded individually; for example, with a figure of a woman, the head, a hat, the arms, feet and body would be made separately, as would have been the base. The reason for this is that there can be no undercutting in a completed moulded shape for the hardening clay could not be extracted from the mould if the design included undercut portions. The various moulds would have been made by cutting up into appropriate sections the original clay or wax figure that had been sculptured by a modeller or designer employed at the factory, or in some cases a model was 'lifted' from the product of another factory. Some of the component separately moulded parts of a Royal Worcester animal model are shown fresh from their plaster of Paris moulds in Plate 4.

The skilled workman who assembled all the separate pieces with slip was called a 'repairer'. He had to ensure that the completed figure looked natural with arms, legs, etc, in an easy posture. It is all too easy to make the parts of a shepherd look like a scarecrow! The repairer or an assistant would also make in the hand or with the aid of sprig-moulds small embellishments such as bows on the shoes or on the dress and they would also usually ornament the base with leaves and flowers. A sprig-mould is normally of small size and the design is cut in reverse in the plaster or other material. A squeeze of clay is then pressed into the prepared mould and lifted ready to be placed on the vase or figure-base with slip. The relief motifs on traditional Wedgwood jasper wares are formed in this way. A sprig-mould is rather like a miniature edition of the press-mould shown in Plate I, except that the indentation would not be so deep and the formed sprigged ornament would be solid not hollow.

BISCUIT–FIRING

Having formed an object by throwing on the wheel, by jollying or by moulding, and having trimmed away any seam-marks, having formed a foot or base (and in the case of thrown wares turned the object on a lathe) and added any required handle or spout, the piece is left to dry. After as much water as a warm atmosphere will take up has been extracted, the object should be checked for any imperfections and if perfect or nearly so! it will find its way to be 'biscuit'-fired. I am assuming here that the object is not of hard-paste, for some but not all such wares are glazed before the one firing the body receives.

With soft-paste porcelains the first or biscuit-firing is the most extreme, all subsequent firings being at progressively lower temperatures. The average English biscuit-firing temperature would be at some 1050 to 1150°C and here the drying and shrinking porcelain, experiencing its highest temperature as it vitrifies, is prone to damage. It can explode, if not previously dried adequately, distort or simply melt into a shapeless mass if the temperature is too high (under-firing will cause troubles at later stages), or it can become stained by smoke or fumes.

SAGGERS

To obviate the last danger the wares were placed or packed in circular protective cases called 'saggers' (Plate 5) which, once filled, were placed in the kiln, one on top of the other, in great piles, each cemented to the next with clay. The kiln fuel was dirty–wood or coal which gives off smoke–and the object of the saggers was to enable the wares to reach the very high firing temperature without the contents coming into direct contact with the flames, fumes and smoke. The thick clay protective saggers also helped to average out the heat and the wares would be

Plate 5 A small sagger with over-fired collapsed 'waster' inside. A 'placing-ring' is shown on the edge. From the Caughley factory site. *H. Sandon Collection.*

heated and cooled more gradually than would otherwise have been the case.

In this biscuit-firing before the wares were glazed there was no great need to separate the objects. Bowls or saucers for example could be stood one inside the other in safety, although some factories used a thin parting layer of Alumina-powder or ground flint to ensure that the wares did not flux together at the normal firing temperature. However, to help the wares retain their shape during the stresses of firing, rings or specially-shaped strengtheners of a like body were made and placed in the rims of teabowls, cups, etc. Factory sites are often littered with such 'placing-rings'. Unglazed teapot lids or jug covers were often fired on their pots, again to help preserve the shape. Such a placing-ring is shown in Plate 5 on the edge of the sagger.

I have explained that the saggers helped to distribute the heat and that they tended to take up the initial heat-shock. It was most important that the wares should be heated and cooled gradually, so the firing of a potter's kiln was a lengthy business taking days rather than hours, and the kiln would not be opened to the cold air until the saggers and their contents had all but cooled. Once taken from the kiln the wares would again be checked for condition, perfect pieces sorted and put on one side for subsequent decoration. The damaged pieces would be discarded, after investigation into the cause of the failure. For example, the teapots might have collapsed because they were thrown or turned to a too thin gauge, then the workmen concerned would be sought out! Some managements paid their throwers and moulders on a piece-rate basis and then only on goods 'good from oven'! This point will explain the workman's marks found on some wares. These identified the work of the different workmen and enabled their output to be checked and counted.

WASTERS

The discarded pieces were originally waste and are called 'wasters' or 'shards'. They were in most cases broken to ensure that workmen did not sell faulty pieces off cheaply on their own account, and to save space when tipped on convenient spare land within, or sometimes outside, the pottery site. To present-day students these once-discarded broken 'wasters' are of the greatest interest, for when the site is available for excavation (alas many are now built over and inaccessible) these 'wasters' show the range of objects made on that site, and in many cases their half-finished state reveals the factory's modes of production. In several cases spoilt unfinished examples from a site provide the only evidence relating to shapes, for many 'wasters' are as yet unmatched by completed pieces in known collections. The Caughley site was particularly rich in such surprises (see G. Godden, *Caughley and Worcester Porcelains 1775–1800*, Barrie & Jenkins, 1969) and the small excavation on the Worcester site was also of the utmost importance.

Most factory sites have been disturbed at one time or another or have been inhabited at later periods, so that only unfinished pieces should be accepted as coming from the factory. Moreover, several managements dealt in wares from other factories or countries and several purchased broken china in bulk to be ground up and incorporated in their own mix. Much Chinese porcelain was found on the Caughley site in the heart of the English countryside. Several false theories have been expounded by persons who have not remembered this elementary fact, therefore accept as firm *evidence* only unglazed or obviously unfinished spoilt factory 'wasters'.

UNDERGLAZE-BLUE

Our story has progressed to the point where the unglazed porcelain has cooled and has been taken from the biscuit-oven, checked for condition and sorted. Those pieces that were to be decorated in cobalt-blue under the glaze were then put on one side and, as required, passed to the blue-painters who would paint free-hand a stock-pattern straight on to the unglazed porcelain. I will leave a fuller account of underglaze-blue decoration and printing to Chapter 4 which is concerned with decoration, but briefly the blue pigment has to be 'hardened on' by firing to drive out the oils which would make the glazing difficult and also to fix the blue.

GLAZING

The blue-painted or blue-printed wares together with the porcelains that were to have overglaze enamel decoration were then glazed. Most pieces could be dipped in a large vat of liquid glaze, and the surplus shaken off–none of today's spray guns! The glaze which looks white, rather like thick milk, settles on the ware and is partly taken into the semi-absorbent body. Finger-marks can be touched in with a brush and, when dry or nearly so, the glaze can be wiped away from the bottom of the foot-rim or other parts where it is not wanted. This is an important task, for in the next process when the now opaque powder-like glaze is fired and becomes translucent, it is at least semi-liquid before cooling and acts like a glue, fixing objects to the sagger or to the supports and kiln-furniture. Some eighteenth-century manufacturers had the inside of foot-rims wiped clear of glaze so that surplus glaze would not run down the foot affixing it to the sagger. In forming this fire-break-like gap the tool very often also clears an area on the inside of the base within the foot-rim. This used to be called 'glaze-shrinkage' but glaze does not shrink, it spreads! It was also thought to be a sure sign of a Worcester origin for the piece. This is not necessarily so, for while most Worcester porcelains of the 1760–90 period show this glaze-free line, it is not normally present on the earlier or later examples and more importantly other factories used the same technique with the same result. The Caughley porcelains nearly always show this so-called Worcester characteristic and I illustrate (Plate 6) such a 'waster' from the factory site. The glaze-free line also appears on some Liverpool porcelains.

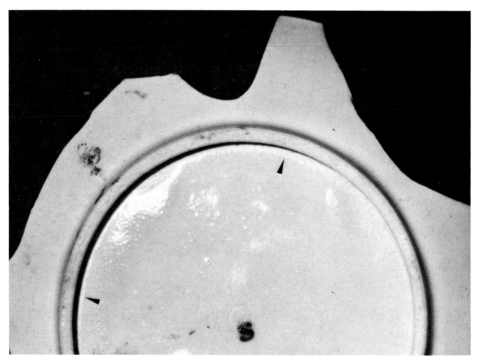

Plate 6 Caughley 'waster' showing the typical 'S' mark, also the glaze-free line inside the foot-rim. *Author's Collection*

Plate 7 A Derby vase, *c.* 1755–60, the companion one turned up to show the darker patches or 'pad-marks' caused by the clay pads on which it was set during firing. *Godden of Worthing Ltd*

One can observe that the flanges of Worcester teapot covers were also wiped clear of glaze, again so that the glaze would not run down the flange and stick the cover to the sagger or kiln shelf, or more likely so that the covers could be sat on circular 'placing-rings' to avoid distortion. Some other factories, notably that at Lowestoft, on the other hand, surmounted the difficulty in other ways and one finds glazed flanges on their teapot covers. Speaking of surmounting, one can quite easily arrange plates, dishes and other objects so that they rest not on their foot-rims or bases but on little triangular shaped stilts or on supports fixed in the sides of the saggers or simply place pads of clay under the base to lift it away from the kiln shelf or sagger-base.

Again, these differing methods of surmounting basic manufacturing problems, in these cases connected with glazing and the 'glost-firing', can be very helpful. Figures made in the eighteenth century at the Derby factory will nearly always show under the base three 'pad-marks'–slightly darker patches (Plate 7)–where roughly circular pads of clay were placed to lift the glazed-figure, vase or other object and to stop the pools of surplus glaze acting as a glue between the figure and the kiln-furniture. Plates and other flat objects made at the Chelsea factory were supported on three or more stilts, the points of which leave little pimple-like blemishes in the glaze (Plate 8) while Bow (and some other) plates and dishes were supported on triangular arms affixed one above the other in the sagger-walls. These left rough lines at three or more places around the rim on the underside (see also Plate 8).

Porcelain is normally glazed because, first, the unglazed body can be slightly porous so that it would take up staining liquids and be unhygienic in use–the glaze acts as a glass-like surface which, when uncrazed, forms a watertight skin. Secondly, the unglazed porcelain is slightly rough to the touch and can have an unpleasant feel. The added glaze flows over the rough body and presents a flat, even, pleasant and clear surface. Thirdly, it forms a near perfect base for any added enamelled decoration or gilding. In short, the glaze seals the body, gives a pleasing surface and facilitates the decorating processes.

On the other hand, the glaze does tend to clog any moulded features and one is amazed to see from unglazed factory wasters how sharp the original moulding was before the added glaze blunted the design. Glaze can also crack or 'craze'. This is normally due to an unbalanced co-efficient of expansion between the body and the glaze, so that the body contracts on cooling at a greater rate than the glaze, so tearing it apart. Ideally the glaze should exactly match the body, expanding and contracting with it. Apart from manufacturing faults, sudden heat or too rapid cooling can craze a glaze when the piece is in domestic use.

GLOST-FIRING

Taking due care and following factory practice the glazed objects would be carefully packed in saggers and the saggers placed in the glost-kilns to re-fire the

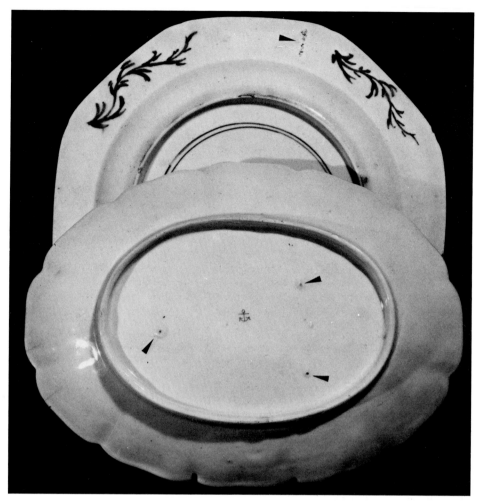

Plate 8 The reverse of a Bow plate and a red–anchor marked Chelsea dish of the 1755 period showing the different types of characteristic 'spur marks' on which the pieces were rested and separated during firing. *Geoffrey Godden, Chinaman*

now glazed wares. As with the biscuit-firing one had to ensure that smoke and foreign bodies did not stain or otherwise disfigure the ware but now one had to ensure that each piece was separated from its neighbour, for as I have explained the melting glaze acts like a strong glue. After glost (or glaze) firing at some 1000°C the wares were taken, after cooling, from the kiln and saggers, examined for condition and if perfect or nearly so, passed on to the warehouse. Glaze, like ceramic-colours had to be fired at the correct temperature and in the right conditions. Over-fired glaze would bubble, be rather matt and would appear uneven, having run in streams down the pot. Thickly applied glaze tends to bubble so that like bubbling boiling water it loses the all-important translucency.

GLAZED WARES

The porcelain object has now been formed, biscuit-fired, glazed and fired again at a somewhat lower temperature. It is now ready to be decorated, although a few pieces would have been sold in the white, devoid of decoration. Such white pieces would have fallen into two classes: those pieces sold to the public for use in this white state, presumably at a rather low price, and secondly those pieces sold to non-factory decorators for embellishment. These independent decorators themselves fall into two classes: the amateur china-painter—and there was quite a craze for this form of 'do it yourself' painting, with the artist so proud of his or her work that a full signature would be added often with the date (see p. 251)—and the many trained and talented ceramic artists who worked alone or in a small studio-like establishment, decorating in a highly professional manner white 'blanks' purchased from the leading manufacturers. Detailed discussion of this work falls within the orbit of Chapter 4.

CHAPTER THREE

Ceramic forms

The proprietors and managers of the newly founded English porcelain factories in the mid-1740s and early-1750s should have acquired a good idea of what articles to produce, for they had and made use of several sources of inspiration:

(1) The imported Chinese porcelains, which by this period almost entirely comprised shapes or objects made solely for the European trade, rather than porcelains made for the Chinese home-market

(2) Contemporary European silver shapes

(3) Contemporary English pewter wares

(4) Contemporary European porcelains

(5) Contemporary earthenwares

(6) Contemporary glass wares.

In practice these categories are not watertight compartments. For example, many of the Chinese porcelain forms were copied from European prototypes–mainly metal objects. As early as 1699 the English East India Company was matching pewter shapes to porcelain–'send 10,000 coarse and fine plates–pewter-fashion'. In other orders these plates were referred to as 'brim-plates' to distinguish the European plate-shape with a flat condiment rim from the Oriental, rimless saucer-like plate. On the other hand, the early English silver teapots were probably copied from Chinese porcelain pots. Each of the European East India companies would have sent its own pattern-pieces of silver, pewter, glass or porcelain to be copied in Chinese porcelain, but once the Chinese potters had received a new shape from say the French or Dutch traders then in subsequent seasons that shape would have been available to the buyers of any nation, for the Chinese were no respecters of copyright–not that any nation had at that time progressed to such design-protection.

One way and another the ceramic shapes by the 1750s were remarkably well established and international, at least for the standard tablewares which represented the daily production of any factory. Let us form some idea of these staple-products, remembering that I am referring here only to basic shapes or objects, not to types of decoration.

TEAWARES

Any collection or gathering of English, or I suspect any other, porcelain will show a preponderance of teawares–cups, saucers, creamers, waste bowls, teapots and similar components. Indeed teawares and tea-services or 'tea equipages', as they were called, represented the 'bread and butter' products of all English factories, with the possible exception of that at Derby.

An eighteenth-century full 'tea equipage' would have originally comprised a teapot and cover, a teapot stand, a tea canister (or 'tea vase') and cover, a milk or cream jug (these often but not always had a cover), a sugar bowl and cover, a slop or waste bowl, a spoon-tray, two saucer-like plates or stands (these were normally of slightly different sizes), 12 teabowls, 12 coffee cups (or often only 6 or 8 coffee cups), 12 saucers. In addition some services were completed with a coffee-pot and cover (some of these pots had their own stand), but such pots were by no means a standard component of tea and coffee sets, which were coffee sets only in that handled coffee cups were included.

Not all buyers would have purchased a 'full' service as listed. Very many would have needed only cups and saucers to go with their silver tea or coffee pots, milk jugs and other pieces. Other purchasers would have bought 'short' sets which comprised the main units plus six or eight cups and saucers. In fact then as now there was nothing to stop the cash customer (a rare bird!) from buying from his or her 'chinaman' exactly what she wanted and no more. It would also seem likely that some pieces, mainly teapots, were sold individually, for in several cases no matching teawares are known. When we read the Worcester price list of about 1760

Plate 9 A rare triangle-marked Chelsea fancy teapot of the mid 1740s. *Sotheby & Co.*

we see that all articles are listed and priced separately. When one purchased a fanciful Chelsea teapot such as that shown in Plate 9 one could hardly expect matching cups and saucers, waste-bowl, etc, and no doubt the teapot served only as a talking-point, a novelty or gimmick and the rest of the teawares were of a more orthodox nature, probably not matching the teapot in any way.

Let us consider the standard parts of a 'full' tea-service, for any collector of English porcelain is going to see and I hope to handle an amazing selection of such units.

TEAPOTS

Eighteenth-century teapots were usually copied in general form from the standard Chinese export-market examples, which were basically circular or globular, although in a few cases English manufacturers divided the body into panels or facets so that one finds octagonal pots, and in some cases tasteful relief-designs were produced by means of moulds.

These delicate relief-moulded patterns seem unique to English porcelains and they can be most pleasing and elegant, especially the Worcester examples of the 1760s. The compact porcelain body permitted the production of really crisply moulded designs, little spoilt by the near-perfect clear and craze-free Worcester glaze, but of course the main praise should be reserved for the unknown designer-modeller who worked the pattern in the first place. These designs, while found on teapots, will also appear on the related teawares.

A standard Chinese-type globular teapot typical of the 1760–80 period is shown in Plate 10. Other pots approached barrel shape as you can see and many slight variations were made by various factories within this period but in nearly all cases we have the circular plan.

By the late 1780s we find the introduction of teapots with an approximately oval plan and by 1800 these oval pots were almost universal in Great Britain. The basic shape, shall we say the oval Chamberlain-Worcester teapot-form, can be found in several versions–with a spiral flute to the body, with upright ribbing, or flutes, or in a plain form. This is true of all approximately oval-plan teapots. I have included in the description 'approximately oval-plan' pots those which are often called 'silver-shape' (Plate 11), a form associated with the New Hall factory but by no means restricted to this one manufactory. I call these New Hall-type specimens 'turreted-pots', as the covers sit within a raised turret-like projection; the time-honoured term 'silver-shape' is unhelpful as practically any porcelain teapot-shape can be matched to a silver example.

This statement is reflected in the next fundamental change which took place in the 1820s when the teapots returned to the old circular plan but had a rococo-type curved elevation and when the majority of pots were mounted on low feet. These moulded rococo-style teapots were capable of very many variations and as a general class they remained in fashion for most of the Victorian era.

Plate 10 A typical Caughley globular teapot (*left*) of the 1775–80 period and a slightly later barrel-shaped teapot. *Geoffrey Godden, Chinaman*

Plate 11 A finely decorated New Hall teapot of the typical 'silver-shape' or turreted form, *c.* 1795–1800. *Geoffrey Godden, Chinaman*

Apart from shapes the main changeable feature over the years was the size of the pots. The early ones made in the middle of the eighteenth century were quite small, reflecting the high cost of tea. The standard teapots then became progressively larger until we get the large pot of the Victorian era. I have used the term 'standard' because teapots, like most basic articles, were made in at least three sizes to suit individual requirements, for example a lone bachelor would not need a large family pot.

The delicate porcelain teapots presented the English soft-paste manufacturers with many problems, for the shock of the near-boiling water poured into a cold pot often caused the body to crack. The Derby teapots were particularly prone to this fault, while in contrast other manufacturers such as the Worcester management were able to make great play of the fact that their wares would withstand boiling water.

Teapots represent a wonderful field of study and many large collections have been formed of just this one article, for so many different shapes were made and so many different patterns employed to embellish the forms. A good range of early teapots are illustrated in Henry Sandon's *Coffee Pots and Teapots for the Collector* (John Bartholomew & Son Ltd, Edinburgh, 1973). Many nineteenth-century examples and marked shapes are featured in my *Illustrated Encyclopaedia of British Pottery and Porcelain* (Barrie & Jenkins, London, 1966) and my *British Porcelain, an illustrated guide* (Barrie & Jenkins, London, 1974).

TEAPOT STANDS

Most eighteenth-century porcelain teapots originally had their own stand but one is rarely so lucky as to find a teapot still complete with its stand. Today, a lone stand without its teapot represents a most desirable find as the little trays are useful, decorative and very collectable in their own right.

As early as 1710 the directors of the East India Company were ordering from China '5000 small deep plates for the teapots', and three years later they were sending a pattern shape formed in tin for the guidance of the Chinese potters: '2000 blue and white small dishes or patty pans to be deep and square, according to the pattern in tin, for the teapots to stand on. 2000 ditto in colours'. It is a matter of question whether these dishes were to match in painted design the teapots but certainly the square shape was not a good match for the circular teapot forms, and with the later English stands there was also some divergence. A standard globular teapot with a circular plan would seldom, if ever, have a plain circular stand.

The basic teapot-stand shape at Worcester from about 1755 to the 1770s or 1780s had an irregular shaped edge and this form was standard too at the Caughley factory into the 1790s (Plate 12) and at some Liverpool factories. On these standard stands stood a large range of teapots, globular and barrel shape. The globular pots from the Lowestoft factory had a strange eight-sided stand which is seemingly unique to that factory. You can see examples in my book *The Illustrated Guide to Lowestoft Porcelain* (Herbert Jenkins, London, 1969), Plates 119 and 175.

Plate 12 A Caughley globular teapot (bearing the 'Fisherman' or 'Pleasure Boat' print) shown with the typical shaped edged teapot-stand, *c.* 1780. *Geoffrey Godden, Chinaman*

With the advent of the turreted teapot in the 1780–90 period (p. 35), larger stands were necessary and these were of a form which matched the shaped sides of the pot. Most factories of the 1790–1820 period produced oval stands for various forms of basically oval teapots but with the introduction of the rococo teapot raised on feet the practice of producing a separate stand almost ceased.

The object of the stand was to form an insulation between the hot teapot and the table-top and also to catch any drips from the spout before they soiled a table-cloth. With these stands it is normal to find some rubbing of the overglaze-enamels resulting from the abrasive action of the teapot-foot. From the rarity of the stands– they are far scarcer than the teapots–one may judge that not all sets were sold with teapot stands and it may be that only the more expensive 'full sets' were so equipped.

TEA CANISTER

The 'full' tea-services of the eighteenth century, at least those from the major English factories, included a 'tea jar', 'tea vase' or 'tea canister', a little covered pot

Plate 13 A charming Lowestoft presentation tea-caddy, dated 1797. *Author's Collection*

sometimes and erroneously called a 'tea poy'. I have said 'little' because the tea was expensive and not much was brought out from its locked store or caddy on to the table.

Britain was certainly importing porcelain 'tea canisters' from China in the seventeenth century and was ordering them by the thousand, both blue and white and with enamelled patterns, in the early part of the eighteenth century whilst the standard Chinese export-market tea-services included this article. It would appear that these porcelain 'tea vases' were filled with the correct type of tea or with a mixture blended to the host's taste and that this was tipped or measured into the teapot on the table. It has been stated that Worcester teasets of the 1760s contained two or a pair of tea canisters, one for Bohea (or Black) tea and one for Green tea, and although some very few inscribed pairs are known they were not part of standard sets which contained only one covered tea canister.

The now rare and often delightful objects (now alas so often missing their cover) seem to have gone out of favour by about 1800 and at some factories before this–I cannot remember seeing a Pinxton example, nor for that matter a Derby example of the post-1780 period but, at the Caughley and Lowestoft works at least, these were made into the 1790s. I cannot resist showing you a charming little Lowestoft gem (Plate 13) which must surely represent a unique presentation piece. By the 1800s the price of tea had dropped considerably and the fashion for a large two-compartmented wooden tea caddy, with its central mixing bowl for the blending of the different varieties of tea, seems to have come fully into fashion.

MILK JUGS

Milk jugs or 'milk-pots' and the related creamers are among the most charming of porcelain objects. It is often difficult to know which is a milk jug and which is a creamer but it matters little. Personally I regard upright jugs as being for milk and the low, long, ewers as creamers.

The simple so-called sparrow-beak jugs (Plate 14) were made at nearly every English factory before 1790. The early relief-moulded Worcester examples of the 1760s can be superb while the later, post-1790 milks from all factories represent a wide field of study. The upright New Hall-type jugs are particularly popular but from about 1820 the general tendency was for the milk jugs to be low, wide and squat.

CREAM EWERS

It has been claimed that early teasets of perhaps the 1760–70 period included both a milk jug and a cream ewer. I do not think this was the case and I do not know of any set with both these articles. It would also be difficult to find low cream ewers matching some of even the most common tea-ware patterns, although very many milk jugs are known of these standard designs.

Perhaps the best-known cream-ewer shape is that called the 'Chelsea ewer', a contemporary eighteenth-century term for the basic form shown in Plate 15. These are, strangely enough, very rarely found in Chelsea porcelain but are well known in Worcester and Caughley porcelain and occur also in Lowestoft, Liverpool, New Hall and Coalport wares plus some other types to which we cannot as yet ascribe a name. All these low cream ewers are attractive and collectable and occur in some considerable variety.

SUGAR-BOWLS

These bowls, variously called in the eighteenth-century 'sugar-pots' or 'sugar boxes' or more recently 'sucriers', were in their various forms part of every tea-service. They were intended, as the name suggests, to hold sugar and for this reason they originally had a cover, although some narrow boat-shaped sugars made at Worcester and Pinxton (and at a third unknown factory) in the 1795–1810 period were open, without a cover. In general the sugar-bowls were deeper but narrower than the open waste-bowl. Being a standard article they were made at all factories

Plate 14 A selection of Worcester sparrow-beak cream or milk jugs bearing typical underglaze-blue prints of the 1765–80 period. *Geoffrey Godden, Chinaman*

Plate 15 A Worcester creamer of the popular shape known as 'Chelsea ewer' and made by several factories in the 1775–1805 period. *Geoffrey Godden, Chinaman*

and at all periods, and in general follow the basic shape of the teapot–for example, an oval teapot of the 1805 period would have an oval sugar-bowl, a rococo-shaped teapot a rococo sugar-bowl.

SLOP OR WASTE-BOWL

These low open bowls or 'basons' were, like the sugar boxes, a standard item of the tea-service. Although made in various sizes they in general seem rather large and this may be because the tea-strainer was not in general use so that each cup would have held more dregs than we are used to finding today. We must also remember that the tea-leaves were somewhat larger than in the modern mixtures.

Little can be said about these slop-bowls; they follow the moulded or painted design on the teapot and they can be very desirable objects. It could well be that during the 1750–70 period some at least were sold with an underplate, see p. 43.

SPOON-TRAY

These little narrow trays or 'spoon-boats', to use a contemporary term, represent one of the rarest and most attractive items of eighteenth-century tea equipment. As the name suggests these trays were to hold the wet teaspoons as, with the fashionable mode of drinking the tea from the teabowl on its saucer, the spoon–if left on the saucer–would at best swing round to hit one in the cheek or at worst fall with a clatter on to the table or floor, hence the inclusion of one communal spoon-tray which held six or so spoons. Or perhaps the hostess after pouring the cup would sugar and stir it for her guests using one spoon only.

These attractive little pieces are found in Chinese porcelain, in Staffordshire salt-glaze stoneware and in most other ceramic bodies, none with such attractive results as the porcelain examples. The fashion for these trays was changing in the 1790s and practically none was made after 1800, for as the handled teacup came into fashion the spoon-tray was no longer needed–the spoon remained on the saucer and only the cup was taken to the lips.

PLATES

Eighteenth-century English tea-services did not include individual place-plates, a standard part of modern sets. They did, however, include two saucer-shaped plates of slightly different sizes.

The original uses of these two plates are open to some doubt. They are often regarded as bread and butter or cake plates and indeed post-1800 services included two handled plates or dishes for such usage but some contemporary eighteenth-century sale-records list these plates as the slop-basin and as the sugar-bowl stand and this may account for the differing size of plates.

However, if the original use for these saucer-like plates was for stands it would seem to have changed to the more normal use as bread and butter or cake plates by at least the mid-1780s and probably some time before this. Certainly when the oval or boat-shaped sugar bowl came into fashion the circular plates remained part of the standard make-up of a service, yet the oval sugar-bowl would not sit evenly upon the circular dished-plate.

TEABOWLS AND SAUCERS

Early English teawares were adapted from Oriental wares; in particular this is seen in the use through most of the eighteenth century of handleless teabowls. Such a bowl can be trimly turned by the manufacturing potter with little trouble, and the walls do not have to be thickened to take the weight and pull of a handle in the firing process. Any potter would surely rather make a teabowl than produce a handled cup. It is little wonder then that the fashion for teabowls continued for so long: teasets with handleless teabowls were cheaper than the better class ones with handled teacups.

In use, however, the thin teabowl presents problems, especially when the bowl is small, as were the early examples. The bowl becomes very hot–but can be held by the finger and thumb, grasping the top rim, or the foot rim, or with the thumb under the foot and the finger on the rim (except that it cannot be picked up or set down in the last two positions). It can also be taken to the mouth on its saucer–if you have a steady hand and if you have previously placed the spoon on the spoon-tray.

It is an over-simplification to state, as is so often done, that all early teacups were handleless; some handled cups were made by the leading firms such as the Worcester partnership and these, by their general low, wide bowl shape (in contrast to the tall, narrow coffee cups), are certainly teacups. These rather rare handled teacups were as a rule only supplied with the more expensive sets.

Teabowls were made into the nineteenth century especially for the cheaper range of teawares but by about 1810 the handled and larger teacup was almost universal.

Of all the porcelain teawares, teabowls and teacups are the most plentiful. Not only were twelve sold with each 'full' set, as against one waste-bowl or milk jug but also very many sets of bowls and saucers were sold on their own: a family with its silver teapot, sugar bowl and cream jug would still need china cups and saucers. Silver teabowls or cups are very nearly unknown for the simple reason that the hot liquid makes the silver too hot to bear by the hand. As early as 1681 we find remarks such as 'that which will turn us best to account are cups of all kinds–sizes and colours' in the instructions to the buyers in China. To the present-day collector teabowls and saucers have great charm, particularly the early relief-moulded teabowls of the 1750–60 period. The more mundane later examples, perhaps bearing an underglaze-blue printed design, represent the most inexpensive of Georgian ceramics.

COFFEE CUPS

The pre-1790 English tea and coffee services were normally sold with twelve, eight or six coffee cups. The exact number varied from factory to factory or according to the purchaser's requirements but separate saucers were not made, the coffee cups being used with the standard (teabowl) saucer. A coffee cup is normally tall and narrow in comparison with a teabowl or teacup and has one handle. In addition it can be found embellished with any of the standard relief-moulded designs or enhanced with any one of a host of blue and white or enamelled patterns.

We call these taller cups 'coffee cups' but there was nothing to stop them being used for tea. They are certainly more convenient to use than the handleless teabowl, and with the smaller exposed surface area the liquid retains its heat longer. While speaking of tea and coffee we must not lose sight of the fact that chocolate was a very popular drink in the eighteenth century and that many cups would have had a dual function; a 1710 instruction relating to Chinese porcelain makes this point: '8000 small cups with one handle, fit for coffee or chocolate', although by the 1760s the chocolate cups tended to be larger, sometimes with two handles and a cover.

COFFEE CANS

A coffee can differs from a coffee cup in that the sides are cylindrical. Small cans or mugs were made at many porcelain factories in the 1750–60 period (at Bow and Worcester for example), but these rare early cans were not issued as part of a standard teaset. Later from Bristol and other factories we find rather large straight-sided cans and saucers ornately decorated in the Sèvres style and these, like the fine Derby examples, were often individual pieces or pairs made for the cabinet rather than for use.

By about 1800, however, the coffee can had almost superseded the shaped coffee

Plate 16 A selection of coffee cans of the 1795–1805 period (*Top l. to r.*) Derby, Miles Mason; *bottom l. to r.* Pinxton, Coalport and Spode. *Geoffrey Godden, Chinaman*

cup at all English factories, yet in the space of some twenty years the coffee can had in turn given way to more fanciful forms of coffee cups. It may be thought that apart from the different bodies and glazes, the straight-sided can offers little help to the enquiring collector. This is not so, for the different handles offer a very reliable guide to origin. I show in Plate 16 a few of these characteristic can-handles.

COFFEE POTS

I have left till last the consideration of porcelain coffee pots, for they were not part of the standard service–only of special long services or where supplied to the customer's express wish, since many families would have had their silver coffee pot.

Porcelain coffee pots are truly elegant pieces of traditional tall form; especially pleasing are the early Worcester examples.

It is strange but true that porcelain coffee pots of the nineteenth century are almost unknown and yet hundreds of thousands of tea and coffee services were made and in use. The reason, as stated above, was probably that silver or silver-plated pots were used instead.

An interesting book which includes illustrations of various porcelain coffee pots is Henry Sandon's *Coffee Pots and Teapots for the Collector.*

BREAKFAST SERVICES

Apart from the standard tea-services, there was a far lesser number of breakfast services which may loosely be regarded as enlarged teasets. Such sets came into favour in about the 1790s. Apart from a rather large size of teacup, we find included the now rare egg cups (sometimes on a special stand), honey-pots (these may be found in the form of a beehive), butter-pots, covered muffin dishes and sometimes small plates. I have before me an account for a Chamberlain-Worcester breakfast service of the 1820 period which lists:

> 1 teapot and stand
> 1 sugar box
> 1 slop basin
> 1 cream jug
> 12 teacups and saucers
> 12 coffees
> 12 breakfast cups and saucers
> 8 3rd size plates
> 1 pint jug
> 1 square sugar basket
> 2 muffins and covers
> 2 butter tubs and stands
> 2 loaf (bread) plates, 9 inches
> 2 egg stands, three egg cups each

While discussing the rarer items such as muffins and butter tubs we can also add unusual objects such as covered custard cups. These rare little pieces were often sold in sets on a tray or stand. There are also covered 'ice cups' or ice-cream cups, spoons, ladles, salts and even porcelain toast-racks.

CABARET OR DÉJEUNÉ SERVICES

These delightful tea equipages were set on a shaped tray and comprised a small teapot, a milk or cream pot, or sugar box and usually two cups and saucers. This sounds simple enough but these services are little treasures, not only because the items are delicate and small, of forms not normally met with but because they are usually decorated in the richest style.

One such set in Mr Christie's sale of Chelsea and Derby porcelains held in April 1771 was catalogued as: 'a large déjeuné, consisting of a teapot, milk-pot, sugar-box, two cups and saucers, the stand for ditto most curiously painted in cupids, with a musical triumph, with a fine blue celeste ground round the compartment, curiously chased with bull-rushes and ornamented with burnished gold.'

Typical if rather early examples are shown in Plates 150, 218 and 219 of my *Illustrated Encyclopaedia of British Pottery and Porcelain*. Other, later ones were made in the 1800–20 period and again in the second half of the nineteenth century by firms such as Mintons and Royal Worcester. The pre-1820 examples are very rarely found complete and when they are you will have to be prepared to reach deep into your pocket!

CABINET CUPS

The superb and often richly decorated cabaret services lead us on to a class of ornamental, often large-size cup and saucer, the cup normally of can-shape with straight sides. These cups may be single- or double-handled and some of these cups originally had covers. These are often so fine that one cannot believe that they were made for use–hence the term 'cabinet-cup'. This was a contemporary classification and yet they served a dual purpose, for again to quote from Mr Christie's 1783 catalogue of Chelsea and Derby or 'Chelsea-Derby' porcelain we find such pieces described in the following manner: 'a pair of very beautiful caudle or cabinet cups, covers and stands, enamelled in compartments with rose coloured cupids and richly finished with burnished gold stripes.' (This was knocked down to Mrs Christie at £2/19/0d.) '…a pair of very elegant caudle or cabinet cups, covers and stands, peacock pattern, enamelled fine blue and gold.' (Caudle was a hot gruel-like drink spiced and laced with wine much drunk by invalids or nursing mothers.)

Others were described only as 'cabinet cups': 'a superb and elegant cabinet cup and saucer enamelled in compartments with landscapes, fine ultramarine blue ground richly furnished with chased and burnished gold.' A further description acknowledges the rather obvious origin of these magnificent articles–the Sèvres factory in France: 'One pair superbly elegant French-shape cups and saucers enamelled in compartments with figures, fine ultramarine blue ground richly finished with chased and burnished gold.'

The tradition for these fine cabinet cups, so suitable as presents, continued up to about 1820, with the Derby, Chamberlain-Worcester & Barr, Flight and Barr and Flight, Barr & Barr, Worcester factories specialising in such objects.

CHOCOLATE CUPS

The same 1783 sale of Chelsea-Derby porcelain also contained chocolate cups as did many other sales: 'six chocolate cups and saucers, enamelled with roses, festoons of green husks and purple and gold border'. These cups are usually larger than a teacup, often with twice the capacity and with one or two handles. Some originally had covers, as is evidenced by the Chamberlain-Worcester accounts: '2 chocolates, two-handled, with covers and saucers. Best Queen's (pattern).' (July 1799.) '6 rich figured chocolates, complete with covers and stands, pattern 305 at £4/4/0d.' (May 1803.)

DINNER-SERVICES

After teawares one might think that the next most important standard ceramic product would be dinner sets or as they were called 'table services' with their long runs of plates and dishes. This was not the case, for with the notable exception of the Bow factory the English manufacturers before 1765 were content to let the imported Chinese porcelains supply the need for inexpensive table services. I say 'content', but in fact they had little choice as they could not compete with the imported wares. The Chinese potters could produce thousands of thin plates without a trace of warping or other blemish while English manufacturers using a heat-prone artificial porcelain could not approach these standards. The Worcester factory, for example, with a normally very workable body and with a skilled workforce, produced some magnificent tureens but the (surviving) pre-1760 plates and dishes can almost be counted on the fingers of one hand!

English manufacturers were undercut in price by the Chinese and came a poor second to their potting skill. This is not to say that no English manufacturer produced dinner-services, several did but not on a large scale, apart from some magnificently rich Chelsea porcelain examples.

The May 1782 sale of Chelsea and Derby porcelains sold by Mr Christie included: 'a complete set of table-china enamelled with groups of coloured flowers, and richly finished with a fine blue and gold vine border, consisting of 60 table [dinner] plates, 24 soup plates, 20 oval dishes in sizes, 1 pair tureens and covers, 4 sauce boats and stands and a salad dish'. (Sold for £44/2/0d.) This is a reasonably representative make-up of a dinner-service of the 1770–90 period. Two points may be made: first, these early sets did not normally include small-size 'side-plates' and, secondly, the twenty oval dishes which were supplied in graduating sizes were vegetable dishes–they were flat and uncovered. The salad dishes are normally somewhat shallower than a punch-bowl and they may have a shaped edge.

On a more mundane and less costly level we find listed in a sale of Worcester porcelain conducted by Mr Christie in December 1769, an underglaze-blue printed dinner-service of a tureen cover and stand, 16 oblong dishes in five different sizes, a pair of sauceboats, 4 oval 'compoteers', 2 round dishes, 48 dinner plates and 24 soup plates. The complete set was sold for a mere £5/7/6d, which underlines my point concerning the remarkably low price of the blue-printed wares. You may have noted in both the sets listed, the inclusion of sauceboats–perhaps the most graceful and collectable of all dinner-service components. These are to be found in amazing variety originating from every pre-1780 English porcelain factory and although some of these noble boats were included with dinner-services very many others must have been sold separately, in pairs or sets of four–as of course were silver or plated sauceboats.

Fine tureens are known from many factories and in many ornate and fanciful forms, such as boars-head tureens, but these were made as special centre-pieces, not as part of a standard service. Early English soup plates made prior to 1770 are remarkably rare.

In the latter part of the eighteenth century the imported Chinese dinner-services were much more complete than our own products, comprising large meat platters,

Plate 17 Sample pieces from a superb Worcester armorial dinner-service of the 1810–15 period. Small tureen $7\frac{1}{2}$ inches high. *Sotheby & Co.*

covered dishes, salts and even hot-water plates and dishes (these were double-walled vessels which could be filled with hot water to retain the heat of the food) as well as the normal tureens (of two sizes), dishes and plates. In their way the Chinese sets and their components seem to emulate pewter or silver pieces.

By about 1800, however, the English sets were or could be superb, especially those from the Worcester factories (p. 209) where the compact, durable porcelain and good glazing, coupled with neat potting and quality painting, as well as the tasteful gilding, captured the market which the Chinese had held for so long. Try to picture a fine mahogany table dressed with sets such as that illustrated in Plate 17. These pretentious services were almost too good to use but equal potting skill went into the less expensive services, some of which were decorated in a very restrained style, with little floral sprays or merely with a gold border. Throughout the nineteenth century most everyday services were of course made in pottery rather than porcelain. The English earthenwares were world renowned and varied, with such strong bodies as the 'stone-china' and 'Masons Patent Ironstone China' wares. The porcelain services from the Minton or Spode factories were far more expensive and met a relatively small upper-class market.

DESSERT-SERVICES

After teawares the main standby of English eighteenth-century factories was not dinner-services but the related dessert-services—a class of porcelain strangely neglected by the Chinese potters or rather by the European traders or East India Companies that were responsible for ordering and importing the Oriental porcelain.

The dessert-service market was a very important one in England and very many of the single pieces found in collections today were originally part of such services, certainly most of the plates with a diameter of less than eight and a half inches, the variously shaped side-dishes and many other pieces. Our cabinets would look very bare if we were to withdraw the dessert-service pieces–for we would lose not only the standard shapes listed above but also most of the openwork baskets, leaf-shaped dishes, a host of tureens and even some figures. I will quote just three lots from contemporary sales to illustrate my point, first, one from the Chelsea sale of February 1770: 'A beautiful complete service for a dessert, consisting of two large basket-work dishes, two oval baskets with handles, two large rosette compoteers, four oval green edge ditto, four vine-leaf dishes, four seven-leaf ditto, four strawberry ditto, four shell ditto, and three dozen of plates, finely enamelled in groups of flowers' (sold for £30/9/0d). Note the inclusion in this service of sixteen leaf-shaped dishes of four different forms. The Chelsea sale catalogues also include very many similar fancy dessert forms sold separately, lots such as 'four small cabbage leaves enamelled in flowers, after nature, for a dessert' (sold for £1/9/0d).

By no means all Chelsea dessert dishes were of leaf-shape. Another service sold in the same sale comprised: '...two large oval baskets, two open-work rosette dishes, two close ditto, four round compoteers, four oval ditto, twelve scollop'd ditto, four silver-shap'd ditto, four leaves in baskets, four round baskets and twenty-four plates with the pea-green edge, all finely enamelled with fruit' (sold for £31/10/0d). In this set we have several baskets. Others were sold separately as 'one large oval two-handled basket for a dessert' (sold for £1/11/6d). The mention of fruit painting on these dessert plates prompts me to introduce a tantalising quotation, a Chelsea service the property of John Follett: 'a small dessert service of beautiful Chelsea china, consisting of a sugar bowl cover and stand, 2 lemons and covers, 2 oval baskets, 15 small fruit dishes, 1 extra large plate, and 2 pairs of partridges on their nests to contain sugar, etc.'

This lot was sold for a mere £4/6/0d! Admittedly this sale was in 1813 and cannot be considered a contemporary reference to the use of the two-piece partridge tureens or covered sugar boxes. One can, however, well believe that the small lemon and other fruit boxes graced a table at dessert although the partridges and other bird-boxes might be more suited to sauces than to sugar; at all events, they were most certainly made for use on the table. While mentioning fruit-shaped Chelsea porcelain boxes I should add that one lot sold in 1771 included: 4 pears, 3 apples, 2 pomegranates, 4 lemons, 6 citrons, 8 melons, 2 figs, 2 artichokes, 5 lettuces, 4 sunflowers and a rose, all sold for a mere £1/5/0d.

DESSERT FIGURES AND CANDLESTICKS

Other articles made to grace the table at dessert were vases, and one finds in Chelsea sale catalogues lots such as 'twelve small dessert vases'. A 1760 adverisement for another sale of Chelsea porcelain sheds some light on the use of at least some of these

Plate 18 A pair of early Derby figures with baskets of the type used on the table. *c.* 1755–60. 6½ inches high. *Sotheby & Co.*

vases when it reads a 'variety of baskets, leaves, compotiers, sweetmeat vases for dessert and some small figures for ditto'. Turning to figures we find these again mentioned in a notice relating to the 1763 sale: '...a large variety of handsome candlesticks, large groups of figures and single ditto of all sizes for desserts...' The groups and figures for dessert would mainly be those which incorporate baskets or other containers such as shell-shape bowls to hold comfits (breath-sweeteners), small fruits or the like (see Plate 18). However, many figures or groups were used purely for decoration on the table. In this last quotation of 1763 there was mention of 'handsome candlesticks'. Remembering that all eighteenth-century lighting was candle-power and mostly at table-level, we can see that the dinner-table must have held candlesticks of one material or another. Many of these in the homes of the wealthy would have been of porcelain but far from being simple pillar-sticks modelled on brass or pewter examples, porcelain candlesticks were decorative and ornate focal-points of the table.

Plate 19 One of a pair of Bow candlestick figures with floral 'bocage', *c.* 1765. 9½ inches high. *Godden of Worthing Ltd*

Here are a few Chelsea candlestick models as listed in the 1770 sale catalogue:

> One pair of large table candlesticks, with dog, fox, grapes, &c
> A pair of candlesticks with a sportsman and companion
> A pair of large ditto, with an ox, ass, &c
> A pair of table candlesticks, goat in a well
> A pair of boar-hunting candlesticks
> A pair of Black-a-moor candlesticks
> A pair of candlesticks for four lights, with groups of figures, representing the four seasons, curiously decorated with flowers.

This last item in particular serves to remind us that the fashion for these table novelties, the fruit and other fancy-shaped boxes, the table figures and groups and the ornate table-candlesticks, came to us from the Continent and several English models would have been copied from Dresden (Meissen) porcelain originals. The example shown in Plate 19 is from the Bow factory.

ICE-PAILS

Still our list of dessert wares is by no means exhausted: we have knife-handles in Chelsea and other porcelains and some of the more expensive dessert-services included open ice-pails, normally of jardinière-form but sometimes oval with two separate compartments. These ice-pails were for cooling the wine-bottle in a bed of crushed ice. From about 1780 we find the three-piece ice-pail with an inner bowl and handled-cover (Plate 20). These were sold in matching pairs, one such pair being included in Christie's 1785 sale of Derby porcelain: 'a pair of elegant ice-pails, basons and covers, enamelled with groups of flowers, fine mazarine-blue ground richly gilt'. These three-piece pails were probably for chilling fruit of various kinds, although if the liner and cover were removed they would serve to hold a wine bottle. These fruit-coolers remained fashionable until the 1820s; they are quite scarce and costly items and rarely found perfect today, yet they are imposing items of decoration on a sideboard or on a pair of tables.

SHELL CENTRE-PIECES

Another popular and imposing item of dessert dressage was the shell centre-piece. Christie's 1769 sale of Worcester porcelain included, for example, 'a curious stand for the centre of a dessert decorated with shells, &c'. Such shell-pieces were made at the Bow factory, at Derby, Plymouth and Worcester. Probably the last examples were made at the Chamberlain factory in Worcester in the early 1790s, although the Irish Belleek factory made rather similar centre-pieces in the 1870s and later.

NINETEENTH-CENTURY DESSERT-SERVICES

By the 1780s and certainly by the 1790s the dessert-table began to simmer down. It lost much of the old flamboyance; the novelties gave way to more utilitarian forms. In place of the fruit-shaped covered boxes or tureens and the partridge tureens there was a pair of circular or oval covered tureens and stands enamelled to match the plates and dishes. Contemporary catalogues and factory records show us that these tureens or rather covered bowls were for cream and sugar. Some were originally equipped with matching porcelain spoons–delicate articles nearly all of which have long ago been broken and discarded.

The centre-piece settled down to an almost standard dish mounted on a low stand, some three or four inches high. The various shaped dishes were still flat–i.e.

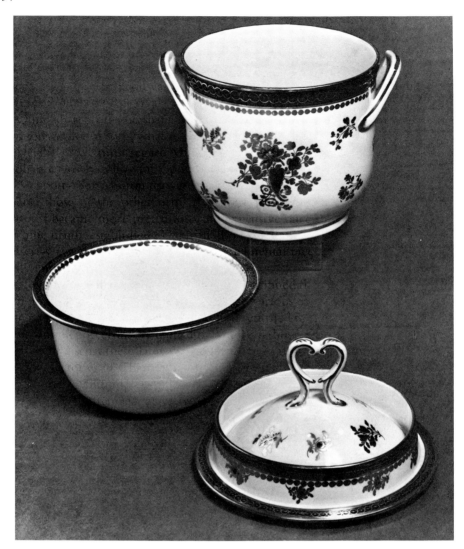

Plate 20 A Caughley ice-pail showing the three sections making up the complete article, *c.* 1790. 10¾ inches high. *Godden of Worthing Ltd*

they were not raised on a separate base or stem. Many dessert-services of the 1790–1820 period were truly magnificent in the painted and gilt decoration they bore. After about 1820 the side-dishes tended to be raised some two inches on feet or a shaped foot. The centre-piece or comport was now mounted on a central stem some six or more inches high.

The post-1840 Victorian porcelain dessert-services almost defy description for they were so varied. The standard sets, if any can be so described, comprised one or two tall comports, some eight inches high, mounted on a central stem, two similar

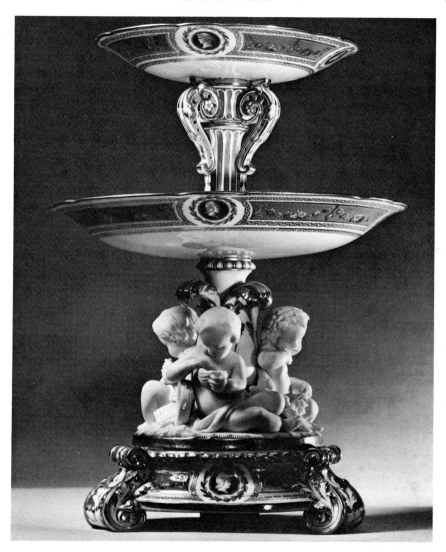

Plate 21 A fine centre-piece from a Minton dessert-service showing the combination of the unglazed parian figures with the glazed and decorated porcelain. *Author's Collection*

comports about six inches high, four low comports some two inches high. The dished-top of the comports matched the outline of the plates, basically of circular plan. The standard sets would have included twelve, eighteen or twenty-four plates, according to the customer's choice and pocket.

The major factories such as Minton, Copelands, Royal Worcester also produced really sumptuous services, the centre-pieces often supported by parian-figure bases, the white matt parian contrasting delightfully with the richly glazed porcelain (Plate 21), and the plates might well have delicately pierced borders.

BASKETS ETC

I have mentioned the three main types of tableware–the tea, dinner and dessert wares but there is a great variety of articles such as jugs of many sizes, tankards or mugs, salad-bowls and various other containers as well as large bowls which are normally described as punch-bowls although they would have been used in many different ways. Baskets of all sizes were a great feature of the early-nineteenth-century English factories; a few Rockingham porcelain examples painted with Sussex views are shown in Plate 89. Some very decorative inkwells or inkstands were also made by the leading manufacturers in the nineteenth century.

Of a more utilitarian nature we find surviving a relatively large number of eighteenth-century toilet bowls and guglets (or handleless water vases) and relatively few egg-cups, egg-drainers, eye-baths, mustard-pots, thimbles, buttons, finger-bowls, spittoons, decanter stands or flasks; yet all were made, with a multitude of other useful objects.

Plate 22 A Derby bulb pot with loose cover, painted with typical floral panel, *c.* 1790. 8 inches long. *Godden of Worthing Ltd*

VASES

Progressing forward to more ornamental pieces, we have a great assembly of vases, of all sizes and of all shapes and bearing every type of decoration. Some of these served as pot-pourri vases, a pleasant odour arising from the pierced cover to scent the room. Most English porcelain vases were, however, for ornamental purposes only, to dress a mantelpiece or cabinet. They had covers and could hardly have been used for cut flowers or the like. From about 1760, however, there was a fine series of low bulb or flower pots showing a distinct Continental influence. At first these were rococo in style (Plate 22), to become in general of half-moon shape from about 1800. The flat-back is undecorated as it faced the wall. These bulb pots and the related circular jardinières (with their separate bases) were very richly decorated and can be magnificent objects. The early-nineteenth-century mantel would not have been complete without a pair of cylindrical spill-vases, or 'match-pots' as they were called, which in rare instances were made to match the bulb pot (Plate 23).

Plate 23 A Chamberlain-Worcester bulb pot with a pair of matching spill-vases, *c.* 1805. *Godden of Worthing Ltd*

Plate 24 A fine quality pair of Minton figures, after Dresden originals, *c.* 1840. 8½ inches high. *Geoffrey Godden, Chinaman*

On the eighteenth- and nineteenth-century mantel there would also have been perhaps a porcelain clock-case and almost certainly a pair of decorative porcelain figures and a pair of animals or birds modelled in the round. These figures, groups and models from nature were produced from the earliest days of the British ceramic industry up to the present time. They will always be in great demand both as cabinet pieces and as dressing for a table, sideboard or other furnishings in a room. Several books have been devoted to this aspect of ceramic art and other specialist books give a good pictorial account of the figure models made at individual factories (see Chapters 5–9) but in this very brief summary I can mention that some factories produced extremely few figures while others concentrated heavily on their production. Eighteenth-century Worcester figures and bird or animal models are extremely scarce and by no means up to the modelling standard of this factory's other products. The Liverpool factories and that at Lowestoft concentrated almost entirely on useful wares while in contrast the Bow, Chelsea and Derby figures and groups are quite common (but not cheap) and certainly outnumber the surviving teapots from these factories. Early-nineteenth-century Worcester figure models are also very scarce and there are hardly any from the important Spode factory, while this factory's main rival, Minton, excelled in Derby and Dresden-style figures of exquisite quality (Plate 24). After about 1850 the inexpensive parian figures and the earthenware models dominated the figure market.

CHAPTER FOUR

Decoration and marketing

Assuming that the formed object is to be decorated, in addition to any moulded ornamentation it may already bear, there are two basic types of decoration to be considered. That applied before glazing and that applied after glazing, these being broadly classed as 'underglaze' and 'overglaze' decoration. Each have subdivisions such as hand-painted or printed designs.

UNDERGLAZE–BLUE

Underglaze painting is normally confined to cobalt-blue, this being the pigment best able to withstand the high temperature of the glost-kiln in which the glaze is matured. The cobalt is so powerful a colouring agent that it cannot be used alone but is used either as 'Zaffre' or 'Smalt'. Zaffre is prepared by heating the cobalt ore and fritting the ground-powder with sand, sometimes with the addition of borax and calcined flint to act as a flux. Smalt was made by adding Potassium Carbonate to Zaffre; the resulting glass-like mass was then pulverised. An extremely useful chapter on cobalt is included in Dr Bernard Watney's standard work, *English Blue and White Porcelain of the 18th Century* (Faber, London, 1963, revised edition, 1973).

The diluted cobalt in liquid form is painted in the normal manner but on to the unglazed porcelain. To give graduations of tint, detail, shading, etc, different strengths of pigment can be used or more usually some overpainting is carried out, so that very dark details may have three applications of the blue pigment. I write 'blue' but when applied it appears nearly black, to become a fine blue only after glazing and firing. The glaze seems to have an important part to play in maturing the blue for when, as sometimes happens, the glaze does not completely cover an article the blue at the unglazed part will appear dark and dirty looking. We write and talk of underglaze-blue but while it is indeed applied under the glaze, on firing the blue rises through the glaze so that the term 'inglaze blue' would be more appropriate. In fact you can paint the cobalt on top of the glaze and on firing it will sink into it to give the appearance of underglaze-blue.

Blue and white porcelains have always been extremely popular and fashionable. This fact probably dates back to the earliest importations of Chinese porcelains, and certainly in the first half of the eighteenth century when the large-scale trade in these

Oriental wares was being developed the directors of the English East India Company instructed their agents or 'Supra-cargos' that 'the china ware must all be of useful sorts most blue and white' or noted 'always preferring good blue and white to any other colour', to quote from directions issued in 1724 and 1731 respectively.

When some twenty years later English manufacturers entered the porcelain market they largely knew what the buying public required and the demand for blue and white designs suited the novice porcelain producers remarkably well. It was relatively trouble-free and inexpensive to produce, indeed the Lowestoft factory produced only blue and white designs for the first thirteen or so years of its existence, c. 1757 to c. 1770. Trouble-free, for only two main firings were required: the normal biscuit and the glost firings, with none of the subsequent firings that would have been necessary had overglaze enamels or gilding been employed (see p. 67). Secondly, the manufacturers did not have to bother about preparing troublesome enamel colours and were spared the cost of the gold. Thirdly, many of the blue-painters could be semi-trained or apprentice painters earning a low wage, as the majority of the blue and white porcelains were of a repetitive nature; one can picture youngsters painting the same mock-Chinese landscape designs on countless teabowls and saucers day after day and week after week. These remarks may appear somewhat disparaging since even the normal run of eighteenth-century blue and white porcelain gives nearly all collectors the greatest visual pleasure. Some pieces are indeed ceramic masterpieces in their way–but by no means all.

From the serious collector's point of view the English blue and white wares have several attractions. They are, or were, relatively common and inexpensive so that a good representative and instructive collection can be formed at a fraction of the price of enamelled pieces. A very wide assortment of shapes were enhanced with blue and white designs and indeed many forms are known only in blue and white. A range of inscribed and dated pieces enables us to plot the development of various pastes and factory styles. The importance of such documentary pieces cannot be overstressed but to the true collector the importance of blue and white probably lies in the difficulties of attribution that these simple everyday wares pose. Take for example a blue and white teabowl and saucer, is it Bow, or Lowestoft, or perhaps Derby? Was it made at one of the Liverpool factories, at Bristol or even in China? To find the answer one must know the type of paste one is holding–soft-paste, hard-paste, bone-ash body, soapstone body, one must have knowledge of the potting techniques used at different factories. These and many other facets of ceramic knowledge go to such a diagnosis, for very few examples of blue and white porcelain bear a helpful factory mark.

If you have mastered blue and white your knowledge of all English porcelain is built on very firm and reliable foundations.

BLUE-PRINTED DESIGNS

I have written so far only of hand-painted blue and white designs but this is hardly half the story. It would appear that in about 1760 the demand for these porcelains, particularly for the less expensive table-wares, led to the introduction of printing so that the standard designs could be run off at speed and one could produce, for example, five hundred blue-printed saucers, each bearing an identical design. Before this can happen, however, the all-important 'copper-plates' have to be engraved. The printing process was first applied in the 1750s over the glaze–on to various earthenwares, enamel wares and Worcester and other porcelains. In about 1760, the same process was adapted to the application of cobalt-tinted pigments to the unglazed porcelain.

THE PRINTING PROCESS

Whether over- or under-glaze the printing process is essentially the same. First, a flat sheet of quite heavy gauge copper, the 'copper-plate', has to be prepared and engraved and/or etched. This sounds simple but the engraver, or the designer behind him (if they are not the same person), has to dream up a pleasing design suitable for placing on a variety of shapes–on teapots, on saucers or small teabowls, on narrow coffee cups, to name some of the component units in a standard teaset. The design had not merely to fit the various shapes but also to sell–it had to induce the buyer to choose a Worcester teaset rather than a Bow or Lowestoft set. The designer-engraver was a key-man indeed.

He most probably drew his initial design on paper, making a series of trials to be submitted to the factory owner, partners or manager. These drawings could be adapted from paintings or prints of the period or copied from popular designs introduced by a rival firm or printed versions of popular hand-painted Chinese or English porcelains, or of course they could be completely new patterns. Once drawn on paper, improved upon and passed at a high level of management, the design could be transferred, probably by 'pouncing', to the face of a copper-plate. Pouncing consists of piercing a series of small holes through the paper to mark the main lines or details of the composition. The prepared paper is then laid on the copper and a porous bag of finely powdered material is rattled on the surface so that the powder drops through the holes or pin-pricks to mark the copper-plate as desired. This temporary image can then be lightly engraved into the relatively soft workable copper with sharp and fine chisel-like engraving tools and further details added until the required design is shown on the copper-plate.

ENGRAVING

This preliminary design must then be worked over. Parts of the design that are to show a bold dark line must be cut deep so that they hold more pigment; parts that have to be shaded must be cross-hatched with a series of closely spaced lines; while delicate shading or the merest outline such as the edges of a rose-petal must be left as the finest and shallowest incised cut into the copper-plate. Many of the finest copper-plates had delicate details added by the etching process with the help of acids. I have spoken of one copper-plate but to introduce a single new teaware pattern some twelve or more different copper-plates must be painstakingly prepared to suit the different size of article, the teapot, its cover and stand, the cream or milk jug, the waste-bowl, the sugar-bowl and cover, etc.

TRANSFERRING

Once the set of plates has been engraved hundreds of articles can be adorned with the same design before the copper-plates need touching-up or re-engraving. The initial engraving is time-consuming and a skilled trade, but after that, low-paid, semi-skilled labour can transfer the design to the waiting porcelain. The procedure in simple terms is to warm the copper-plate and to charge it with a thick, oily, treacle-like mixture containing the cobalt-pigment. Having forced this into the engraved lines the surplus pigment is cleaned from the face of the copper leaving the 'ink' only in the recessed lines according to their depth or thickness. A special tough yet thin tissue-like paper is then laid over the charged and re-heated copper-plate and pressed firmly on to it so that the pigment is transferred from the lines on to the paper.

This transfer-tissue is then trimmed, discarding surplus pieces of the paper or dividing the design as required to fit the pot. The inked paper can then be carefully positioned on to the unglazed but biscuit-fired article. The paper is then pressed firmly and carefully to transfer the pigment on to the ware. This paper is subsequently soaked off, the ware dried and the pigment lightly fired or 'hardened-on', to burn off the oil and fix the design. Factory wasters often illustrate the importance of the 'hardened-on' process, for when one washes such pieces the unglazed pattern remains, but with pieces that were discarded before the all-important light-firing the pattern dissolves almost at the sight of water.

The next stage is to glaze the object bearing the hardened-on design. This process is simple and has been explained on p. 27. The ware is then glost-fired (p. 30). If on examination the wares are cleanly fired with a well matured blue and clear covering glaze, the objects can be passed to the warehouse, later to be made up into sets and dispatched to wholesale or retail outlets. Examples that have a slightly 'flown' glaze, or which display a blue that has run, would be separated and ultimately sold as 'seconds' or 'thirds' at a reduced price.

This verbal account of the underglaze printing technique may well give the impression that it is complicated but in practice this is not so. It enabled tasteful well-drawn designs to be applied by cheap labour. In all probability the following two notices of 1763 and 1772 refer to such blue-printed porcelains, both in this case Worcester:

the most valuable part of all, and which principally calls for notice, is the extraordinary strength and cheapness of the common sort of blue and white Worcester porcelain...

Complete tea services of blue and white Worcester china from £1 to £1·5s the set, consisting of 43 pieces.

The blue-printed porcelains are often decried as mass-produced wares. I do not agree with this dismissal. Originally the process enabled the articles to be produced at a price the customer could afford, and we must remember that a factory's success depends not on the quality of the relatively few superb pieces it produces for the rich but on the success of the low-price, 'bread and butter' goods made for the mass-market. Chelsea failed while the Worcester factory has continued to the present time.

I also contend that most blue-printed designs of the 1760–90 period are superior to the run-of-the-mill hand-painted designs. These are mainly repetitive and they degenerate with endless copying, while the printed designs retain the original quality. If there is a fault in the printed designs it lies in the fact that the engraver had time to rework and perfect his design so that in some cases there is a certain tightness or lack of spontaneity–the pattern can be too perfect!

A good range of blue-printed patterns as well as hand-painted wares are illustrated in my out-of-print booklet *An Introduction to English Blue and White Porcelains* (Godden of Worthing Ltd, 1974), while the whole field of blue and white is admirably covered in Dr Watney's *English Blue and White Porcelain of the 18th Century*.

OVERGLAZE DECORATION

Overglaze designs are those patterns or motifs added to the glazed and fired blanks. In some ways the coloured pieces present less trouble to the manufacturer than the inexpensive blue and white pieces. The reason for this lies in the fact that the enamels (as overglaze pigments are called) do not have to endure the high temperature of the glost-kiln. They are matured at the relatively low temperature of some 700°C in a small 'muffle-kiln'. A visit to any factory site provides evidence of the high kiln-loss of blue and white wares and of the almost total lack of wasters or failures in the enamelled designs.

I do not intend to explain how the colours were mixed or otherwise prepared from metallic oxides and applied, for the painting process varied little from the normal painting technique. I must point out, however, that, when applied, the pigments bear little or no visual relation to the fired-colour and that in some cases the pigments have to be applied in a given order and fired between the application of the separate colours, as they mature at different temperatures.

STOCK DESIGNS

With a few exceptions all designs, blue and white or enamelled, are stock-patterns which are linked to a pattern-book or to **pattern-pieces** retained within the factory.

The exceptions to this general rule mainly comprise the pieces made to the special order of a customer. While some motifs permitted a certain licence, in that flower compositions or scenic designs with standard borders could be changed at the whim of the artist, most patterns remained reasonably constant.

The eighteenth-century housewife shopping for perhaps a new tea-service no doubt had a larger choice than her present-day counterpart but if she shopped in the city of Bath or in Bristol or Cheltenham she would have seen, as today, largely the same selection of patterns. The reason for this is simple: the painting of stock designs enabled the management to employ mainly semi-skilled hands at low rates. It also enabled the retailers to re-order time and again popular designs, and the customer was able to purchase replacements. Obviously new designs were added to a factory's range, slow-selling patterns were discarded, popular ones retained or slightly up-dated, but it was not until the 1780s or early 1790s that the system of adding pattern numbers to the wares was adopted and before that the designs were designated by a name or by description (see p. 257).

OVERGLAZE PRINTING

The general practice of issuing repetitive designs was by no means limited to the British manufacturers. The same was true of the Continental factories, and there is evidence that the tons of Chinese porcelain shipped to London by the East India Company comprised under ten separate designs each year! This situation obviously opened the way for mass-production techniques of which the most important was the English practice of adapting the printing process to ceramics. I have already discussed printing in blue under the glaze but before this was introduced, in about 1760, there was overglaze printing, from the mid-1750s, on pottery tiles, enamel wares and on porcelain. The technical details of engraving the copper-plate have already been outlined and the earlier use of engraved design differed only in the fact that the inked transfer paper was applied to a glazed and fired blank and that no 'hardening-on' would be required before the design was fired.

The late W. B. Honey (Keeper of the Department of Ceramics at the Victoria and Albert Museum when I started collecting in the late 1940s), a noted authority and discerning writer, has rightly observed that 'transfer-printing is one of the few entirely English contributions to the art of porcelain...the earliest work done in the technique has a peculiarly English eighteenth-century charm, which a closer acquaintance can only increase...' Quite apart from the need to reduce costs and speed production, try to visualise the amateur appearance that would result from a factory hand having to paint hundreds of copies of the printed design shown in Plate 25. Not only would he have to paint the figures as best he could but in order to live he would have to paint rapidly, for the factory hands were all employed on a piece-rate basis. As it is, the printed design is by the doyen of ceramic artist-engravers, Robert Hancock (c. 1730–1817). His work can be found on enamels, on Bow porcelain, and notably on Worcester porcelain. This one artist engraved a

Plate 25 A Worcester coffee cup and saucer bearing Robert Hancock's famous Tea-Party overglaze-print, *c.* 1765. *Geoffrey Godden, Chinaman*

wonderful array of designs—each one a charming little masterpiece. The standard work on Hancock and his designs is Cyril Cook's *The Life and Work of Robert Hancock* (Chapman & Hall, London, 1948, with a supplement privately published in 1955). In the eighteenth century, besides Hancock, many other talented engravers were employed at various factories or supplied engraved copper-plates on a freelance basis.

Robert Hancock's prints are complete in themselves and were not further embellished at the factory. The normal colour of the design is black. At the time of production this was known as 'jet' and somewhat misleadingly these Worcester porcelains were described as 'jet-enamelled' not printed. In the Worcester porcelain sale conducted by Mr Christie in December 1769 we find listed: 'A compleat tea and coffee equipage, jet enammelled L'amour, 43 pieces.' (Sold for £1.18s.)

The purchaser of this black-printed teaset bearing the L'amour design was James Giles, a talented London decorator of Worcester and other porcelains. The rare and delightful examples of Worcester jet-printing that are tastefully coloured-over are now often attributed to the Giles decorating studio in London, but we have no proof to substantiate this popular belief.

Early Worcester prints are superb. They are now rare and deservedly costly. In general the Hancock-type overglaze printed designs were made only within the period *c*. 1756–74. There was some overglaze printing after this but by then fashion would seem to have favoured printed designs in underglaze-blue.

PRINTED OUTLINE DESIGNS

Apart from the superb Hancock prints on Worcester and other porcelains, designs that are complete in themselves, some simple printed designs appear on Bow porcelains. These patterns mainly comprise Chinese figures and they would seem to be little more than outlines for the apprentice boy-painters to colour in. This ceramic technique has continued down to modern times and was much used in the nineteenth century when very finely engraved floral compositions were coloured in by hand–the purchaser and present-day owner fondly believing they had or have an entirely hand-painted object, not a mass-produced printed design coloured over by a young boy.

SALE OF ENGRAVED COPPER–PLATES

The master-engravers were key-men who could sell their services and their copper-plates to the highest bidder. Thus quite apart from the normal copying of one factory's popular designs by another, precisely the same design could appear on porcelains of a different manufacture when the original engraved copper-plates were sold. Several of the Worcester copper-plates, including at least one signed by Robert Hancock, were found at the Coalport factory, although there is no evidence at present that they were ever made use of at the Caughley or Coalport factories.

ENGRAVERS TO THE TRADE

From about 1780 specialist engraving firms began to supply sets of engraved copper-plates to potters who did not have their own highly-paid engraver. Obviously, if a small factory required only four or five new printed designs each year then it was far cheaper to buy the plates ready engraved. The majority of nineteenth-century printed pottery designs originated from a few specialist engraving firms.

BAT–PRINTING

The engraved designs of which I have previously written were in the main made up of straight lines or cross-hatching, but from about 1800 a new style of engraving and/or etching technique of printing was applied to English ceramics. The engraved pattern was made up of dots rather than lines, the dots being smaller or larger, closer or more widely spaced according to the depth of colour required.

Plate 26 A Spode cup and saucer showing the delicate effect of the bat-printing process, *c.* 1810. *Geoffrey Godden, Chinaman*

Instead of transfer-paper the image was transferred from the copper-plate to the glazed article by means of a pliable bat of glue and isinglass, or like substance, hence the term 'bat-printing'. The copper plates were charged with oil or a similar medium, the glue-bat transferred this to the article and powdered colour was then dusted over the article to adhere to the oiled parts. This indeed is how the New Hall and Spode firms managed to print in gold, and that is the method described by William Evans, a practical ceramic painter and decorator, in 1846. The engraved or etched copper-plate could now be most delicately engraved, as the plate had not to be charged with the old thick colouring compound and no heat was needed to soften this before it would transfer. Certainly these bat-printed designs of the approximate period 1800–20 can be a real delight and they are generally under-rated. Look for a moment at this Spode cup (Plate 26), originally part of quite an inexpensive teaset.

GILDING

Apart from printing and painting in enamel colours there is a further class of overglaze decoration–gilding, a rather neglected subject. Gold ornamentation on early porcelain was not as rare as some authorities would have us believe. Much of the imported Chinese and Japanese porcelain was enriched with gilding. For example the instructions given to the supra-cargos of the East Indiaman *Loyal Bliss* in 1712 include mention of gilt wares: '20,000 plates in colours and gold, 10,000 with a border inside and gold edges...' When English manufacturers commenced production in the mid 1740s and early 1750s, the gilding process must have caused some concern and added greatly to the cost of the article. This cost was not so much due to the value of the gold as very little was in fact used, but more to the trouble of applying it, re-firing the object and then burnishing the gold which appears brown and dull and slightly rough until the final polishing process.

We must bear in mind that gold is applied as the last form of embellishment. A Worcester plate may bear decoration made up of underglaze-blue (matured at a high temperature in the glost-kiln), enamel decoration added after glazing and matured in a muffle-kiln at approximately 700°C, and finally some parts of the pattern may be picked out in gold. This is fixed at a lower temperature still, in the last firing process. The gold is consequently the least permanent form of decoration and will be the first to show wear.

The application of gold to ceramics was a separate craft carried out by the gilders rather than by the painters. In the eighteenth century and for at least the first part of the nineteenth century, pure or almost pure gold was used. At some early factories, or by some decorators, the gold would appear to have been applied in leaf-form adhering to the glaze only by the application of size or a like substance. It was not fixed by firing. This standard technique is fine for picture frames or for other objects that are not handled or washed but for porcelains a more permanent method is required. One can still find now white figures or groups which show in protected crevices traces of the original unfired (or cold) gilding or of unfired colours.

The earliest fired gilding was of the type called 'honey-gilding' because the powdered gold or gold-leaf was mixed with honey before being painted on the glazed ware. After firing the gold fluxed slightly with the glaze and became a permanent part of the decoration. The dull fired gold could then be burnished by being rubbed quickly with a polished and smooth bloodstone or agate mounted on a short handle. From the nineteenth century to the present time the burnishers have been women but we have no evidence that females were so employed in the eighteenth century. The honey-gilding did have a certain body or thickness which permitted 'tooling' or 'chasing' of floral or other motifs with a metal point, in the Sèvres style. The tooled or chased design usually shows bright against the only slightly burnished or 'sanded' dullish gold, giving contrast. Some of the Chelsea and Worcester tooled gilding of the 1760–70 period can be extremely fine and was probably more time-consuming to complete than the main painted decoration. Tooled gilding on a dark blue ground has a magnificently rich effect, and perhaps the painters themselves were responsible for the tooled butterflies, insects and flowers that are drawn or incised into the gold. Certainly if not the painters then only the most skilled gilders would be so employed. Most useful wares would have borne only simple burnished gold borders or other enrichments, while the cheaper 'bread and butter' lines would not have been gilt at all.

The great difficulty with the necessarily low-fired gilding is to induce the gold to adhere to the glossy-glaze, a difficulty by no means always overcome. Some factories, notably that at Bow in about 1750, used a brown-coloured undercoat or fluxing agent, which at one and the same time added depth to the gold and assisted the fixing. Similar but lighter coloured underlays can be seen on some later porcelains such as Bristol where the gold has worn or flaked away.

In about the 1785–95 period the old honey-gilding gave way to mercury-gilding. The gold, being mixed with mercury to form a paste-like substance, can be painted, stippled or otherwise applied to the porcelain. The mercury is vaporised in the muffle-kiln leaving the gold to be sanded to a dull polish or burnished to a fine polish as required. Mercury-gilding to a trained eye is rather harder and more brassy than the soft honey-gilding and in some cases (Minton of the 1825–35 period and Rockingham) the colour has acquired a distinct coppery tint.

The Regency period saw some magnificent gilding on English porcelains although we must admit to some copying of then current Paris porcelains where vase-handles, etc, were gilt to emulate ormolu, and matt or frosted dull gold effects were used to great advantage contrasting well with the bright, burnished gilding. The leading firms–Spode, Minton, Davenport, Daniel and the Worcester companies–employed very talented gilders who also made good use of raised-gilding or relief designs in gold. The relief design was first worked with a mixture of colour and ground-porcelain, the relief-work then being gilt, 'sanded' to a dull polish and sometimes chased or tooled. The technique, the introduction of which is attributed to Henry Daniel (p. 185), when used with restraint can be superb but often the effect is spoilt by excess. Magnificent gilding of this type is best seen on the reverse side of Daniel, Davenport or Minton vases (Plate 27) of the 1820–40 period–the side normally turned to the wall!

Obviously time-consuming, quality gilding of the type I have just described is only found on the most expensive products of the leading firms. There were short-cuts for the less expensive wares. Peter Warburton patented in 1810 three methods of printing in gold and a rare and attractive class of gold-printed New Hall porcelain is to be found with the mark 'Warburton's Patent'. The Spode company also printed in gold, normally on a deep-blue ground. Messrs Minton introduced a patented technique of acid-gilding (see p. 229), a tasteful style subsequently taken up by many late Victorian firms, and in the 1870–80 period we find the introduction of German or 'bright-gold' on some wares of the smaller potters. This liquid gold did not need burnishing but the effect is watery and cheap.

Returning to eighteenth-century gilding, the fact that it needed only a soft-firing in a muffle-kiln meant that some of the independent decorators could quite easily enhance slightly decorated wares with gilding, or gild white porcelains. Several London decorators, from about 1780, added gilt borders, etc, to Chinese blue and white porcelains, and they may also have added gilding to some English blue and white wares. The Giles Studio in London during the 1760s and 1770s is also a source of some tasteful gilt designs found on Worcester and perhaps Caughley porcelains.

Plate 27 A detail of the raised gilding on the reverse of a Minton vase of the 1840s. *Geoffrey Godden, Chinaman*

I find some of the simple eighteenth-century and early-nineteenth-century gilt patterns far more pleasing than the fashionable and very expensive apple-green ground Worcester porcelains. There is one superbly gilt Worcester teapot in the Victoria and Albert Museum, which to me is preferable to most enamelled pieces, and I always give a little bow of acknowledgement to its gilder as I pass. In a less ornate style the gilt patterns of the 1785–1810 period can be extremely pleasing (Plate 85), as can the white and gold Caughley or Worcester porcelains, see Plates 32 and 57.

I do not wish to fill the remaining part of this book with a class by class coverage of the various styles of ceramic painting. The huge range can be seen in most well-illustrated modern reference books; my own two works *An Illustrated Encyclopaedia of British Pottery and Porcelain* (1966) and *British Porcelain, an illustrated guide* (1974) contain well over a thousand illustrations between them. Stanley Fisher's book *The Decoration of English Porcelain* (Derek Verschoyle, London, 1954) also contains much relevant information. More recent discoveries have shown several of the author's attributions to be incorrect, nevertheless his main views are helpful and of importance.

DECORATION

Some consideration of styles of decoration will be given later in the coverage of individual factories. In general I would suggest that the minimum of decoration is the most successful for useful wares and in this regard I, like many present-day collectors, favour the early porcelains of the 1750–55 period to the more flamboyant wares of the next decade. There is, however, a case for richly decorating vases and such ornamental pieces which were made to dress a mantel or cabinet.

Many manufacturers made the error of completely covering the surface of the object with ground-colours or other painted decoration–a fault not confined to the Victorian period–so hiding the attribute of porcelain: the wonderful white or near white body, a material having a real beauty of its own. The decoration should complement and enhance the porcelain and the white body set off the added decoration. Of all the overglaze enamel decorations I respect most the floral patterns, the scattered sprays (rather than large masses) and the restrained Oriental-style designs (Plates 35, 39 and 48). These seem to me well suited to the medium on which they are painted and could hardly offend the eye or appetite of the person eating from such porcelains.

We must all make our own judgements of what we like or wish to collect. Apart from individual taste there are many good reasons for collecting a particular style of decoration. One collector I know seeks porcelain painted with named views–a reasonably common interest–but here it is extended to revisiting the location and photographing the scene or building as it appears today, over a hundred and fifty years after the scene was first painted on his porcelain. A keen gardener might collect wares painted with botanical specimens. Many people collect porcelains painted with a yellow ground or with yellow bands for their decorative merit or because these pieces suit so well the furnishing of a room. Such people need a healthy bank balance for yellow is the rarest of ceramic colours and the most costly. If you are wealthy you can also consider the rare porcelains painted with shells or feathers, for such pieces are always of the finest quality. For the less wealthy there are endless interesting styles of decoration or types of porcelain to consider, ranging down to crested Goss china at a pound or two a piece. There is, however, no need at all to specialise in any one type and most collectors follow the healthy practice of buying simply what appeals to them. Bernard Leach, the doyen of modern potters, had the right idea when he replied to the question–'why on earth did you buy that?'–'because I like it'. There is no better answer.

DISTRIBUTION OF FINISHED WARES

We have discussed in general terms the different types of decoration found on

English porcelain and before turning our attention to the major factories we should have an idea how the finished wares were distributed and how they reached the customer. We must remember that in the eighteenth century, roads as we know them today were non-existent; they were little better than muddy, rutted tracks. The easiest and cheapest mode of transport for goods–if not for people–was by water and the porcelain factories were mainly situated at ports–London, Bristol, Plymouth, Liverpool, Lowestoft, or on important rivers. The River Severn, for example, permitted raw materials to be shipped to Worcester, to Coalport and the nearby Caughley factory and it also formed the main artery for the dispatch of the finished wares. Derby was likewise well served by river transport as were the Staffordshire Potteries, particularly so after the establishment of the Midland canal system.

Many people have a mind's eye picture of hawkers travelling the country districts and markets with their wares. This system may have been employed for the commoner types of pottery but the more sophisticated porcelains were not hawked in this manner.

Prospective buyers living for example within twenty miles of a porcelain factory would have been inclined to purchase their wares direct from that source–particularly when a special order was to be placed. Both the main Worcester factories had separate retail establishments in that city where a full range of wares were on display and where orders could be placed. The original order and sales books for the Chamberlain factory still survive and make most interesting reading.

Other cities and towns would each have had one or more 'chinamen'. One may have stocked Derby porcelains, another acted as agent for Worcester, Caughley or Bristol wares so that the buyer in at least the main centres of trade had quite a good choice not only of English porcelains and earthenwares, but of Chinese blue and white porcelains and of glass, papier-mâché and other related goods. On the evidence of the Chamberlain records it would seem that these retail-shops would not only have carried a stock of the more saleable patterns and stock items but they would also have had available a selection of sample-pieces to assist the buyer to choose a tea or dinner service to suit his or her taste. Orders could then be relayed back to the factory. In March 1790 we find for example listed 'Patterns sent to Mr P. Bushly, Yorks'. These were pattern cups and saucers but the price quoted is for the full teaset.

1	cup and saucer–Prince of Wales' border	sett at	£13–10–0	
1	do.	new Royal Festoon	,,	£8– 8–0
1	do.	new Royal Star	,,	£7– 7–0
1	do.	new gold festoon	,,	£6– 6–0
1	do.	Brosley blue & gold sprigs	,,	£5– 5–0
1	do.	plain blue & gold sprigs	,,	£3–13–6
1	do.	plain gold sprigs	,,	£3– 3–0

In some cases the order books also give details concerning transport, for example when Chamberlain supplied porcelain blanks to William Billingsley's decorating establishment at Mansfield they were dispatched from Worcester 'per canal to Nottingham...', underlining my point about the advantages of water-transport.

PATTERN-PIECES

Apart from sets of pattern-pieces some factories also produced pattern-plates in which the surface or border is divided into segments, each part bearing a different and numbered design. The customer could then visit the local 'chinaman' and order a service to be made with border number 10 or 11, stipulating, for example, a scenic or floral centre, or give orders that his armorial bearings or crest be added to the chosen standard pattern.

LONDON SHOWROOMS

Several of the major porcelain manufacturers had London showrooms or wholesale warehouses. Not only did these London establishments serve the nobility but even in the eighteenth century there was quite a thriving export trade and the overseas buyers could in London find the pick of English pottery and porcelain. The London factories of Bow and Chelsea had local retail establishments and the 'Worcester China Warehouse' in Aldersgate Street was issuing price-lists of available porcelain by about 1760–delightful scallop-shell dishes in blue and white from 4d to 1s each, depending on size, or the charming double-handled sauceboats (Plate 28) from 2s to 4s each!

William Duesbury of Derby opened his 'large and elegant suit of rooms' in Bedford Street, Covent Garden in June 1773. The trade-card, a copy of which is in the Victoria and Albert Museum, includes engravings of typical wares for 'the nobility Gentry and Public in General'. The Caughley or 'Salopian China Warehouse' was at 5 Portugal Street, Lincoln's Inn Fields, and was later taken over by Spode.

Apart from the London establishments of various manufacturers it would seem to have been fashionable for the chief firms to have offered their products to the public by auction–not only at 'Mr Christie's Great Room in Pall Mall' but at several other auction rooms. Many notices of these London sales are printed in J. Nightingale's fascinating book entitled *Contributions towards the History of Early English Porcelain from Contemporary Sources* which was privately printed at Salisbury in 1881. This rare book is among the most useful and interesting of our ceramic source-books.

INDEPENDENT DECORATORS

Another means of supply for the porcelain-buying public in London were the independent decorators, of which James Giles is the best known, but by no means

Plate 28 A relief-moulded early Worcester double-handled sauceboat, showing the painter's mark on the base, *c.* 1755. *Geoffrey Godden, Chinaman*

the only practitioner. Giles advertised in January 1768 that he had Worcester porcelain 'useful and ornamental, curiously painted in the Dresden, Chelsea and Chinese tastes...as the Proprietor has a great variety of white goods by him, Ladies and Gentlemen may depend upon having their commands executed immediately and painted to any pattern they shall chuse'. The sources of supply were many, the choice varied. See p. 110 for a fuller coverage of James Giles.

TOY WARES

I have already stated that the finer porcelains were not hawked about the country as was the cheaper utilitarian pottery and in this regard it is convenient to scotch the idea that the charming little miniature pieces such as the teaset shown in Plate 29 were travellers' samples. These were made and sold purely as children's playthings as contemporary accounts well illustrate. Chamberlain of Worcester, for example,

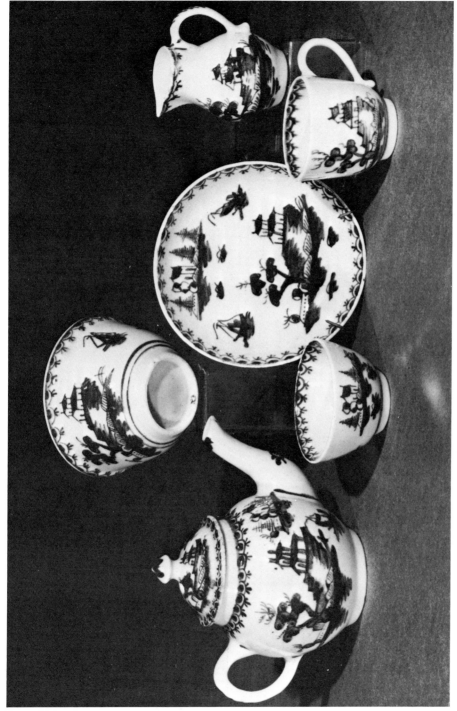

Plate 29 Part of a Lowestoft miniature or toy teaset painted in underglaze-blue, *c.* 1765. Teapot 2 inches high. *Author's Collection*

ordered various articles from Thomas Turner of the Caughley factory (p. 86) in 1789, and noted: 'The toy china is too small but send a few.' Chamberlain ordered such items as '2 Toy teasetts, pleasure boat (pattern) 4/8d' and 'toy' dinner and teasets were included in the 1799 sale of Caughley porcelains on Thomas Turner's retirement.

In several cases the patterns found on these delightful toy wares, and indeed the shapes themselves, do not occur on full-size wares, so they can hardly be travellers' samples! If travellers did in fact travel the country with porcelains, it was purely to the wholesalers and retailers–the 'chinamen' of the period–not direct to a private customer. The housewife, I believe, had a very good selection of fashionable porcelain on display in every sizeable town.

CHAPTER FIVE

The major eighteenth-century factories

In the next four chapters we will discuss the various English porcelain manufacturing factories or firms. My coverage in this chapter is somewhat brief for in most cases detailed and reliable modern books, which I have listed, are readily available to give the full story of the major eighteenth-century English porcelain manufacturers, and these works give a very good pictorial coverage of the firms' output and styles. I do not seek here to compete with these specialist books and I prefer instead to concentrate on giving information on the lesser known wares in subsequent chapters.

The following coverage is arranged in alphabetical order, for the several factories that were established in the 1745–55 period continued for so long a period that a chronological coverage would present great difficulties and lengthy overlaps.

BOW, *c.* 1747–1776

The Bow porcelain factory, originally termed 'New Canton', is one of the earliest English porcelain factories if not the first. It was situated in what we would now loosely term the East End of London, or more accurately it was on the north side of Stratford High Street at Stratford Langthorne in the parish of West Ham in Essex.

An interesting early reference to this factory appeared in Daniel Defoe's *Tour of Great Britain* published in July 1748: '…the first village we come to is Bow where a large manufactory of porcelaine is lately set up. They have already made large quantities of tea cups, saucers, etc which by some skilful persons are said to be little inferior to those brought from China…' Here in this account, presumably written in 1747, we have the main facts: the works were on a comparatively large scale; it was no back-street pottery employing six or seven persons. The main products were of a useful nature and could be compared with the fashionable Chinese porcelains; indeed in this factory's blue and white wares the Oriental influence is quite startling.

The reference to the factory being 'lately set up' is of interest. Some four years earlier, in December 1744, a patent was taken out by Edward Heylyn and Thomas Frye, persons at a slightly later date undoubtedly connected with the Bow factory, although Alderman George Arnold, a very successful London businessman, was probably the main investor, and until 1750 the partnership traded as Arnold & Co. This patent was for

> a new method of manufacturing a certain mineral, whereby a ware might be made of the same nature or kind and equal to, if not exceeding, in goodness and beauty, china or porcelain ware imported from abroad...The material is an earth, the produce of the Cherokee nation in America, called by the natives Unaker...The articles are put into a kiln and burned with wood, called 'biscuiting', if they are very white, they are ready to be painted blue...they are then dipt in glaze...

It is believed that no porcelain was made under this first patent and you will note that the wording is tentative and reads 'whereby a ware might be made...' One could also note that the wares were apparently intended to emulate the imported Chinese porcelains and that underglaze-blue designs were favoured. As I have shown, the factory was seemingly in being and producing useful wares such as cups and saucers by 1747 or at least 1748, and in November 1749 Thomas Frye took out a further patent. Bones as such are not mentioned but then one would not want to give away trade secrets and we find instead the all-embracing grouping 'animals, vegetables and fossils by calcining, grinding and washing'. Chalk, limestone, sand and flints are all mentioned but no novel new process is publicised nor would one expect this to be the case, and certainly by the period of this patent in November 1749 the Bow factory was well established and producing porcelains on conventional lines.

The Bow body is of the English artificial type being soft-paste with a high percentage of bone-ash (calcined and ground animal bones) in the mix to increase the workability and the strength. It is what we call a bone-ash body–like that employed at the Lowestoft factory. Analysis of a typical early example would give a result similar to this table:

	%
Silica	43·58
Alumina	8·36
Lime	24·47
Phosphoric Acid	18·95
Oxide of Lead	1·75
Magnesia	0·60
Potash	0·85
Soda	1.20

The bone-ash content is shown by the high percentage of Phosphoric Acid which indicates some 45 per cent bone-ash. Other Bow pieces analysed by the late Herbert Eccles contained between 48 and 28 per cent bone-ash.

From the late 1740s through the 1750s the body tended to be rather creamy in tint (except when overlaid with a slightly blue glaze) and has a compact appearance. It is heavy and on occasions can seem remarkably hard.

From the 1760s the standard body became more open or floury, lighter in weight as well as in colour. The potting is normally rather thick and consequently the pieces will feel heavier than contemporary Chelsea, Derby or Worcester porcelains. The glaze is rather soft, prone to knife scratches and in some cases to staining and crazing.

The factory made a great feature of blue and white, nearly always comprising table-wares decorated in the popular Oriental style. The pieces with powder-blue ground can be extremely fine. These blue and white Bow wares do not bear a true factory mark but normally they bear the painter's personal tally-mark or reference number painted under the base (not on the inside angle of the foot-rim, a position favoured by the Lowestoft painters).

Some blue designs bear ornate Chinese-style character marks, such as those shown here. Some blue-printing was practised but in the main the factory produced hand-painted designs in underglaze-blue for some thirty years from the late 1740s until its closure in 1776.

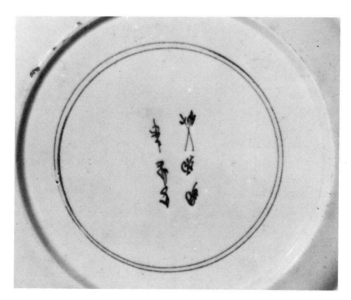

The later wares, decorated in overglaze enamels, often bear an anchor and dagger rather boldly painted in red enamel, but one would not expect pieces made before 1765 to bear such a mark—if marked at all, they would bear various letters or devices such as an arrow-like sign incised into the body.

A long range of decorative figure and animal models were made, particularly in the 1760s and 1770s. In general these are somewhat heavier in appearance than the finely modelled Chelsea examples and small areas of underglaze-blue often augment the overglaze enamels. Turning a Bow figure one may often find at the back a square hole made to hold a metal candle-holder fitment. The Bow figures were press-moulded (see p. 20) so that they are thickly walled (or on occasions solid) and heavy for their size in comparison with the slip-cast Chelsea or Derby pieces of the same period.

The Bow porcelains seem to have enjoyed a good export market in North America and there is evidence of American clays being used at this London factory. It seems highly likely that some of their workmen found employment in the Philadelphia porcelain works of Messrs Bonnin & Morris.

The Bow factory closed in 1776. Many books inform us that William Duesbury of the Derby porcelain works purchased the concern or its working materials but I do not know of any evidence to support this belief. Certainly if such a purchase took place it had no visual influence on the Derby products, and we can say that the history of this London factory closed in 1776, when England was losing America. In its modest way it was a success, producing for nearly thirty years a very pleasing range of seemingly inexpensive porcelain–mainly for the tables of the middle class– and surviving for a relatively long period the real competition from the imported Chinese porcelains, from the slick Chelsea productions and from the well-potted Worcester porcelains with their superior body.

For further reading you should consult Dr Watney's *Blue and White* book and *British Porcelain*, edited by R. J. Charleston (E. Benn, London, 1965), the chapter on Bow written by Hugh Tait of the British Museum. This authority was also the author of the splendid British Museum catalogue of the 1959 Bow exhibition held at that museum. A representative selection of illustrations of Bow wares are shown in my *British Porcelain, an illustrated guide*.

BRISTOL, *c.* 1749–1752 and *c.* 1770–1781

We have to consider two distinct types of Bristol porcelain. First the soft-paste wares of the 1749–52 period, which used to be called 'Lowdin's' and are now more correctly termed 'Lund's-Bristol', and secondly the hard-paste porcelains of the 1770–81 period. Strangely, both classes were continued at different ceramic centres, respectively at Worcester and at the New Hall works in the Staffordshire Potteries.

The first porcelain made at Bristol (a city with several claims to ceramic renown– for its excellent tin-glazed delft-type ware and other earthenwares) was of the soapstone type. In March 1749 Benjamin Lund with William Miller (a grocer and banker) were granted licences to mine this mineral (steatised granite) in the neighbourhood of the Lizard. Little or nothing is known of how this 'soapy-rock'

(A) A part Lowestoft tea and coffee service painted with the two-bird pattern in the Redgrave style combining underglaze-blue with overglaze enamels. Coffee pot $9\frac{3}{4}$ inches high, *c.* 1780–85. See p. 123.

(B) A New Hall initialled presentation jug of typical shape painted with floral sprays by a well-known hand. $7\frac{1}{2}$ inches high, *c.* 1790–1800.

See p. 149.

first came to be used in a ceramic mix or if earlier trials had been made before Lund and Miller set up their small works at Redcliff-Backs, Bristol. Benjamin Lund would seem to have had no previous experience in ceramics, being a dealer in copper and brass. If they were the first to try it they were lucky, for its inclusion in a porcelain mix results in a very workable, compact and crisp body, one with a pleasant visual appearance. The Worcester factory was to be founded on this Bristol recipe.

A very interesting contemporary reference to the local soapstone was made in the diary of Dr Richard Pococke when he visited the Lizard on 13 October 1750 'to see the soapy rock...which is mostly valued for making porcelain and they get five pounds a ton for it, for the manufacture of porcelain now carrying on at Bristol'. In November 1750 Dr Pococke visited the works at Bristol where he recorded: 'I went to see a manufacture lately established here by one of the principal manufacturers at Limehouse which failed'. We have yet to identify any porcelains from the London Limehouse works of the late 1740s but it could just be that soapstone was used there and that the manufactory, under new sponsors, was moved closer to the source of the raw material in Cornwall. Dr Pococke was probably not referring to either Lund or Miller when writing of a potter from Limehouse. Dr Pococke also recorded seeing 'very beautiful white sauceboats adorned with reliefs of festoons which sell for sixteen shillings a pair'.

This description has enabled us to identify some of the products of this early West Country factory–these now very rare but delightful festooned sauceboats. Other pieces have been identified by the relief-moulded place-name 'Bristol' or 'Bristoll' to be found under the base of some sauceboats, low creamers and on one model of a standing Chinese sage in the *Blanc de Chine* style. These marked key-pieces of which probably under twenty are known today give us a very good idea of the early Bristol porcelains. Much, perhaps two-thirds of the output, was decorated under the glaze in blue, normally with Chinese-style water scenes with boats, islands and the like (Plate 30). They are somewhat sparsely decorated as if, rightly, to show to the best effect the quite pure porcelain body, still a novelty in the early 1750s. Also noteworthy are the relief-moulded borders and panel surrounds. Such designs were to be such a feature of the Worcester porcelains, of Lowestoft and of other factories but here perhaps we see the first essays in this so attractive and so English mode of ceramic decoration.

The porcelain body is not all that translucent but, in use, as long as the body is white, unblemished and stable the translucency of say a sauceboat is of little consequence–one does not hold it to the light.

The glaze is good, tight and does not craze, but it is prone to bubble and spot where thickly applied or where it has run in the firing. The cobalt-blue is often somewhat lighter in tone than on the slightly later Worcester pieces and there is a tendency for the blue to have run slightly in the firing, giving a somewhat smudged or hazy effect. However, for their period (1749–52) the available marked pieces show a good mastery of the then new art of porcelain manufacture, and one is not surprised to find that the partners found themselves being courted for a take-over bid by a consortium of rich merchants and others from Worcester who wished to participate in the porcelain adventure and obviously were in need of know-how and a supply of raw materials. This development will be explained on p. 135. Here I simply record the fact that in June 1751 the Worcester partners drew up their articles of association to purchase the secrets of the Bristol works, the proprietors of which were not to continue to make porcelain or to disclose the processes to others. The raw materials, moulds and other working materials, as well as some (or all) of the Bristol workforce, were transferred to Worcester where the transplant prospered. The final moments of the Bristol venture are recorded in the *Bristol Intelligencer* of 24 July 1752 where we read that the local manufactory was 'now united with the Worcester Porcelain Company where for the future the whole business will be carried on'.

'United' yes: the great difficulty left to us is to distinguish between Bristol and early Worcester porcelain. It is as difficult as differentiating between Worcester or Chelsea or Derby porcelain made in 1755 from that made in 1756, for there is a seemingly uninterrupted continuation. Some collectors will argue the point *ad infinitum* but really it makes very little difference if one of these delightful early pieces was made at Bristol in 1751 or at Worcester in 1753.

The late Herbert Eccles analysed one of the typical low sauceboats of the type shown in Plate 30. The result, published in the Victoria and Albert Museum booklet *Analysed Specimens of English Porcelain* (1922), reads:

	%
Silica	67·62
Alumina	4·61
Lime	2·64
Phosphoric Acid	2·00
Magnesia	13·28
Soda	1·61
Potash	1·15
Oxide of Lead	8·01
	———
	100·92

The Magnesia content is the important one, representing as it does some 40 per cent of soapstone, although the amount of Oxide of Lead is surprisingly high and unusual.

There are remarkably few of these early Bristol pieces outside the larger museums but the following books will offer some help–Dr Watney's *Blue and White* book, *The Illustrated Guide to Worcester Porcelain* by Henry Sandon (Barrie & Jenkins, London, 1969); *Worcester Porcelain* by Franklin A. Barrett (Faber, London, 1953, revised edition 1966) and H. Rissik Marshall's work *Coloured Worcester Porcelain of the First Period* (Ceramic Book Co., 1954).

Plate 30 A rare Lund's-Bristol relief-moulded blue and white sauceboat with the moulded mark 'Bristol', *c.* 1750. 8¼ inches long. *Geoffrey Godden, Chinaman*

BRISTOL HARD-PASTE PORCELAIN, *c.* 1770–1781

William Cookworthy seems to have carried out early, probably unsuccessful, experiments in hard-paste porcelain in the mid-1760s at Bristol before establishing his famous Plymouth works in 1768. However, he returned to Bristol in 1770 establishing there a factory which continued production for some eight years only. Richard Champion succeeded Cookworthy late in 1773 and it was Champion who later sold the patent-rights to produce translucent bodies containing Cornish Kaolin and Petuntse–the true or hard-paste type of porcelain (see p. 15).

The name of William Cookworthy is a very important one in English ceramics. He found in Cornwall the vital raw materials and had the necessary knowledge to make use of his discoveries, although it is doubtful if he profited greatly from the venture. Nevertheless, all three English hard-paste factories owe directly or indirectly their existence to this man–the father of the English china-clay industry. John Penderill-Church is the author of an interesting little book on this pioneer, *William Cookworthy 1705–1780* (Bradford Barton, Truro, 1972).

The Bristol true porcelains are somewhat neater and cleaner than the related earlier Plymouth porcelains–the glaze is noticeably better but the body did tend to tear slightly in turning, causing slight faults. The modest waste-bowl shown in Plate 31 illustrates well some of these characteristic defects. First, the body shows 'wreathing', a series of little ridges ('A') running like a spring or the thread of a screw around the piece. These marks are formed by the pull of the fingers or turning-tool as the piece is thrown or trimmed. Secondly, we can see at 'B' the small tears where the body was dug into during the turning or trimming process, and thirdly at 'C' we can see a 'firing crack' or opening of the body. Such firing cracks can occur in almost all porcelains but they are quite usual on these early hard-

Plate 31 A hard-paste Bristol bowl of the 1770s showing (A) turning ridges, (B) body tears and (C) firing crack. *Geoffrey Godden, Chinaman*

paste wares. A 'firing-crack' differs from a later impact crack in that it is slightly open and glaze has flowed into the opening. Such cracks are caused by the body contracting unevenly during the firing process. Unless very disfiguring or serious, these manufacturing faults are normally overlooked by collectors or rightly regarded as a helpful indication of origin or age.

In general the Bristol factory concentrated on tasteful enamelled designs often with a decided Continental air. To me the most attractive of the enamelled Bristol designs are the well-painted simple floral patterns or festoons of flowers painted with wet-looking colours. The gilding is restrained and elegant. Less successful are the rather poorly painted copies or adaptations of Chinese figure designs. These are normally painted on the simpler teaware shapes and this general class has given rise to the term 'cottage-Bristol'.

Apart from table-wares, mainly tea and dessert service forms, the Bristol factory made some very attractive figures, some of which bear the impressed mark 'T' or 'To' of the repairer (see p. 25), but the factory is perhaps best known for the very rare oval biscuit (unglazed) floral encrusted plaques, some of which bear initials or even armorial bearings in the centre.

The enamelled wares often have a copy of the Dresden crossed-swords mark (below) in a rather dull underglaze-blue. By the side of this the painter or gilder would add his personal tally-number in overglaze enamel or gold. Such a mark is here shown but very many examples of Bristol hard-paste porcelain are unmarked. The blue and white wares are decidedly scarce. In comparison with Worcester pieces (and such wares were copied at Bristol) they are rather unsatisfactory. One fancies that if they were not the product of a rather short-lived and collectable factory they would cause little or no excitement, although an advertisement in Aris's *Birmingham Gazette* of 1 February 1779 makes the claim: 'The blue and white is now brought to the greatest perfection equal to Nankeen, which with the very great strength and fine polish [glaze] renders it the best for use of any china now in the world.' Alas, this is an unwarranted claim but it does show us today that these underglaze-blue designs were made up to the final period of the factory's existence. We are in fact not very sure of the date of closure; the works were seemingly being run down as early as 1778 and Champion was in Staffordshire trying to sell his rights in November 1780. The Bristol factory closed in 1781 but probably production had ceased some time before this.

The blue designs were, in the main, Chinese-style landscapes, and some not very successful blue-printing was practised. When Bristol blue and white is marked one would expect the simple cross to appear rather than the crossed-swords mark, but remember that this simple cross device can occur on other wares, especially as a painter's tally-mark.

The late Herbert Eccles analysed a Bristol enamelled saucer and published the following result:

	%
Silica	69·96
Alumina	24·43
Lime	1·50
Phosphoric Acid	0·17
Magnesia	trace
Potash	1·36
Soda	1·92
Oxide of Lead	1·50

This is remarkably close to his analysis of a fragment of eighteenth-century Chinese hard-paste porcelain.

The literature on Bristol is sparse. We have two classics of the 1940s: F. Severne Mackenna's *Cookworthy's Plymouth and Bristol Porcelain* (F. Lewis Ltd, Leigh-on-Sea, 1946) and the same authority's *Champion's Bristol Porcelain* (F. Lewis Ltd, Leigh-on-Sea, 1947). Of more recent vintage we have Dr Watney's *Blue and White* book. Some typical Bristol forms and styles of decoration are featured in my *British Porcelain, an illustrated guide*.

CAUGHLEY (or 'SALOPIAN')
c. 1775–1799 and continued by the Coalport management

The Caughley porcelain works or the 'Royal Salopian Porcelain Manufactory' was situated on high ground in open countryside to the west of the River Severn, some two miles south of Broseley in Shropshire. The place-name is pronounced 'calf-ley', and it was to an existing pottery or earthenware factory there that Thomas Turner came in the early 1770s. Thomas Turner had formerly worked at the Worcester porcelain factory. He is mainly known as an engraver but he probably had a good all-round knowledge of porcelain production or was able to bring with him key personnel from Worcester. Certainly Robert Hancock, a fellow engraver from that factory (see p. 64), advertised in July 1775 that 'having disposed of his share in the Worcester work, he is now engaged in the Salopian china manufactory...the sole province of dealing in this manufactory, except in the London trade, being assigned over by Mr T. Turner & Co.'

The '& Co.' in the firm's trading style included Ambrose Gallimore who had been granted a sixty-two-year lease of the original Pottery in 1754. At least one example of Caughley porcelain is known with a circular printed mark which reads 'Turner Gallimore. Salopian'. The former pottery was rebuilt in about 1772 and a quite large open-plan porcelain factory was erected on the site. This had three kilns, as is evidenced by contemporary estate maps. The site was conveniently situated–clay for the saggers was readily available, as was coal, mined in the next field! and the site was reasonably near the River Severn, linking to the north with the Midland canal system and to the south with Worcester, Bristol and the coast shipping. The Caughley factory was also secluded; it still was in the last few years when I enjoyed many a pleasant picnic there with my wife while searching for 'wasters'.

For a long period the Caughley wares were regarded as inferior imitations of Worcester; if an example under discussion was finely made it was classed as Worcester, if poor it was relegated to Caughley. While it must be admitted that many shapes and patterns were made at both factories their classification is by no means as simple as the old rule would suggest. I submit that much Caughley is superior to Worcester of the same post-1775 period and I think pieces in my reference collection in Worthing substantiate my opinion. Happily, the old view permits us sometimes to purchase Caughley pieces for much less than would be charged for a Worcester example of the same type!

The Caughley factory produced in some twenty-four years between about 1775 and 1799 a very wide and interesting range of porcelains from buttons to large dinner-services. Many of the standard patterns are even now not particularly rare or costly and the Salopian wares can be considered one of the most collectable classes of English porcelain.

The basic Caughley body is of the soapstone type, very similar in make-up and appearance to Worcester. An analysis of one of my 'S' marked pieces bearing the standard blue-printed 'Fisherman' design gave the following result:

	%
Silica	75·25
Magnesia	11·06
Alumina	5·54
Potash	2·14
Phosphate	1·78
Lime	1·75
Soda	1·68
Ferric Oxide	0·49
	99·69

Worcester porcelain is very close to this analysis. The Caughley body often shows an orange tint by transmitted light, although it can also be quite greenish like the Worcester porcelains. The Caughley glaze is a good close-fitting one, colourless when applied at normal thickness but when gathered in pools it can have a greeny-blue tint. On many examples it is *very* slightly matt as if the piece has been breathed upon.

The body and glaze was in practice extremely workable like that used down-river at Worcester. This workable and stable body, coupled with the wide application of printed patterns in underglaze-blue (probably three-quarters of the factory's output comprised blue-printed designs), enabled Thomas Turner to compete not only with the established and renowned Worcester porcelains but also with the fashionable and by now inexpensive Chinese porcelains. Two typical Blue-printed teapots are shown in Plate 10. Speaking in terms of blue and white, Caughley, Worcester and the imported Chinese wares practically monopolised the market in the 1775–95 period and from 1785 the Worcester firm had almost ceased to produce these traditional blue and white wares, leaving Turner to fill the gap. This he did very successfully.

The Caughley factory seemingly produced only relatively simple overglaze designs. These can be very attractive, combining deep underglaze-blue with gilding, and of course the cost was quite low so that the durable wares must have sold readily in the vast middle-class market which Turner catered for with such success. I find particularly attractive some of the simple gilt Caughley tawares. This vast class of decoration is very neglected and does not, as yet, find the same

Plate 32 A Caughley teapot showing one of the simple gilt designs of the 1790 period. *Geoffrey Godden, Chinaman*

favour as even the simplest of the underglaze-blue designs. I illustrate a tastefully gilt example in Plate 32.

It is often thought that Thomas Turner was preoccupied with copying Worcester shapes or designs, and collectors have jumped to the conclusion that it was Caughley that copied Worcester pieces. This is by no means proven. With the most popular of Caughley printed designs the 'Fisherman'–or 'Pleasure boat' design, to give it the original title–it seems more than likely that Worcester copied Caughley. Other designs found on both types of porcelain may have been introduced by Turner himself while engraving for Worcester before he moved north to Caughley, so that in a sense they are Turner's own designs. I would also make the point that very many Caughley designs do not occur on Worcester or any other porcelains; they are unique to the Caughley factory.

There is a very interesting class of Caughley porcelain that displays a decided French influence, sometimes in the adaption of Continental forms but more commonly in the use of simple sprig motifs in the style of Chantilly and other

Plate 33 A French-style Caughley porcelain custard-cup painted in underglaze-blue, *c.* 1795. *Geoffrey Godden Chinaman*

French porcelains that enjoyed an international market (see Plate 33). These simple floral motifs could be in underglaze-blue or in overglaze enamels. Once again Thomas Turner successfully copied popular designs that could be produced at little cost, an almost certain road to success.

Much Caughley porcelain was shipped down to Chamberlain's Worcester decorating establishment to be embellished before being forwarded to Turner's London warehouse or shipped back up-river to Caughley for distribution from there.

I cannot in this general book deal with the mass of accounts and other records which we have relating to Caughley porcelain or with the tons of 'wasters' found within recent years at the factory site. I certainly cannot give detailed information on the slight variations between the very similar Caughley and Worcester shapes and patterns; all this is given at length in my specialist book *Caughley and Worcester Porcelains 1775–1800* (Barrie & Jenkins, London, 1969). I can however make some basic points:

(a) The Caughley glaze was cut back from the inside of the foot-rim like Worcester. This fact is shown time and again in 'wasters' from the factory site (Plate 6) and by clearly marked completed pieces. This is *not* a sure sign of Worcester origin, see p. 28.

(b) The shaded printed-crescent mark was *not* used at Caughley; it is a Worcester mark.

(c) The 'disguised numeral marks' similar to those shown are Worcester marks *not* Caughley.

(d) You cannot tell Caughley from Worcester by judging quality alone.

Caughley wares were not sent to the main Worcester factory to be decorated. All underglaze-blue decoration is Caughley work although *some* enamelling and gilding was added at Chamberlain's works. Most other reference books make exactly opposite suggestions but my points are accurate and are supported in detail in my specialist book on the Caughley and Worcester porcelains.

The Caughley factory marks comprise the word 'Salopian' impressed but in practice this mark is found only on dishes, plates and such flat-based objects. The initial 'S', however, occurs printed in underglaze-blue on a multitude of objects large and small. On pieces bearing a blue-printed design the 'S' will be printed too but sometimes a hand-painted and small 'o' or 'x' was added resulting in 'So' or 'Sx' markings. On hand-painted blue designs the 'S' is also painted and the extra letters do not occur.

The capital initial 'C' from Caughley was also employed both in hand-painted and more often printed versions. On the rare powder-blue ground pieces mock-Chinese characters (not numerals) occur. With the exception of the very rare and early 'Gallimore Turner' mark (p. 86) Thomas Turner did not use his own name as an identification, relying on the initial 'C' for the then little-known place-name Caughley or the county designation 'Salopian' (Shropshire) or its initial letter 'S'.

It seems likely that in the late 1790s the basic soapstone-type body was changed to a type of hybrid hard-paste; this development is covered in the next chapter.

In October 1799 Turner sold the Caughley works as a going concern to the partners working the nearby Coalport factory–John Rose, Edward Blakeway and Richard Rose. Turner sold much of his stock by auction in Shrewsbury but the Caughley factory was continued by John Rose for some fifteen years and the story of this later period is told in the Coalport section.

Most books published before the late-1960s are rather unreliable concerning the Caughley wares as the authors did not have access to the finds since made on the factory site, so that pieces we know to be Worcester are shown as Caughley, incorrect facts are given on the factory marks and other important matters. Our current knowledge is I believe well explained in my *Caughley and Worcester Porcelains 1775–1800*, which features over three hundred helpful illustrations. Several magazine articles also shed light on our new knowledge; these include *Collectors Guide* of October 1967, August 1968 and the same magazine's special 'World of Antiques' issue of October 1968, also the *Connoisseur*, May 1969 and *Burlington Magazine* of January 1969. The catalogue of the 1972 Bicentenary Exhibition held at the Shrewsbury Art Gallery is also a most helpful record.

Good collections of Caughley porcelain can be seen at the Victoria and Albert Museum in London and at the Clive House Museum at Shrewsbury while my own reference collection at Worthing (p. 242) includes a representative selection of wares and factory 'wasters'. A Godden tape-recorded talk linked with this collection is available (see p. 277).

CHAMBERLAINS, c. 1788–1852

To the name Chamberlain we normally add the place-name 'Worcester', giving rise to descriptions such as 'A fine Chamberlain-Worcester figure-painted vase'. We cannot use the place-name alone for from the 1780s to the present century there were two and sometimes three different firms producing fine porcelain within the city of Worcester.

Robert Chamberlain, the founder of the firm we are discussing, was apprenticed to the main so-called Dr Wall porcelain company. In fact he is said to have been its first apprentice in the 1750s. Robert was to specialise in the decorating side of the Dr Wall concern and, in the 1770s, it would appear that he and his son Humphrey were in charge of this all-important department. However, after Thomas Flight took over the works in 1783 Robert Chamberlain and his son left, and in about 1786 they established their own decorating establishment in Worcester. At first and for a period of about two years they, with their team of decorators, seem to have been employed in embellishing the Flight porcelains by contract or other arrangement but in 1788 or early in 1789 the Chamberlains broke with the Flight management at the former Dr Wall factory and they now were supplied with blanks (undecorated porcelain) by their former colleague Thomas Turner of the Caughley porcelain factory (see p. 86). Thomas Turner had also loaned Robert Chamberlain a large sum of money and they were in fact at this early period business partners, the Chamberlains not only decorating for Turner but also affording a valuable retail outlet for Caughley porcelains in Worcester. Some of this Caughley porcelain was enamelled and gilt to Turner's express orders and was returned to him or forwarded to his London warehouse on completion. Other Caughley wares were purchased outright by the Chamberlains and sold by them after being embellished. On 27 June 1789 the Chamberlains opened their retail shop at 33 High Street, Worcester. These premises were in fact previously used by Flight's, so that the Chamberlains must

Plate 34 A Caughley 'cabbage-leaf' jug decorated in Chamberlain's Worcester decorating establishment and shown in the accounts of September 1789. *Geoffrey Godden, Chinaman*

have gained some of Flight's former customers who returned to a shop that had now changed ownership. In reading contemporary documents one gains the strong impression that Chamberlain and Flight were very keen rivals and that they were hardly on speaking terms, enticing away each other's decorators! The typical Caughley 'cabbage-leaf' jug shown in Plate 34 would appear to be that ordered at the Chamberlain shop by a Mrs Hooper on 26 September 1789. The order book reads ' 1 pint jug fawn and gold ciphered SMH'. These initials appear in gold on the front of this early example of Chamberlain's decoration on a Caughley porcelain blank.

In about 1791 and certainly by 1793 the Chamberlains had decided to branch out and become porcelain manufacturers as well as decorators. For some years, however, they continued to decorate some Caughley porcelains but by 1796 the majority of the porcelains were of Chamberlain's own manufacture and he was receiving Royal orders and had built up an export trade.

The early Chamberlain porcelains, especially the tea-services, were decorated in a simple manner, with floral sprigs etc, or with Chinese-style designs (see Plate 35) but many vases and other ornamental pieces were decorated in the richest style– rivalling the contemporary Flight or Derby porcelains. The post-1800 history of the Chamberlain partnership is given in Chapter 8 and I have purposely started the story in this present section to make the point that the Chamberlain decorating establishment and manufactory were established in the eighteenth century and that very fine pieces were being produced. Some have regarded Chamberlain's as a second-class factory, but this is not so. In workmanship and decoration the Chamberlain wares excel many other types; it is a very under-rated factory and the wares will repay the attention of collectors.

Plate 35 An early Chamberlain teapot following a basic New Hall shape, see Plate 11, *c.* 1795. 5¼ inches high. *Geoffrey Godden, Chinaman*

'How can I recognise Chamberlain's porcelains?' A good question. The early Chamberlain body is discussed in Chapter 6 and this hard-looking body is quite helpful to the trained eye of a person who has seen and handled key-pieces. From about 1794 pattern-numbers appear painted under the base of useful wares, near the foot-rim. From about this period we find hand-painted name-marks painted *inside* the covers of teapots and sugar-bowls but not normally on other pieces from the teaset. These painted marks normally comprise 'Chamberlains', 'Chamberlains Worcester' or 'Chamberlains/Worcester/Warranted' (the words one above the other), with the number of the pattern added below. Later, in the nineteenth century various printed name-marks were employed, see p. 196. The best guide, however, is the shape, for very many of the early pieces were unmarked and a very good selection of the characteristic forms will be featured in a forthcoming Godden book devoted to the Chamberlain porcelains. The Chamberlain-decorated Caughley porcelains of the late 1780s and early 1790s do not appear to bear any special mark and they are normally regarded purely as Caughley pieces although it would seem more correct to link the name of the decorator to the place of origin, 'Caughley-Chamberlain'.

For further information on Chamberlain wares see p. 193.

CHELSEA, *c.* 1745–1769

Chelsea is the most famous English porcelain factory and yet we are still not at all sure of its exact location in the Chelsea district of London or of the exact year of establishment.

What we do know is that it was producing quite sophisticated pieces by 1745, such as the moulded Goat and Bee jugs, some of which bear this date incised under the base (see p. 95). They are obviously not trial pieces nor early experimental wares. These jugs and other objects of the same period owe much in inspiration to contemporary silver-wares and we should remember that Nicholas Sprimont (1716–71), the manager of the factory for most of its history, was originally a silversmith.

The Chelsea-body varied greatly during the factory's life, but it was always of the soft-paste variety. This and the related glazes have a warm, friendly feel and prior to about 1755 the glaze was whitened with oxide of tin: such pieces have a waxy cream-like appearance.

Apart from the very early examples which were often unadorned with enamels or gilding, the Chelsea porcelains were the most richly decorated of English eighteenth-century ceramics and in general the management seems to have set its sights on the higher-class market, producing ornate pieces for the rich.

Extremely few examples were decorated in underglaze-blue, this relatively inexpensive class of production being left almost entirely to the Bow factory. Many of the Chelsea products were sold by public auction, mainly in London. These fashionable gatherings afford us today valuable information on changing styles and

Plate 36 (Left) The base of a Chelsea 'goat and bee' jug showing incised triangle mark, 1745. *Rous Lench Collection*

Plate 37 (Below) The base of a Chelsea cup showing the rare and early trident mark in underglaze-blue, *c.* 1745–48. *Sotheby & Co.*

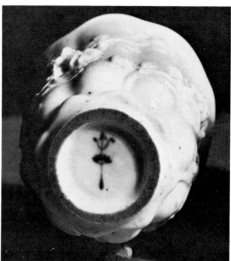

models as several of the original printed catalogues have survived and are quoted in several specialist books on Chelsea wares.

The various periods of Chelsea porcelain are conveniently classified by reference to the marks then employed, normally the anchor in various forms and colours. Before discussing these, however, I must mention two early marks, rather odd-men-out. First, we have the incised triangle mark as found on the Goat and Bee jugs and other pieces of about 1745 (Plate 36). Do note that I said 'incised' not impressed or ground-in; in other words the triangle-device should have a spontaneous appearance with a slightly ploughed-up look–as if you had drawn such a mark with a matchstick in butter or cheese. The other early mark which we regard as of Chelsea origin is painted in underglaze-blue (although this colour may not have been used in the decoration) and comprises a trident piercing a crown (Plate 37).

We can now discuss the succession of anchor marks. The first version of the Chelsea anchor was relief-moulded on a small applied oval pad; this is called the 'raised-anchor' mark and its probable period of employment was but three years, 1749–52. The raised-anchor can be picked out in red enamel (Plate 38). Such examples may represent transitional pieces made in the raised-anchor period but decorated in the following red-anchor period. The standard body was a glassy, frit-paste with the waxy cream-like whitened or semi-opaque glaze. This same body and glaze was carried over to the next period, *c.* 1752–6, known as the 'red-anchor' period, because a *small* anchor was neatly painted in a red enamel. Note how in the

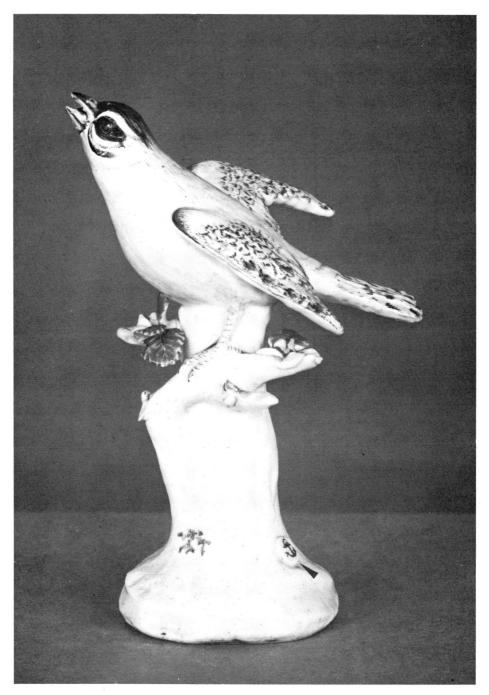

Plate 38 A Chelsea bird model showing the raised anchor mark which, in this case, is picked out in red, *c. 1749–52. Victoria and Albert Museum (Crown Copyright)*

(C) A superb quality two-piece bulb-pot or flower container in hybrid hard-paste porcelain tentatively attributed to Enoch Wood. 10 inches high, *c.* 1800–1805.

See p. 175.

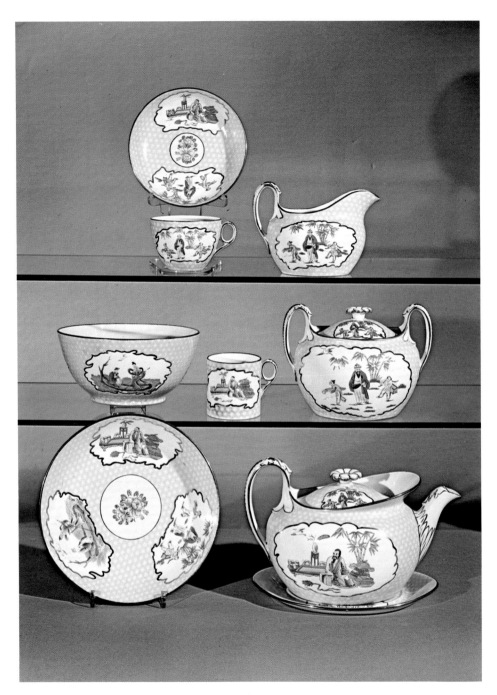

(D) An attractive Wedgwood bone-china part-teaset showing typical forms. Printed name mark and pattern number 566. Teapot $6\frac{1}{4}$ inches high, c. 1815.

See p. 187.

bowl shown in Plate 39 the anchor mark is tucked away near the foot-rim and how small it is. Large, blatantly positioned marks should be treated with caution.

If a red-anchor saucer-dish or plate is held to a light, small light coloured 'moons' or stars can be seen (Plate 40). These seem to have been caused by small air-pockets within the piece and although some Longton Hall porcelains display the same faults, they are a good guide to pre-1760 Chelsea porcelains. When defects appear on the surface, like exploding 'stars' or spots in the glaze, the painters very often camouflaged these by over-painting them with insects, or floral-sprays, for manufacturing processes had by no means been perfected and slight faults were accepted. Foot-rims would normally need to be ground flat before the plate or dish would 'sit' on a table. The three little pimple-like marks under a Chelsea dish or plate are not defects but rather the marks left by the 'stilts' or 'spurs' on which the piece rested in the glost-kiln, so raising the glazed plate from the kiln-shelf or from another plate, to prevent the glaze gluing the pieces together (see p. 30 and Plate 8). Notable very pleasing and characteristic enamelled designs included animal fable subjects (Plate 41), attributed to the hand of O'Neale, and botanical studies, although flower-sprays remained the standard mode of decoration supported by the

Plate 39 A red-anchor marked Chelsea bowl of the early 1750s showing the relatively small size of the mark. Diameter of bowl 7 inches. *Geoffrey Godden, Chinaman*

Plate 40 A Chelsea saucer of the 1750s showing by transmitted light so-called 'moons' or lighter patches. *Geoffrey Godden, Chinaman*

simple Japanese-style patterns which were perhaps copied second-hand from Continental copies of the Oriental originals.

The next main period of Chelsea porcelain is the gold-anchor period, *c.* 1756–69. Here the mark is in gold–providing the piece bears some gilding. This is by far the longest period, but I must point out that some late red-anchor and early gold-anchor wares of a more ordinary nature bore an anchor painted in brown enamel (this tends to be of a rather larger size than the red anchor), and some of the very rare blue and white pieces bore a blue anchor. In general the gold-anchor marked porcelains are very richly decorated (often with ground colours) and ornately gilt, so much so that in my early days it was popularly thought that the colour of the anchor was related to the quality of the piece not to its period of manufacture. This is not the case. Indeed modern taste prefers the earlier rather sparsely decorated wares to the more richly decorated and once extremely popular and expensive gold-anchor examples.

In this gold-anchor period or late in the red-anchor period the body was changed to a bone-ash type containing about 40 per cent bone-ash. A gold-anchor plate analysed by the late Herbert Eccles gave the following result:

	%
Silica	45·52
Alumina	12·06
Lime	26·00
Phosphoric Acid	14·27
Soda	0·73
Potash	0·93

The change is more apparent in the lead-glaze which, being thickly applied, tends to break up into that network of fine lines we call crazing. It is also clear or only

Plate 41 A Chelsea fluted dish painted with fable panel in the O'Neale style, *c.* 1752. *Messrs Sotheby &*
Co.

slightly coloured rather than being whitened by the addition of tin oxide. These different glazes can readily be contrasted by examining pieces in available collections.

While Chelsea porcelain has always enjoyed a very high reputation, at least in England, it must be stated that the potting is very often thick, the pieces are on the heavy side and the glaze is far from perfect–if we accept that such a covering should be translucent and well fitting, free of crazing.

I have pointed out that the various periods into which we divide up the Chelsea porcelains are related to the different types or colours of the anchor marks: the raised anchor, the red anchor and the gold anchor. We must remember, however, that the dates given are dates of convenience to us today. They are approximate only and there was probably some overlap when two different marks were used. One must also remember that by no means all Chelsea porcelain is marked; probably less than half was marked and that is why a study of the body, the glaze and the potting features is so important and why collectors should familiarise themselves with marked and authentic pieces.

I have added 'authentic' because so many fakes and reproductions are on the market. These pieces normally boast a prominent anchor (usually in gold) about twice the size of the real Chelsea anchor. Always question any anchor mark measuring over a quarter of an inch in height. The fakes are nearly always in a glittery hard-paste porcelain but some were made well over a hundred years ago so that they are 'antiques' in their own right and have acquired a pedigree. Remember always, a mark is easy to fake and several factories other than Chelsea used this device. Until you are quite sure of your subject you are well advised to buy your Chelsea from a reputable source, forsaking the bargain find in some back-street shop. You should bear in mind too that wares bearing a painted or printed designation 'Chelsea' are not from that factory. Such markings usually relate to the style of decoration applied to some twentieth-century porcelains or even earthenwares (see also p. 256).

I cannot discuss here the many fine figures and groups produced at Chelsea or the charming little 'toys', the seals and scent bottles, but these aspects of the factory's production are well covered in specialist books, for example *English Porcelain Figures of the 18th Century* by A. Lane (Faber, London, 1961) and G. E. Bryant's classic work *Chelsea Porcelain Toys* (Medici Society, London, 1925). Other very useful books on Chelsea porcelain in general include *Chelsea Porcelain, the triangle and raised-anchor wares*; *Chelsea Porcelain, the red-anchor wares*; *Chelsea Porcelain, the gold-anchor period*, all three by F. S. Mackenna (F. Lewis Ltd, Leigh-on-Sea, 1948, 1951 and 1952 respectively). The Chelsea section (by J. V. G. Mallet) in *English Porcelain 1745–1850*, edited by R. J. Charleston, is also most instructive, and a good selection of Chelsea porcelains are featured in my *Illustrated Encyclopaedia of British Pottery and Porcelain* and my *British Porcelain, an illustrated guide*.

In August 1769 the Chelsea premises, plus all the working materials, were put up for sale, after a life of some twenty-five years during which some superb porcelains were made. The factory in fact continued for a further period until 1784, as it was purchased and continued by William Duesbury of the Derby factory. These later wares of the 1770–84 period are termed (I think incorrectly) 'Chelsea-Derby' and they are the subject of the next section, p. 103.

Before leaving Chelsea I must at least mention a separate class of porcelain which we normally think of as an offshoot of Chelsea. I refer to the so-called 'Girl in the Swing' pieces, named after the model shown in Plate 42. It is a typical example with its rather wooden modelling and overgrown leaves, many of which are larger than the girls head! These porcelains which show on analysis an unusually high lead content (about 16 per cent) were perhaps sold through the 'Chelsea China Warehouse' in St James's, the manager of which reported in January 1751 that 'My China Warehouse is not supply'd by any other person than Mr Charles Gouyn late Proprietor and Chief Manager of the Chelsea-House, who continues to supply me with the most curious goods of that manufacture, as well useful as ornamental.' We cannot be sure now if these goods were of Gouyn's new and separate manufacture–the 'Girl in the Swing' porcelains–or if he was supplying the St James' warehouse with old stock from the main factory.

Certainly, we do not know where the 'Girl in the Swing' class of figures were made or even the exact duration of the concern. This is usually regarded as a mere six years from *c.* 1749 to 1754 but it may have lasted slightly longer. The wares are extremely rare and costly, exciting much interest when a specimen comes on the market. While some of the 'toys' such as fancy scent bottles of the type shown by Miss Kate Foster in her paper printed in the *Transactions of the English Ceramic Circle* (vol. 6, part 3, 1967) are attractive as are the very scarce teawares, the figures have little charm or technical excellence and one wonders what demand they would attract if they were made today and offered in the normal retail markets. Nevertheless, if you see any little figures or birds standing on a base like that shown

Plate 42 The celebrated 'Girl in the Swing' figure from which this class is named, *c.* 1750. 6¼ inches high. *Victoria and Albert Museum (Crown Copyright)*

in Plate 43, then you are almost certainly looking at the rarest class of English porcelain.

Strangely the figures and bird models outnumber the table-wares but this is probably only because we as yet know so little about these wares. The 'Girl in the Swing' useful wares await identification, for as yet only one type of enamelled decoration—floral sprays—seems to have been recognised. I should mention that Dr Watney has, in the *Transactions of the English Ceramic Circle* (vol. 8, part 2, 1972), suggested a possible link between some pieces we attribute to Derby of the 1750s and the 'Girl in the Swing' class. Much research needs to be carried out on the source of this rare group.

Plate 43 A 'Girl in the Swing'-class bird model on typical shaped base, *c.* 1750. 5¼ inches high. *Geoffrey Godden, Chinaman*

The extent of our present knowledge of this rare class of London porcelain is set out in the *Transactions of the English Ceramic Circle* (vol. 5, part 3, 1962), in an interesting paper by R. J. Charleston and the late Arthur Lane. Some typical pieces are featured in my *British Porcelain, an illustrated guide.*

CHELSEA-DERBY, *c.* 1770–1784

The Chelsea premises and working materials were put up for sale in August 1769 and were sold to James Cox but were resold to the well-known and established Derby porcelain manufacturer William Duesbury in February 1770. He must have been well pleased with the great prestige which this new acquisition gave him.

William Duesbury continued production at Chelsea and employed several of the former hands, as is evidenced by the wage-records and other documents quoted by Llewellynn Jewitt in his book *The Ceramic Art of Great Britain* (Virtue & Co., London, first edition, 1878). The porcelains made at Chelsea within the Duesbury period, 1770–84, are referred to as 'Chelsea-Derby'. However, the Derby influence is hardly marked and Duesbury himself in his advertisements and sale notices rightly and understandably referred to the goods being offered as Chelsea porcelain, his trade-card reading 'Duesbury & Co., Manufacturers of Derby and Chelsea Porcelain'. The position is today complicated by the fact that a large class of figures and groups which seem to have no links at all with the Chelsea factory are also called 'Chelsea-Derby', although they appear to be purely of Derby manufacture and of a period before Duesbury took over the Chelsea factory!

It would be very convenient if we could designate all porcelain made at Chelsea before the buildings were demolished in 1784 as 'Chelsea', regardless of the ownership of the works, and all porcelain made at Derby as 'Derby' but at the moment we seem terribly muddled in our thinking. The situation was, and is, admittedly complicated for there was some interchange of moulds, clay and workmen between the two factories, and the very real difficulty of distinguishing between the Chelsea and the Derby porcelains of the 1770s probably gave rise to the joint term 'Chelsea-Derby' as an easy way out of the problem.

The pair of large vessels shown in Plate 44 are of interest as they were almost certainly those included in a Duesbury & Co. sale held in May 1781 and described then as 'a pair of uncommonly large octagon jars (near two feet high) decorated with natural flowers and finely enamel'd with figures, landscapes &c, richly ornamented with chas'd and burnished gold, the figures represent a votaress of Baccus and Innocence washing her hands at an altar'. These vases bear the gold-anchor mark and should, I believe, be classed as Chelsea, although they were made in 1780 or 1781, some ten years after the works were sold to Duesbury.

The table-ware designs which we normally attribute to the Chelsea-Derby period are quite different in general feeling to these vases. They are decorated in a restrained classical manner, with swags and festoons of flowers etc, and seem much

Plate 44 A pair of so-called Chelsea-Derby vases, a pair sold in May 1781. 22 inches high. *Messrs Christies*

more associated with the Derby factory than with Chelsea. The wares are thinner in the potting than the earlier gold-anchor period Chelsea wares and the gilding often has a tendency to peel from the body, a fault found with Derby wares of about this period. The accounts relating to the early period of Duesbury's ownership of the Chelsea factory were available in the nineteenth century and some of these are quoted in Llewellynn Jewitt's *Ceramic Art of Great Britain*. These show that small 'toys' such as seals, thimbles and scent bottles were being made in large quantities, also many vases and busts on pedestals. We also find entries such as '48 compotiers [dishes] all made with the Darby clay, 24 ornemental plates, made with ditto'. Such Chelsea-made objects of 'Darby clay' puzzle us today but I believe they should be regarded as true Chelsea and certainly they were decorated at this famous London factory.

The Chelsea works under Duesbury appear to have been gradually run down as workmen were transferred to Derby or were otherwise lost to the London factory. The main value of the purchase was probably prestige and the right to use the Chelsea gold-anchor mark (Duesbury had in fact previously on occasions used the anchor device on his own wares), but as time wore on Duesbury no doubt found that he could not efficiently manage both factories, so in 1784 the last of the Chelsea buildings was demolished and the remaining useful materials transferred to Derby.

Apart from the so-called 'Chelsea-Derby' figures–which I regard as purely Derby–the 'Chelsea-Derby' wares are often marked. These marks are normally in gold and comprise the following basic devices:

The crowned-anchor mark is quite rare and should probably be regarded as a Derby mark, while in general the gold anchor occurs on pieces which I regard as of Chelsea manufacture. The conjoined D and anchor mark is found largely on porcelains which I believe are of Derby manufacture, the mark perhaps signifying the joint management controlling both the Chelsea and Derby factories. This broad and general classification by marks will be questioned by many and I cannot myself believe that the matter is closed. We will be debating for years the true origin of the porcelains classed as 'Chelsea-Derby'. These porcelains of the 1770–84 period do not bear a pattern number.

Typical 'Chelsea-Derby' porcelains are featured in several books on Derby porcelain such as F. B. Gilhespy's *Crown Derby Porcelain* (F. Lewis, Leigh-on-Sea, 1951) or his *Derby Porcelain* (Spring Books, London, 1965). Some other examples are shown in my *British Porcelain, an illustrated guide*.

COALPORT, *c.* 1796 to the present day

The Coalport porcelain works were established and in production at least by June 1796 but I must delay our discussion of these little-known early wares to Chapter 6. The post-1820 examples are featured in Chapter 8.

DAVENPORT, *c.* 1793–1887

The Davenport works at Longport in the Staffordshire Potteries were established in the 1790s but the early products would appear to be limited to earthenwares. The Davenport porcelains are discussed in Chapter 6.

DERBY, *c.* 1750 to the present day

Although I have indicated before that the production of porcelain in the city of Derby has been spread over two hundred years or more, it has not been a continuous progression on one factory site. There are several periods and types of Derby porcelain and we are concerned at the moment only with the eighteenth-century pieces, later developments being revealed in Chapters 8 and 9.

The early history of the Derby works is not at all clear but on the evidence of some white jugs with the incised initial 'D' and in one case also the date 1750, the factory was in production at this period. I must point out in passing that these jugs now seem very similar to some early Chelsea and 'Girl in the Swing' porcelains of the same period. One Andrew Planche 'china-maker' had a largely unknown but probably important part to play in the establishment of the porcelain industry in Derby, with John Heath. However, the prime-mover was undoubtedly William Duesbury who started his ceramic career as an independent decorator and after building up the reputation of the Derby factory as the 'Second-Dresden' (to use his own description!) he was able in 1770 to purchase the Chelsea works.

The earliest Derby porcelains were made in about 1750 by 'Heath & Co', that is by John Heath and Andrew Planche. We have an unsigned agreement dated 1 January 1756 showing that William Duesbury 'Enammelor' then agreed to join Heath and Andrew Planche 'china-maker' as co-partners to produce 'English China'. Duesbury continued until his death in 1786 when he was succeeded by his son of the same name.

The early Derby porcelains are of soft-paste porcelain, which is somewhat open in texture and lighter in weight than contemporary Bow or Chelsea. The figures and other moulded wares are slip-cast (p. 21), a fact that accentuates the light feeling of the wares. The glaze is normally free of crazing and is tight-fitting and thinner than the Chelsea glazes with less tendency to pool, or run. Great care was taken to keep the bases of figures clear of glaze so that they would not stick to the kiln-furniture and would need little or no grinding after the pieces came from the kiln. To accomplish this, the glaze was stopped short of the bottom edge, or the edge was chamfered or trimmed at an angle giving rise to the description 'dry-edge'. Later, from about 1755, the Derby wares were kept clear of the sagger or other kiln-furniture by being placed on three or more clay-blobs or 'pads'. These separators left showing slightly darker 'pad-marks' or 'patch marks', which are a good guide to a Derby origin, see p. 30 and Plate 7.

Duesbury's early pre-1770 porcelains are rarely gilt; they are not as pretentious as the Dresden and Chelsea pieces which inspired so much of his productions, especially the figures and groups. It is these figure models that built Duesbury's reputation in the early days. His useful wares are now quite scarce and not really startling and while some blue and white porcelains were produced they do not have the charm and 'life' of some other makes, nor do they show the crisp workmanship of the Worcester examples. The rare enamelled table-wares are normally painted

Plate 45 Two typical Derby biscuit (unglazed) groups of the 1790s. 10 and 12½ inches high. *Godden of Worthing Ltd*

with flowers in rather dry-looking colours; the flowers grow on very thin cotton-like stems. Other pieces are painted with simple Chinese-figure designs.

The figures and groups of the general type often classed as 'Chelsea-Derby' are, as I have noted, almost certainly purely of Derby manufacture. In the 1770s we have the introduction of the beautiful white biscuit (unglazed) Derby figures and groups (Plate 45). These are of superb workmanship and only the finest unblemished examples were sold in this white state.

The slightly faulty models were glazed and coloured to mask the defects; we therefore have the situation that originally the undecorated examples cost more than the gaily coloured pieces. In general these white models with their wonderfully sharp modelling are not appreciated as they should be. You should bear in mind that by no means all unglazed white figures are of Derby origin, for the idea came from the French Sèvres factory and many other Continental manufacturers made such wares but these to British eyes are too white and cold looking and in many cases the hard-porcelain has an unpleasant feel–I am not

Plate 46 A finely decorated Derby saucer of the puce-mark period (see p. 109) painted with monochrome scene, *c.* 1790. Diameter 5½ inches. *Geoffrey Godden, Chinaman*

speaking here of the early Sèvres examples which are delightful but rather simpler than the Derby pieces. A good account of the Derby biscuit wares is given in a paper by Timothy Clifford in the *Transactions of the English Ceramic Circle* (vol. 7, part 2, 1969).

By the 1780s the Derby body had become very smooth and almost waxy to the touch. It was coated with a soft, warm and pleasant-feeling glaze (whitened rather than clear) which tended to form a scum-line at the edges near the foot-rim. The useful table-wares now became a more important feature of the factory's production. Very tasteful simple forms were embellished with fine quality painting, notably landscape subjects (Plate 46) and floral designs (but what flower-painters!– one, William Billingsley, is perhaps better known than Duesbury himself). Unusual seascapes, battle-scenes and the like can also be found. These expensive Derby porcelains of 1780–1800 may be regarded as the finest of the period–surpassing in delicacy and charm the Worcester porcelains and totally outclassing the Caughley, Liverpool and Lowestoft wares. Derby's nearest rival was the almost related small works at Pinxton, nearest in geographical terms as well as in quality, see p. 128.

Before about 1774 the Derby porcelains were seldom or never marked, except for those pieces which bear the Chelsea anchor-mark, but now a mark became more usual and by 1800 one can almost say that if a piece is not marked it is not Derby. The first real standard Derby porcelain mark comprised the cursive capital letter 'D' under a crown. This normally occurs painted in blue enamel but it can occur in other tints. Being hand-painted, many slight variations in drawing may be expected, all within the period c. 1774–82. This mark is by no means common.

The Derby porcelains made before the 1770s should not be called 'Crown-Derby'. This term, if used at all, relates to the post-1770 period and the description 'Duesbury Derby' is preferable for eighteenth-century wares. Many Derby porcelain useful wares made before say 1790 bear an incised cursive 'N'. This is under the glaze and added during manufacture. Although its significance is now uncertain it serves us today as a useful guide to a Derby origin. By this period the Derby body contained some 40 per cent of bone-ash. A very rare mark comprises the words 'Duesbury London' painted in a neat manner, one word above the other. This mark no doubt relates to the London showrooms but, by its rarity, by no means all pieces sold there could have been so marked.

The next standard painted mark (found also incised on figures) is the first of a series of so-called 'crossed baton' marks. Here, placed between the crown and the initial 'D', are two crossed sticks or batons with three dots added at each end. This mark would seem to have been introduced in about 1782. At first it was very neatly painted, very often in a puce coloured enamel (rarely in blue, black or gold), and with this mark we get for the first time pattern or other numbers added below the mark. Perhaps this application of pattern numbers to Derby porcelains of the 1780s marks the first use of such numbers on any English ceramics–see p. 257. The red-painted version of this mark is of a post-1800 period and as time progressed the mark was sometimes very hastily painted, as you can observe by comparing the neat puce colour mark of the 1790–1800 period (above) with the red mark of the 1820s–a typical specimen of which is shown overleaf.

Continental copies of Derby porcelain occur with standard Derby marks, but the porcelain is hard and the gilding flat and no one should be fooled by them—providing authentic pieces have been examined. The later so-called Stevenson & Hancock porcelains made at the separate King Street works in Derby can mislead some people, as at first the old Derby mark was employed and even when the additional initials 'SH' appear some new collectors do not realise their significance.

The second William Duesbury succeeded his father in 1786, but he in turn died in 1797. I propose to leave the present discussion of Derby porcelains at this point and to take it up afresh when we move on to deal with the nineteenth-century porcelains in Chapter 8. Useful specialist books on the Derby wares are: *Crown Derby Porcelain* by F. B. Gilhespy (F. Lewis, Leigh-on-Sea, 1951); *Derby Porcelain* by F. B. Gilhespy (MacGibbon & Kee, London, 1961); and *Derby Porcelain* by F. A. Barrett and A. L. Thorpe (Faber, London, 1971).

A good general display of Derby wares is to be seen in the Derby Museum, in the museum gallery at the Royal Crown Derby works, and of course there is a very good selection at the Victoria and Albert Museum in London.

GILES, *c.* 1760–1780

We are not really dealing with a make of porcelain in this short section but rather with an independent decorator, independent in that he was not employed by a factory but decorated on his own account blanks purchased from various sources.

There were in the eighteenth century many such independent decorators. Probably the best known of these decorators was James Giles, but few books give any clear account of his work and the available information is rather scattered. I must exempt from this statement the excellent account of Giles's work given by H. Rissik Marshall in his book *Coloured Worcester Porcelain of the First Period* (Ceramic Book Co., Newport, Mon., 1954) but this is a very scarce and expensive book.

James Giles was born in 1718, the son of James Giles. An apprentice record of June 1729 describes James Giles senior or his son Abraham (the record is not clear which is meant) as a 'china-painter' bound to Philip Margas. Two points are interesting here, first that there was a trade of china-painting at this early date long before the English had learnt to make porcelain but this is perhaps explained by my second point—that Margas was a leading 'chinaman' or dealer of the period and was a very large purchaser of Oriental porcelains imported by the English East India Company.

James Giles junior was apprenticed to John Arthur, jeweller, of St Martin-in-the-Fields, London, in 1733 and by November 1747 he was described in a Poll list as a 'chinaman' at Berwick Street. At this period the porcelains he dealt with would most probably have been Chinese but he could have stocked some early Bow or Chelsea wares.

If we are to believe the history accompanying the 'Craft' bowl of Bow make, now in the British Museum, Giles or Gyles as his name was sometimes written, had a kiln for firing enamelled porcelains at Kentish Town in about the year 1760 and he may have been practising as a independent china-painter a few years prior to this. Mortimer's Directory of 1763 lists James Giles 'China and Enamel Painter' at 82 Berwick Street, Soho. (Enamel in this context perhaps refers to the decoration of glass.) The entry continues: 'This ingenious artist copies patterns of any china with the utmost exactness...either in the European or Chinese taste...' Giles also had by 1767 a warehouse in Cockspur Street which he was wont to call the 'Worcester Porcelain Warehouse' and in a 1767 advertisement he claims to have available 'a great variety of articles of the said manufactory, useful and ornamental...'

A sale notice relating to Giles's decorated porcelain held in May 1770 gives us a good idea of the range of his decorating achievements on Worcester blanks: 'the whole consisting of elegant dessert services, fine tea sets, caudles etc, curiously enamelled in [with] Figures, Birds, Flowers, etc, and ornamented with mazarine and sky blue and gold. Every article in this sale is the sole property and has been enamelled in London by and under the Direction of the Proprietor of the said warehouse, who having at present a large quantity of white china, continues to execute all orders to any pattern, at the shortest notice...'

This decorator was obviously in no small way of business and was apparently capable of embellishing Worcester (and other porcelains) in the most elaborate manner.

In broad terms we can divide the work we attribute to the Giles Studio into the following classes:

> Dishevelled birds in landscape
> Teniers-type figure subjects
> Fruit painting–usually including some sliced fruit
> Landscape and figure designs, often in monochrome

but of course such designs can occur on factory-decorated wares or on pieces painted by other decorators depending on their skill and markets. Giles, or his painters, also enamelled other orthodox styles, such as boldly painted floral compositions–often featuring a large full-blown tulip and, as he advertised to 'execute all orders to any pattern...', armorial and other devices may occur and perhaps 'matchings' to other services made by other firms.

On some very rare examples from the Giles Studio we find two or even three different types of decoration–such as on the Worcester bowl shown here, Plate 47, and which commanded a world record price when sold at auction in 1973. These

Plate 47 Two views of a three-panelled Worcester porcelain bowl decorated in the London studio of James Giles. Turquoise ground, *c.* 1770. Diameter 6½ inches. *Messrs Christies*

pieces obviously help us to tie up the differing styles to the one London decorating establishment. Such important pieces are rightly highly valued, in fact any decoration that can be classed as Giles's is in great demand.

No signed specimens of his painting are known to me and the identification of his work has been largely built up by the study of four plates which were given to the Victoria and Albert Museum by Mrs Dora Edgell Grubbe, a descendant of Giles. These specimens you will find referred to in several books as the 'Grubbe' plates. They are of Worcester manufacture of the 1765–70 period and it is well documented that Giles purchased Worcester blanks to decorate. There seems little or no doubt that these Grubbe plates were painted by Giles, or at least were decorated in his workshop or studio. It is often forgotten that he must have employed several painters and gilders and we do not have any evidence that he himself painted the objects so readily accredited to him. I have already referred to the coloured-over Worcester printed designs and if indeed this enamelling was carried out in the Giles Studio such simple colouring-in would hardly have been his own work.

It is fashionable to ascribe to Giles examples of Chinese porcelain obviously painted in this country with European flowers and other subjects. I think it most doubtful that the flower pieces were decorated in the Giles Studio and we must remember that this was but one of many such establishments. In general the Chinese pieces are of earlier date than the Worcester porcelains attributed to Giles and certainly they are quite different in style. If they were painted by James Giles they must surely represent his earlier work and you will recall that the Giles family had connections with one of the leading dealers in Oriental porcelains.

Having given up the shop or warehouse in Cockspur Street Giles retained the Berwick Street premises, 'where he continues to paint and enamel all sorts of china'. Apart from decorating Giles probably acted as a normal 'chinaman' selling the wares of various manufacturers, at this period mainly Derby porcelain but also glassware and even Chinese lacquer ware. His surviving account-books of the 1770s show he dealt with the Bow, Caughley, Derby, Liverpool (Philip Christian) and Worcester concerns. The sale catalogue of his stock also suggests that he decorated, or at least dealt in, some Continental porcelains including Frankenthal and Nymphenburg wares. He sold to Thomas Pitt a pair of presumably Derby biscuit groups and these can hardly have borne any added decoration. He also purchased from the Worcester factory much blue and white porcelain. It has been suggested that he embellished this with gilding but at this period very little blue and white bears gilding and such additions were mainly fashionable after Giles's death in 1780. It does seem, however, that his studio was responsible for some simple and attractive gold designs on Caughley and Worcester blanks. These are quite different from the sumptuous pieces we traditionally associate with Giles's decoration.

I have in mind here simple gilt designs such as that seen on the charming Worcester teapot (Plate 57) and indeed this same design appears as one panel on a plate decorated with other patterns firmly associated with the Giles Studio. Perhaps we pay too much attention to the more pretentious Giles decoration and neglect his more ordinary decoration on Worcester porcelain.

Much research still remains to be carried out on these London decorated porcelains. The known facts are to be found in the following publications, which will give you a good groundwork to build upon:

Paper by Aubrey J. Toppin published in the *Transactions of the English Ceramic Circle* (vol. 1, no. 1, 1933)

Paper by W. B. Honey published in the *Transactions of the English Ceramic Circle* (vol. 1, no. 5, 1937). He illustrates as Plate 11, the four 'Grubbe' plates now in the Victoria and Albert Museum

Coloured Worcester Porcelain of the First Period by H. Rissik Marshall (Ceramic Book Company, Newport, Mon., 1954)

Worcester Porcelain and Lund's Bristol by F. A. Barrett (Faber, London, revised edition, 1966)

The Illustrated Guide to Worcester Porcelain by Henry Sandon (Barrie & Jenkins, London, 1969).

An important document consists of Mr Christie's catalogue of the sale of 'Elegant Porcelaine of English and Foreign manufacture, part of the Stock in Trade of Mr James Giles, Chinaman and Enameller, quitting that business, brought from his shop in Cockspur Street...' The sale was held on 21–25 March 1774. Details of this sale catalogue are given by R. J. Charleston in his paper published in the *Transactions of the English Ceramic Circle* (vol. 6, part 3, 1967). A well illustrated article by Mrs A. George is contained in *Collectors Guide* of June 1974 under the title 'James Giles's London Atelier'.

In March 1977 Mrs George of Messrs Albert Amor Ltd, the well known London dealers in antique porcelains, held an important loan exhibition of porcelain and glass decorated at the Giles workshop. This magnificent array is featured in the excellent exhibition catalogue, entitled *James Giles China Painter 1718–1780*. It is a most useful source of information on this branch of ceramic decoration.

LIVERPOOL, *c.* 1754 into the nineteenth century

There were in the city and port of Liverpool many potters producing a variety of earthenwares and stonewares for the home trade as well as for export to North America and other markets. Several of these, at one time or another, turned their attention to the manufacture of porcelains.

The Liverpool porcelains are of variable quality, some equal Worcester and specimens may well be misplaced in Worcester collections, but other examples are very inferior copies of contemporary Worcester or Caughley or Chinese wares. It is perhaps too easy to group together all Liverpool porcelains–we do not so group

Bow and Chelsea under a London heading and there is the danger of placing any problem example under the all-embracing designation 'Liverpool'.

The fact that few collectors readily understand the different types of Liverpool porcelain, coupled with the low regard given to the pieces by many collectors, means that the real student or specialist can find many bargains or at least interesting examples to enhance his collection. Be warned, however, the study is not easy; very few pieces are marked and our key pieces are not as certain as we would wish, although our knowledge has greatly increased in recent years with the discovery of factory wasters.

The following brief notes are arranged in the chronological order of the establishment of the different works.

Richard Chaffers & Co., c. 1754–1765

This pottery was established on Shaw's Brow, Liverpool. A soapstone-type soft-paste porcelain was being made by about 1756 but for some two years prior to this a bone-ash-type body may have been made. In general, these Chaffers's porcelains are the most accomplished of all the Liverpool makes, closely rivalling Worcester. Much blue and white was made for the middle-class markets and these blue and white wares with the related enamelled designs display the popular Oriental influence.

Richard Chaffers died in 1765 and his pottery was continued by Philip Christian & Co., qv.

Samuel Gilbody, c. 1754–1761

By 1758 this young Liverpool potter was advertising 'China Ware of all sorts, equal for service and beauty to any made in England'. He was perhaps the first English

Plate 48 An attractively painted Gilbody (Liverpool) tankard, *c.* 1754–61. 5 inches high. *Formerly Author's Collection, now Victoria and Albert Museum*

manufacturer to claim his products were beautiful as well as serviceable and certainly today we can readily admit they have charm and quality of workmanship and painting. Gilbody is one of the few Liverpool makers to have produced figures but as yet these are extremely rare—I say 'as yet' for more may be discovered as we search them out.

I have chosen to illustrate a delightful mug decorated very much in the Lund's-Bristol or early Worcester style (Plate 48). This damaged piece gave me pleasure for many years and has now passed on to the Victoria and Albert Museum collection where I trust it gives equal pleasure to a wider gathering.

Our identification of Samuel Gilbody's productions owes much to the site finds of Alan Smith, as featured in the *Transactions of the English Ceramic Circle* (vol. 7, part 2, 1969).

William Ball, c. 1755–1769

The soft-paste soapstone-type body produced by William Ball is most pleasing or at least its wet-looking covering glaze is very attractive. Specimens are normally painted in a bright blue and usually comprise the standard popular types of Chinese-style landscapes with figures. As with the other Liverpool porcelain manufacturers Ball seems to have concentrated on useful wares—such as teasets.

As a class these Ball porcelains are rare but charming. Once seen, the body (often with slight turning-tears) and the oily-looking glaze should be easily remembered.

William Reid & Co., c. 1755–1761

In this section we encounter the difficulty experienced in our study of Liverpool porcelains with the lack of key-pieces. Once, only a very few years ago, I would have written in a dogmatic manner that the Reid pieces were unmistakable; in fact I wrote: 'These Liverpool porcelains are easily identified once one has handled a single typical example. The body is almost opaque and may be likened to pipe-clay. The glaze has a proportion of tin oxide added, giving it an opaque bluey-white appearance...' This is all quite true but the trouble is that recent excavations carried out by Paul Bemrose at Newcastle-under-Lyme in Staffordshire have brought to light 'wasters' of a type very like the wares we have all been regarding as Liverpool.

Research continues on this great problem and if the pieces we call Reid are shown to be of Staffordshire origin, then someone will make his name by discovering what William Reid made at *his* Liverpool pottery. If you wish to see illustrations of the Staffordshire finds—and they are most interesting, you can consult Mr Bemrose's paper in the *Transactions of the English Ceramic Circle* (vol 9, part 1, 1973).

Philip Christian & Co., c. 1765–1776

Christian took over Chaffers's factory on the latter's death in 1765 and the production of soapstone-type body continued. The underglaze-blue tends to be slightly grey and rather pale but is finely painted. The overglaze colours tend to be rather dull in tone but good flower painting occurs.

Pennington & Part, c. 1770–1799

Seth Pennington and his partner John Part produced some bone-ash-type porcelains but the wares normally attributed to this partnership are on the poor side with crudely engraved designs printed in a dark blue. The glaze tends to spot, and slight defects can be seen in many pieces which seem to have been produced down to a price rather than up to a quality. These porcelains are typical of the old idea of all Liverpool porcelain being of poor quality, but this is too sweeping a picture.

Thomas Wolfe & Co., c. 1795–1800

I will discuss the Liverpool porcelains made by Thomas Wolfe, John Luccock and Miles Mason at the Islington Pottery in Chapter 6, as they are of the hybrid hard-paste type.

The Liverpool porcelains made at the Herculaneum Pottery are of nineteenth-century date, see p. 186.

For our present picture of the Liverpool porcelain manufacturers and their products we are in the main indebted to the researches and writings of Dr Bernard Watney. You should certainly study his *Blue and White* book, revised edition, also his Liverpool chapter in *English Porcelain*, edited by R. J. Charleston. The *Transactions of the English Ceramic Circle* also contain some most important papers on Liverpool wares; these contributions include: 'Liverpool Porcelain' by T. Knowles Boney (vol. 4, part 1, 1957); 'Four Groups of Porcelain, possibly Liverpool' by B. Watney (vol. 4, part 5, 1959); 'Four Groups of Porcelain, possibly Liverpool' by B. Watney (vol. 5, part 1, 1960); 'The Porcelain of Chaffers, Christian and Pennington' by B. Watney (vol. 5, part 5, 1964); and 'Samuel Gilbody...' by Alan Smith (vol. 7, part 2, 1969). My own modest work *An Introduction to English Blue and White* illustrates some typical Liverpool porcelains decorated in underglaze-blue.

Our understanding of Liverpool porcelains is based on very slender clues and subsequent research may well result in the reclassification of some classes. The discovery of new dated or otherwise documentary specimens is awaited with interest. Our confusion is confounded by the fact that the types of body appear to have changed at the various factories from time to time–indeed the Liverpool potteries produced every known type of English ceramics.

LONGTON HALL, c. 1750–1760

For very many years we have believed that the first porcelains produced within the Staffordshire Potteries area were those at the Longton Hall factory which was established in 1750 or perhaps in 1749, but it seems now that this honour must be presented to the Newcastle-under-Lyme works of the approximate period 1745–55 (see p. 125). However, the Longton Hall porcelains are still of great interest to

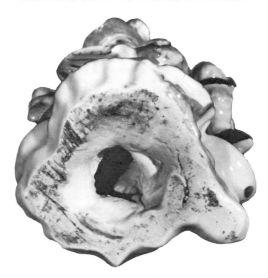

Plate 49 The underside of a Longton Hall porcelain figure showing fire-cracks and typically rough finish, *c.* 1755. *Geoffrey Godden, Chinaman*

collectors and well worth study. Once again we owe much of our present-day appreciation of the history of the Longton Hall factory to the researches of Dr Bernard Watney as published in the books listed at the end of this section.

The name Longton Hall stems from the situation of the pottery at the building known as Longton Hall between Stone and Newcastle-under-Lyme. We used to associate only one man with this factory–William Littler–but the works would seem to have been established in 1749 or in 1750 by William Jenkinson, who claimed to have obtained (we know not where) 'the art, secret and mystery of making a certain porcelain ware in imitation of china...' In October 1751 William Nicklin and William Littler were taken into partnership. Nicklin, a lawyer by profession, may have supplied the very necessary funds, for the trading style Nicklin & Co. was apparently employed in 1751. William Littler almost certainly supplied the expertise, being an experienced 'earth potter' making saltglazed wares. The early Longton wares would have included the white figures and animal models which we term the 'snowman'-class on account of the smothering mass of white glaze that clogs the modelling.

In 1753 Jenkinson retired and Nathaniel Firmin and his son Samuel joined the partnership. They with Robert Charlesworth in 1755 were a source of new working capital but this quickly came to an end and in September 1760 a great sale of Longton Hall porcelain was held in Salisbury. This marks the end of the Longton adventure but Littler later turns up at West Pans in Scotland (see p. 132).

The Longton Hall porcelain is of the glassy soft-paste type showing on analysis a high percentage of lead. The glaze on occasions seems to have been clouded with oxide of tin or a similar whitening agent and a scum-line can often be seen at the glaze edge. In general the pieces are thickly potted and often rather crudely

Plate 50 A typical Longton Hall leaf-dish painted by the so-called 'castle' painter, *c.* 1755. 8 inches. *Messrs Sotheby & Co*

finished—especially the insides of figures as seen looking into the hollow base (Plate 49). Chelsea-type 'moons' can also appear in Longton porcelain (see p. 97). Natural forms were popular—leaf-shaped sauceboats, fruit-shaped boxes, leaf-dishes (Plate 50), etc. Most pieces were enamelled over the glaze but blue and white useful wares were also made and many specimens bore a rich blue ground—one that was very prone to run in the glaze. Some Longton Hall porcelain—mainly mugs—were embellished with the overglaze printed designs at Liverpool.

Longton Hall porcelain is generally unmarked. When a mark does occur it comprises what appears to be two crossed 'L's with dots below as shown here.

Other small marks, crosses, letters, chemical signs also occur but these are probably workman's marks and as such are not helpful, for similar tally-marks are found on many types of porcelain.

Within approximately a ten-year period, in the 1750s, the Longton Hall works managed to produce a relatively large range of wares. A very good selection is shown in Dr Watney's standard work *Longton Hall Porcelain* (Faber, London, 1957); his contribution on Longton Hall to *English Porcelain 1745–1850*, edited by R. J. Charleston is also important, as is his *Blue and White* book. Some typical pieces are shown in my *An Illustrated Encyclopaedia of British Pottery and Porcelain* and *British Porcelain, an illustrated guide*.

LOWESTOFT, *c.* 1757–1799

The charming and unpretentious Lowestoft porcelains were my first love. I still remember the thrill of buying from a leading West End dealer a complete tea-service for what I thought at the time was a King's ransom price of twenty-five pounds! This was when I was fourteen or fifteen and only later did I realise how generous that dealer–the late David Manheim–had been to this young upstart of a collector. The Lowestoft porcelains have always given me the greatest pleasure, and even excitement, when I managed to find a rare specimen lurking in some unexpected place.

I should explain to you that many people still refer to a class of hard-paste Chinese export market porcelain as being 'Lowestoft'. Most of us now know better but you may find this term sometimes used to describe eighteenth-century Chinese wares. Sometimes the contradictory term 'Chinese-Lowestoft' is employed. The real Lowestoft porcelain is soft-paste and like the Bow body, it contains a relatively light percentage of bone-ash–some 40 to 45 per cent.

The modest factory was situated in Bell Lane at the resort and fishing town of Lowestoft, the most easterly part of the British coastline. Lowestoft and its nearby rival Yarmouth were important places for coastal shipping and also for trade to Holland. However, the ambitions of the proprietors of this porcelain factory seem to have been very limited and simple–to produce a range of useful wares for the locality rather than to try to compete with the leading manufacturers of the day. This policy gave rise to the production of a number of special pieces, inscribed with names, places and dates, made to commemorate family occasions. This side of the production is exemplified in the little circular 'birth tablets' made to mark the birth of local children. These modest aims paid dividends, for the factory existed for over forty years, outliving Chelsea and several other great names in the history of British ceramics.

Many rather unlikely stories surround the establishment of the Lowestoft factory. It is said that an unsuccessful attempt to make porcelain from local clay was made in 1756. A successful attempt seems to have been made in 1757 under the partnership of Philip Walker (a local potter), Robert Browne (Factory Manager in 1771 to be succeeded by his son of the same name), Obed Aldred and John Richman. Walker and Robert Browne junior were the key figures in the concern. They were curiously described in a Directory of 1795 as 'China manufacturers and Herring curers' and in many ways their porcelains have an attractive amateur appearance.

The Lowestoft factory seems unique in that for some thirteen years, from 1757 to about 1770, only blue and white designs were issued, no dated overglaze coloured pieces being known before 1774, a fact that underlines the modest aims of the proprietors: to produce useful table-wares for the local middle-class market.

An advertisement in the *Norwich Mercury* of 2 February 1760 gives notice that Walker & Co. (the factory's trading style at that time):

Plate 51 An oval Lowestoft relief-moulded butter-dish, one side mould being assembled upside-down as shown by downward growing plants, *c.* 1765. *Author's Collection*

will be offering for sale a great variety of neat blue and white china or porcelain at the manufactory in town.

'Tis humbly hoped that most of the shopkeepers in the County [Suffolk] and the County of Norfolk, will give encouragement to this laudable undertaking by reserving their spring orders for their humble servants.

We can see here that the blue and white wares were sold direct from the factory. The strange aspect of this advertisement is that it would appear to herald the first endeavour of the management to market their wares.

These blue and white patterns remained the staple of the factory until its closure, and we have contemporary reports that women were employed in this branch of the trade. The employment of female labour was another innovation of the period.

The standard blue and white designs in the main comprise attractive, almost child-like Chinese-style landscape designs often reserved in panels amid relief-moulded borders and floral motifs. Some of these moulded designs incorporate the initials 'IH' of Hughes (the modeller) with a date 1761 or 1764. Look at the typical Hughes-type relief-moulded example in Plate 51; you should also notice how the mould has been placed upside-down so that the sunflower-like motifs are growing downwards!

Plate 52 A Lowestoft flask painted in underglaze-blue with ship-building scene, *c.* 1780. 5½ inches high. *Author's Collection*

Apart from the Oriental-type designs many formal floral patterns are to be found and very rarely pieces painted with local views–such as the delightful flask in Plate 52 painted in underglaze-blue, a piece perhaps commissioned by the shipbuilder or the boat-owner, or perhaps as a present to repay past favours?

Turning from this unique piece with its hand-painted design we have a repetitive class of ware bearing blue-printed designs. Such pieces date mainly from the 1770s, and with a few notable exceptions these printed designs are copies of popular Worcester or Caughley prints. The engraver had a strange hesitant touch and often the shaded or darker areas are painted in by hand. The Worcester crescent mark was often copied on such printed pieces.

Mid-way between blue and white and the enamelled pieces we have a class of Oriental-inspired patterns incorporating both modes of decoration. These are referred to as the Redgrave patterns as this family, or rather several families of this name, are believed to have been responsible for these simple but attractive designs in underglaze-blue with overglaze red, green and gold (see colour plate A).

Studying our list of dated examples—and we have a yearly sequence of nearly two hundred pieces from 1761 to 1799 (with the exception of 1785)—we find our first dated *enamelled* example is as late as 1774. From this date onwards we have a good selection of enamelled wares. Especially notable are some pieces boldly painted with tulips, but many figure subjects occur—both European and Oriental-style patterns, and of course a wide range of simple floral designs. In the 1790s we have a now scarce class of attractive mugs, inkwells and the like inscribed 'A trifle from Lowestoft' or with the names of nearby villages Bungay, Holt, Wangford, etc.

Also of great rarity are the Lowestoft figure models, a pair of putti and a pair of standing musicians. Also small cats, a swan, a sheep and a ram and perhaps one or more dog models. Rare and desirable as these models are, I prefer the simple pieces made to use on the table. Although small, the Lowestoft factory produced a surprisingly assorted selection of articles, the many sauceboat and smaller cream-boat forms being particularly noteworthy.

The date of closure is open to some doubt. Most books give this as 1802 or 1803 but I believe that it closed down in 1799, making it a purely eighteenth-century concern. To support my contention I will point out that our series of dated specimens ceases in 1799. Some later pieces by Lowestoft decorators are of earthenware not porcelain, suggesting that these former employees could not then purchase Lowestoft *porcelain* blanks. We also have the very important point that the wage records of the Chamberlain management show that this Worcester factory gave employment to many Lowestoft painters and modellers in September 1799. The Lowestoft factory must have either closed at this period or have been about to, after the loss to Chamberlains of its key personnel.

No true Lowestoft factory mark exists. The early blue and white porcelains made before about 1774 often bear a painter's number—this in itself is not helpful as several factories used such painter's identification numbers—but at Lowestoft they were usually placed inside the foot-rim as you can see below.

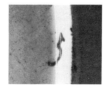

The later blue and white pieces do not bear a painter's mark, nor do the enamelled pieces (although one solitary example is known to me). Some copies of Worcester blue and white bear a crescent mark and some Continental-inspired designs bear a copy of the Dresden crossed swords mark. Some Continental hard-paste copies of inscribed Lowestoft porcelain occur but most of these are unlikely to deceive you–once you are familiar with the true Lowestoft soft-paste and the rather naive style of painting found on the originals. Fortunately the more ordinary Lowestoft wares–their most charming and typical products–have not been copied, although recent very high prices may tempt someone to try their misplaced skill!

Good collections of Lowestoft porcelains can be seen at the Castle Museum, Norwich, at Christchurch Mansion, Ipswich, at the Fitzwilliam Museum, Cambridge and at the Victoria and Albert Museum in London. There are also some representative pieces on show in my reference collection at Worthing. If you are unable to see these collections in the flesh many examples are featured in my *Illustrated Guide to Lowestoft Porcelain* (Barrie & Jenkins, London, 1969). W. Spelman's book *Lowestoft China* of 1905 is now unreliable but the illustrations of moulds and factory wasters make it a valuable source book. Dr Watney's *Blue and White* book contains a valuable chapter on Lowestoft as does *English Porcelain 1745–1850*, edited by R. J. Charleston, the Lowestoft section by G. C. Bolster. Other pieces are shown in my *British Porcelain, an illustrated guide*. The detailed and excellent catalogue of *Lowestoft Porcelain in Norwich Castle Museum* by Sheenah Smith (Norfolk Museum Service, Norwich, 1975) is a must for all serious students of Lowestoft porcelains.

Several interesting articles or papers on different facets of Lowestoft wares are listed below.

'Inscribed and Dated Lowestoft Porcelain', paper by A. J. B. Kiddell in *Transactions of the English Porcelain Circle* (no. 3, 1931).

'Lowestoft China', two articles by A. J. B. Kiddell in *The Connoisseur* of September and October 1937.

'Miniature Lowestoft China', article by D. M. Hunting in *Antique Collector* of December 1949.

'Early Lowestoft', paper by D. M. Hunting in *Transactions of the English Ceramic Circle* (vol. 3, part 1, 1951).

'Lowestoft China Teapots', article by D. M. Hunting in *Antique Collector* of December 1951.

'Lowestoft Figures', article by G. Godden in the *Connoisseur Year Book*, 1957.

'Transfer-Printed Lowestoft Porcelain', paper by John Howell in *Transactions of the English Ceramic Circle* (vol. 7, part 3, 1970).

'Lowly Lowestoft', article by G. Godden in *Art and Antiques Weekly*, 23 November 1974.

'Some Notes on the Introduction of Polychrome Decoration at Lowestoft', paper by John Howell in *Transactions of the English Ceramic Circle*, vol. 9, part 3, 1975.

Lowestoft Porcelain in Norwich Castle Museum, catalogue by Sheenah Smith (Norfolk Museum Service, 1975), vol. 1, Blue and White.

A Godden tape-recorded talk with illustrated supplement is also available (see p. 277).

NEW HALL, *c*. 1781–1835

The New Hall works in the Staffordshire Potteries must certainly rank as a leading eighteenth-century concern, although it seemingly produced only useful wares. For reasons which I hope will be clear, I am postponing discussion of these interesting wares to the next chapter.

NEWCASTLE-UNDER-LYME, *c*. 1744–1754

There is not a single finished piece that was definitely made at this early factory, only one or two pieces that may have been made there. Our researches are in their infancy; in fact before 1973 there were no published references to this manufactory, or rather to its products, at all.

The story opens in 1969 when Paul Bemrose MA, the Curator of the Newcastle-under-Lyme Museum, with his team of helpers started excavations on the site of 'The Pomona Inn' in Newcastle-under-Lyme. The inn marks the site of an early pottery, one in which we believe a type of porcelain was made–the first produced in Staffordshire. The excavations were difficult and very limited but a mass of related wasters were found, some of which appear to be of a porcelain body. Many of these wasters were painted in underglaze-blue. The wasters appeared to have been overfired and the kiln opened too quickly. All were perhaps the result of just one faulty firing. As yet we are unable to tell if so high a proportion of wares were so spoilt that the production of porcelain ceased after a short period or indeed if it ever reached a marketable quality. While several wasters can be considered a very near match to some wares which we have hitherto considered to have been made by William Reid at Liverpool, the question is still open. We must await the excavation of more Newcastle site fragments or the discovery of complete pieces matching the wasters at present available.

In the meantime we can set out the few known facts concerning the proprietors. The pottery, which we can conveniently call the Pomona Pottery, was established by Samuel Bell junior. He is believed to have produced only pottery (see a paper, 'Bell's Pottery, Newcastle-under-Lyme', by A. T. Morley Hewitt published in the *Transactions of the English Ceramic Circle*, vol. 4, part 1, 1957). Bell died in 1744 and the no doubt desirable property was placed on the market. Luckily a 1746 newspaper letting advertisement is preserved in the Staffordshire Record Office and this includes some very interesting points.

To be Lett at Lady Day next at Newcastle-under-Line [sic] Staffordshire

A very commodious house (late in the occupation of Mr Bell, and now in the possession of Mr Steers) with three parlours, a hall, and two kitchens, on the ground floor, chambers and garrets answerable, lately built and fash'd, a large garden, well planted with all sorts of useful fruits, sundry warehouses, workshops, laths, throwing wheels and other utensils useful in making fine earthenware or china; three pot-ovens, one lately built on purpose to burn china; good stabling and yards; all entire in itself.

For further particulars enquire of Mr Crowther at St Katherine's near the Tower; to Mr Bell, in Aldermary Church-Yard, Bow-Lane, London, or of Mr Brittain, at Newcastle aforesaid, where the premises may be seen.

N.B. It's cheap country for coals and provisions.

We here see that in 1746 Mr Steers was in occupation of Samuel Bell's Pomona Pottery which boasted three ovens or kilns, one of which had been 'lately built on purpose to burn china'. We might also observe the mention of Mr Crowther and Mr Bell in London who were possessed of 'further particulars' and both may well have had an interest in the property.

Some of the site wasters made up into a bowl dated under the base '25th July 1746', and this much broken and incomplete piece is the earliest known example of English blue and white decorated porcelain. The maker was probably William Steers, a merchant from Hoxton in Middlesex who had some four years earlier filed a petition for a patent claiming the invention of a new method of making a transparent body in imitation of porcelain. Steers seems to have left Hoxton by March 1745, and by early 1746 he was probably working Bell's former potworks on the Pomona site. He had, however, left by June 1748 when he recommenced paying rates at Hoxton.

The Pomona Pottery would seem to have been bought in about 1747 by Joseph Wilson, a potter who we believe had also worked the mysterious Limehouse Pottery. An important link here is shown in a letter written by Dr Richard Pococke on 14 July 1750, after a visit to Newcastle-under-Lyme: 'Newcastle-on-Lyme is a small well built town...they have a handsome church and a market house for it is the market town and capital of the pottery villages: there are some few potters here, and one I visited whom I saw at Limehouse who seemed to promise to make the best china-ware but disagreed with his employers...'

Dr Pococke does not seem to be saying that the ex-Limehouse potter was making china-ware at Newcastle, rather that while at Limehouse he seemed destined to make the best china-ware the Doctor had seen. Nevertheless the link between the two potteries is of great interest. The potter concerned would appear to be Joseph Wilson and both he and Joseph Wilson & Company paid taxes at Limehouse in 1748. Apart from Dr Pococke's unnamed mention we find a Joseph Wilson at Newcastle-under-Lyme in November 1751 when the following entry occurs in the church register: 'Joseph, son of Mr Wilson, potter, was baptised'. Joseph Wilson is

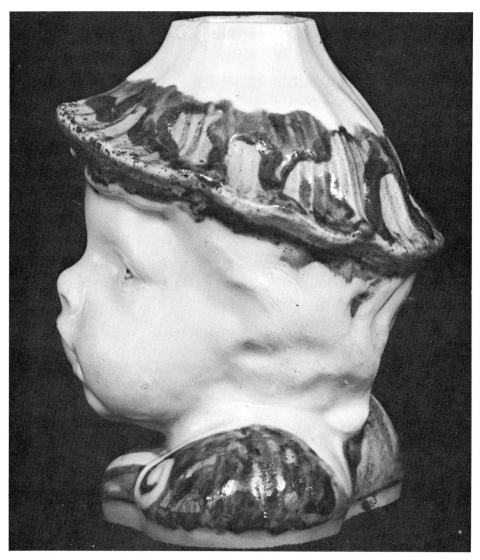

Plate 53 A Liverpool (?) porcelain tea-caddy (missing its conical cover) of the 1750s (see p. 128).
Photo: Godden of Worthing Ltd.

also mentioned in an abstract of a property agreement relating to the sale of the
pottery in 1754.

Dr Pococke continued in his letter to describe the types of wares made at that
time at Newcastle. He does not mention porcelain or china, although he mentions
some 'which when they are quite plain and well done look like china teapots'. The
site wasters in many cases were of earthenware bodies and I should point out that
even the porcelain pieces were not readily identifiable as of this body–they showed
little translucency and were rather creamy in tint but then they were spoilt over-

fired fragments not necessarily representative of the articles offered for sale. Here lies the trouble; we have still to find some finished examples of this manufactory. Some earthenware pieces seem to match shapes in the porcelains we have formerly attributed to William Reid of Liverpool. These include a moulded cup with prunus decoration, some leaf-shaped dishes and perhaps a key-piece which is, or was, a conical cover reportedly identical in shape to that which surmounts the rare little Chinese toy tea-caddies such as that shown in Plate 53, alas without its cover. I have to say 'perhaps' a key-piece for most unfortunately this waster was seen but lost when the trench caved in; such was the condition of the trench that efforts to locate this cover had to be abandoned. A pair of these caddies complete are illustrated as Reid's Liverpool porcelain in the 1973 revised edition of Dr Watney's *Blue and White* book.

These notes have been based on a paper read to the *English Ceramic Circle* by Paul Bemrose in November 1971 and published in the Circle's *Transactions* (vol. 9, part 1, 1973). This paper should be read by all keen collectors and ceramic students. They should carefully study the illustration of the wasters and keep a good look-out for pieces that match these fragments. The porcelains would have been made by William Steers, and perhaps Joseph Wilson continued production between *c.* 1747 and 1755.

Apart from Paul Bemrose's paper the only other account of this factory and the site wasters is contained in the 1973 edition of Dr Watney's *Blue and White* book. In a rather controversial manner I illustrated as Newcastle a series of porcelains formerly thought to be of Reid's Liverpool make, in my *Introduction to English Blue and White Porcelain*, but obviously much research remains to be carried out on these rare pieces.

PINXTON, *c.* 1796–1813

This Derbyshire porcelain factory can hardly be considered one of the *major* eighteenth-century English porcelain factories but it is convenient to include it in this section. It was quite a modest concern, perhaps best thought of as an offshoot of the Derby factory, some fifteen miles away. John Coke of a well-known local family would seem to have acquired an interest in porcelain-making in the mid-1790s. It is believed that William Duesbury of the Derby factory tested some local clays for John Coke and that William Billingsley, the talented Derby porcelain painter, followed up the enquiry and proposed to Coke that he (Billingsley) should manage a new factory at Pinxton. In July 1795 Billingsley met and discussed with Coke the possibilities of establishing a manufactory at Pinxton, mainly, it would appear, to produce teawares. Various very interesting letters from Billingsley to John Coke, together with factory accounts, are published in C. L. Exley's excellent little book *The Pinxton China Factory* (Mr and Mrs R. Coke-Steel, Sutton-on-the-Hill, 1963).

Plate 54 A typical Pinxton porcelain oval sugar-basin, *c.* 1795–1800. 5¼ inches high. *Geoffrey Godden, Chinaman*

Work started on the new factory in October 1795, with a trial firing in April 1796. Billingsley arrived at Pinxton in October 1796. The Billingsley-Coke partnership was dissolved in April 1799, after which Billingsley established his decorating establishment at Mansfield and later moved to Brampton, near Torksey, then to a succession of other now famous ceramic centres. Coke continued alone until September 1801 when he took Henry Bankes into partnership but this was terminated in January 1803. Later, from 1806, John Cutts, a Derby-trained landscape painter leased the factory from John Coke. Some available accounts are inscribed 'Brought of John Cutts. Pinxton Works, Derbyshire', but in March 1813 Cutts wrote to Josiah Wedgwood in Staffordshire regarding his forthcoming employment there. He noted '…I am under the necessity of removing from this place this Lady Day or otherwise engaging the premises for another year', and after

Cutts joined Wedgwoods as a porcelain-painter the Pinxton factory was closed.

We therefore have a possible duration of seventeen years for the Pinxton works, 1796–1813, but it is by no means certain that porcelain was *produced* during the whole of the period. I believe during the Cutts period at least the works were used merely as a decorating establishment–embellishing blanks made in earlier years, or white porcelains purchased from other sources.

The Billingsley-period (1796–9) Pinxton porcelain and glaze is very similar to that made at the Derby factory. The body is a glassy one containing bone. It has good translucency and the covering lead-glaze is warm and pleasing to the touch. One can almost say that unmarked Derby-type porcelain is of Pinxton make, so similar are they in appearance. The later wares are not so trim or of such a good body and, as I have stated, it is possible that no porcelain was made in the Cutts period between 1806 and the closure in 1813.

The often characteristic Pinxton shapes are shown in the books listed at the end of this section. The decoration often comprises small-scale landscapes (Plate 54)–sometimes named local views–also some good flower painting, the best of which may have been by William Billingsley, although most standard patterns were of a very sparse nature–simple sprig motifs or elegant gilt designs. Ground-colours were sometimes applied. These are rather pale and can be unevenly applied, but the quite rare Pinxton porcelains have great charm and are among the most pleasing productions of the period.

Some very few pieces are marked 'Pinxton'; other pieces have a script capital 'P', sometimes followed by a pattern number, but most examples are unmarked or bear only the pattern number. Some Pinxton wares bear small-sized impressed letters, and a notation in the factory account book of 25 February 1797 seems to refer to the purchase of these type-face letters: 'By 20 letters to mark ware at $1\frac{1}{2}$d, 2/6d'. Similar impressed letter markings were employed at the Derby factory. Some pieces attributed to Pinxton bear one of the marks shown below. The body of such pieces is very coarse compared with the early Billingsley-period porcelains and I am by no means sure that pieces bearing these marks or the painted capital letter 'A' were made at Pinxton. Recent research suggests that wares very similar to Pinxton were made by Billingsley at Brampton in the early 1800s.

What we may call the Pinxton collector's source-book is C. L. Exley's *The Pinxton China Factory*, the late Mr Exley's researches and manuscript having been edited for publication in this manner by F. A. Barrett and A. L. Thorpe. The book is well illustrated, and the Exley collection is itself on display in the Usher Gallery Museum, Lincoln. Other Pinxton pieces are in the Derby Museum and the Victoria and Albert Museum. For those collectors on the South Coast I hope to show some representative examples in my reference collection. Apart from Mr Exley's book you can consult the Pinxton chapter (by A. L. Thorpe) in *English Porcelain 1745–1850*, edited by R. J. Charleston, and of course you have a selection of pieces featured in both my large general works. Two interesting articles on Pinxton porcelain are featured in the *Connoisseur* of January and February 1963.

PLYMOUTH, *c.* 1768–1770

The rare Plymouth porcelains are of the true or hard-paste type and this was the invention of the local Quaker chemist William Cookworthy. As early as 1745 Cookworthy had been interested in the manufacture of porcelain, strangely using clay from North America. We do not know if these early experiments met with any success, but success was to crown his endeavours when he came to use raw materials found nearly on his own doorstep. These were the vital Petuntse and Kaolin as used by the Chinese, see p. 15.

William Cookworthy took out a patent for making porcelain in March 1768. The patent was no idle boast for one finished piece pre-dates the patent by three days, showing that he was indeed possessed of the knowledge of how to produce hard-paste porcelain and to fire it at the very high temperature required, some 1400°C. However, the Plymouth works were closed in 1770, after which Cookworthy continued to work his patent at Bristol (see p. 80). Indeed it seems probable that some experiments were carried out by Cookworthy at Bristol before his works were successfully established at Plymouth. Apparently the early porcelains would stain in the kiln, a not uncommon fault found even on the so-called successful Plymouth porcelains.

Cookworthy was quite ambitious; he was not content to make only useful wares and blue and white porcelains emulating the Chinese imports. No, he also produced complicated figure models and groups, also shell-shaped centre-pieces and the like. His downfall may have been the difficulty he experienced in firing flat-wares–plates and even saucers. The blue employed on the blue and white wares fired to a rather unattractive inky-black tone and the overglaze enamels tended to remain on the surface of the glaze. Although these Plymouth porcelains are important, being the first successful essays in English hard-paste porcelain, I much prefer the technically poor relations–the soft-paste wares.

The Plymouth porcelains are normally unmarked, but the sign for tin–the numbers 2 and 4 conjoined–was often employed. The 'repairer's' mark 'T' or 'To' may also occur on figures or other articles formed from a series of separate components. Many copies of Plymouth porcelain may be seen–often bell-shaped mugs painted with exotic birds in landscapes. Such fakes bear the tin-mark, and other fakes bear full inscriptions such as 'Plymouth Manufactory', which occurs on a pair of shell-shaped salts in my ceramic 'rogues' gallery'.

For further information you could consult F. Severne Mackenna's *Cookworthy's Plymouth and Bristol Porcelain* (F. Lewis, Leigh-on-Sea, 1947), Dr Watney's *Blue and White* book and the well illustrated general books such as *English Porcelain 1745–1850*, edited by R. J. Charleston, or my two big books.

SPODE

The Spode factory was certainly established in the eighteenth century but porcelains were probably not made until the 1790s and as they are the first of the English bone-chinas I shall defer discussion of these wares until Chapter 7.

WEST PANS (SCOTLAND), *c.* 1764–1777

This section, like that on the Newcastle-under-Lyme manufactory, owes its origin to comparatively recent research and again you will not find mention of it in books published before the mid-1960s, nor in some books published at later dates.

West Pans is near Musselburgh in Scotland and the proprietor was none other than William Littler–better known for his connection with the Longton Hall factory in Staffordshire. A bill-head for 1766 reads:

BOUGHT OF WILL.ᵐ LITTLER

China maker at West Pans near Musselburgh

in Scotland

Where is made all kinds of usefull and ornamental china. Particularly very fine mazareen and gold enamelᵈ china, also all kinds of stone ware, such as fine gilded and Japan'd Black and Tortoise shell ware &c

We do not know for certain if Littler made porcelain in Scotland as opposed to earthenware. Researches have identified a class of seemingly Longton Hall porcelains which appear to have been decorated later in Scotland, and present feeling in the late 1970s is that Littler did make some porcelain at West Pans in the 1764–77 period, wares that we previously attributed to Longton Hall. I do not, however, regard this as settled; these pieces now thought to be of West Pans manufacture are too early in style for this to be so and too primitive in appearance to have been saleable.

The items listed below the quoted October 1766 bill-head were supplied to the Duke of Atholl and the account was preserved in the Blair Castle papers:

To two large cabbage leaves fine mazareen & gold china	£2/ 0/0
Six pansey leaves do.	£2/14/0
A butter tub and stand	£1/ 0/0
2 dozen dessart plates	£5/10/0
For the additional work and expense of ye crest on each piece of ware	18/0

Plate 55 Two Longton Hall or West Pans porcelain tankards now bearing only the typically run and rich underglaze-blue, *c.* 1760. *Messrs Sotheby & Co.*

These leaf-shaped dishes, the matching plates and the butter dish of 'fine mazareen and gold china' would seem to be very similar to the pieces shown in Plates 357 and 359 of my *Illustrated Encyclopaedia of British Pottery and Porcelain*, with their rich streaky blue borders. However, some of this class bears the crossed 'L's mark (below), a mark that does not seem to fit this Scottish pottery. The mugs shown in Plate 55 bear the typical Littler streaky blue; they also display some slight traces of the original over-gilding.

We cannot, however, be quite certain that these listed pieces were of china or porcelain although they probably were. The question of body arises from the discovery of earthenware copies of Longton-type leaf dishes, plates, etc. These relief-moulded earthenwares were embellished with a blue-glaze giving an overall blue appearance. On this blue-glaze gilt floral sprays were added on at least some pieces of this class.

While speaking of earthenwares we could recall that Littler's bill-head read: 'also all kinds of stone ware, such as fine gilded and Japan'd Black and Tortoise shell ware'. The stoneware could well have included white salt-glazed wares. The description 'fine gilded and Japan'd Black' may relate to the glossy black wares we so readily refer to as 'Jackfield', although they seem to have been made at many pottery centres. Many of these black pieces bear impermanent enamelled and gilt decoration of the type Littler may have applied. Tortoiseshell ware is normally creamware treated with different semi-translucent coloured glazes. We may therefore assume that Littler at West Pans made, decorated, or at least sold, porcelains, stonewares, Jackfield-type black-glazed wares and creamwares.

As to the establishment of the new Littler enterprise near Edinburgh, we read of one such venture in the *London Chronicle* of 25–27 December 1764: 'We hear from Edinburgh that some gentlemen are about to establish a porcelain manufacture in Scotland, and have already wrote up to London to engage proper persons to carry it on.' Some six weeks later the *Daily Advertiser* reported: 'Four persons, well skilled in the making of British china, were engaged for Scotland, where a new Porcelain manufacture is going to be established in the manner of that now carried on at Chelsea, Stratford and Bow.' These newspaper accounts may relate to what was to become the West Pans Pottery but it would seem that Littler was settled in Musselburgh slightly before these reports, for the list of Honorary Burgesses gives under 30 October 1764: 'Mr Wm Littler, China Manufacturer at West Pans.'

In February 1766 Littler applied to the Musselburgh Town Council for permission to build houses for his workpeople, to erect a windmill to grind flint and other materials, also for liberty to take 'as much clay as his manufactory required...' This last request was apparently not granted but he may have had some clay available on his own original site; in fact a council minute of December 1765 refers to clay let to William Littler, china manufacturer. This clay would hardly have been suitable for the making of porcelain but pottery of various types could have been made from it.

Several examples of enamelled porcelain recently attributed to West Pans bear crest-motifs relating to local families. Littler advertised to supply just such pieces but many other wares must have been decorated in a more normal manner. Perhaps such standard pieces are still regarded as purely of Longton Hall make. Littler may have had available a large assortment of his Staffordshire porcelains, even completely finished pieces. An advertisement in the *Caledonian Mercury* of 4 February 1765 lists at this early date a remarkable selection of wares to be sold by auction at the Palace of Holyrood. The advertisement reads in part:

> ...a neat collection of the productions of the Scotland manufactory china ware, it being made at the West Pans, near Musselburgh, and a good part of the china is not inferior to the foreign china both in transparency, beautiful colours and uses; consisting of fine mazareen blue jars and beakers, neatly enamelled and gilded; great variety of figures, chandeliers, candlesticks, flowers mounted in flower pots

representing natural flowers; various sorts of beautiful leaves richly enamelled being calculated for the use of desart services. Also tea pots, cups and saucers, milk jugs, sugar cups and coffee cans, quart jugs and mugs, potting pots and sundry sorts of sauce boats. All these articles both in blue, white and enamel, with many other sorts, too tedious to mention. This being the first offered to public sale and for the sake of ready money, will be sold reasonable...

N.B. A good assortment of enameled cream coloured ware, which will be sold very cheap.

Other slightly later advertisements of wares offered as of West Pans manufacture are quoted by Dr Watney in a paper listed below. Dr Watney has carried out limited excavations on the site and has found some evidence that porcelain was made at West Pans. He has also shown that Littler was seeking a partner to put new funds into the apparently failing works in June 1777.

Many people have added to our knowledge of the West Pans venture and the available facts are ably summarised in the following illustrated papers: 'William Littler of Longton Hall and West Pans, Scotland' by Arthur Lane (with appendix by Dr Bernard Watney) in the *Transactions of the English Ceramic Circle* (vol. 5, part 2, 1961); 'West Pans Story–The Scotland Manufactory', a joint paper by Mavis Bimson, John Ainslie and Bernard Watney in the *Transactions of the English Ceramic Circle* (vol. 6, part 2, 1966). For those who do not have access to these *Transactions* there is a brief account in Chapter 4 of Dr Watney's *Blue and White* book, revised 1973 edition.

WORCESTER, 1751 onwards

As I mentioned when discussing the early Bristol porcelains (p. 82) a body of men from Worcester under Dr John Wall made a successful take-over bid for the Bristol enterprise in June 1751. A list of the Worcester partners and the full agreement for the carrying on of the 'Worcester Tonquin Manufacture' is given in Henry Sandon's excellent book, *Illustrated Guide to Worcester Porcelain* (Barrie & Jenkins, London, 1969).

As this 'take-over' included working materials, moulds and some of the former Bristol work people (even Benjamin Lund, one of the Bristol partners, came up to Worcester), the new enterprise, now centred at Warmstry House in Worcester, was able to make a flying start, obviating the teething troubles experienced by other new porcelain manufacturers. Right from the start the Worcester wares display remarkable quality–in body, glaze, workmanship and in decoration. The soapstone-type porcelain which on analysis shows some 30 per cent soapstone proved to be extremely workable and to behave very well in the kiln during the firing processes. To the touch it is compact but does not feel over heavy; it is smooth and pleasant. Pieces are rarely warped and foot-rims are normally true and did not

Plate 56 Three views of the celebrated Worcester cream-boat bearing the word 'Wigornia' relief-moulded under the base, *c.* 1752. 2½ inches high. *Photo: Tilley & Co.*

need grinding flat. From the start attractive relief-moulded designs were produced. Superb sauceboats and cream ewers were made in a profusion of different moulds. I show one such little piece (Plate 56)–one which set a very temporary world record price for English porcelain when it was sold in 1973–no less than twenty thousand pounds–and it stands no more than two and a half inches high. Happily, it can be seen at the Dyson Perrins Museum at the Worcester works, having come 'home' after spending many years on the other side of the Atlantic. You may ask why such a sum was given for this little ewer or cream-boat. Apart from its obvious charm it boasted one special feature: the word 'Wigornia' (the Latinised name of Worcester) was relief-moulded under the base and as far as we know at present, this is the only piece with this mark to have survived. I would not be surprised if other specimens turn up because the name would have been part of the mould and if you mould a shape you tend to re-use the mould for a run of similar pieces. However, this piece was believed to be unique, a fact which accounts for the price, with two or more wealthy collectors or museums competing for just one known object.

Other small creamers of this general type but without the mark may be purchased for a small fraction of the cost of the 'Wigornia' example–especially those decorated in underglaze-blue, and for the average collector without thousands of pounds readily available, these more ordinary examples will give just as much visual pleasure as the marked creamer. I make this point for as a general rule eighteenth-century Worcester porcelain does tend to be costly. It rightly attracts discriminating collectors from all over the world. Examples decorated with an apple-green ground or with very rare yellow ground are always expensive but the range of the factory's products is so large that (to me) equally attractive pieces can still be found at modest price-levels.

Much delightful Worcester, painted or printed in underglaze-blue, is I believe still under-valued although prices have rocketed in recent years. The overglaze-printed pieces (p. 64) are likewise often reasonable as are the white and gold designs. These simple gold designs show off to good effect the graceful shapes and the workmanlike finish, and in general they are typical of the Worcester taste and potting skill. Look at the teapot in Plate 57, now priced at say sixty pounds against over two hundred if it were smothered with the typical Worcester blue-scale background or over a thousand pounds if the pure porcelain had been hidden under a yellow ground!

I am deliberately avoiding retelling the history of the factory as this is well set out in so many books which you can readily consult (see p. 142). Instead I shall make some general points that are not made in the conventional books.

You may be told by some authors that a sure sign of a Worcester origin is glaze shrinkage inside the foot-rim. Yet, as I have already noted, glaze does not shrink, it spreads during the firing process. This fact gives rise to the practice after about 1760 of wiping the glaze away from the inside of the foot-rim so that the molten glaze would not run down the foot and glue the piece to the kiln-furniture. However, you should note and note carefully that other factories employed the same method of wiping glaze away from the inside of the foot: most Caughley displays this feature (Plate 6) as do some Liverpool porcelains and many nineteenth-century factories followed the practice. You must also observe that the pre-1760 Worcester porcelains do *not* normally show this feature. So, to sum up, a glaze-free line inside the foot-rim is not an infallible guide to a Worcester origin.

It is often stated that the Worcester paste by transmitted light is green. This is generally true but it can vary to a considerable degree and some Caughley porcelains display a very similar greenish tone as both factories seem to have drawn their raw materials from the same source.

While some Worcester porcelains are really superb and neat in all respects, it must be acknowledged that *some* pieces–especially those made in the 1770–80 period–are of quite ordinary quality, made to cater for the vast market for low-priced useful wares. The Worcester management, like others, sold off slightly faulty pieces, 'seconds' and even 'thirds', at reduced prices and one can find pieces with a badly run blue design or examples showing a blister where another piece has fallen against it in the kiln. Make no mistake, Worcester porcelain is *nearly* always faultless but not always.

Some eighteenth-century Worcester is of extreme rarity, and not only figures. Strangely the manufacturers seem to have experienced great difficulty in firing large plates and dishes before the mid-1760s or even the early 1770s. The teasets had two saucer-shaped plates but the number of known flanged dinner plates can almost

Plate 57 A Worcester teapot of typically elegant form decorated only with a slight gold design, *c.* 1765–70. 6 inches high. *Geoffrey Godden, Chinaman*

be counted on the fingers of one hand. The management seem not to have competed with the imports of Chinese dinner-services which were a staple item of the Chinese export-market porcelains. Instead, the Worcester management concentrated happily on the production of a host of table accessories, sauceboats, cream-boats, leaf-shaped dishes, shell-shaped dishes, pickle-dishes, and of course the relief-moulded teawares. These pieces, so English in their way, were decorated with Oriental-inspired figure or landscape patterns painted with such charm that to British eyes at least they have far more appeal than the wares that inspired them.

I have already spoken of the over-glaze-printed designs (p. 65). Worcester was probably the first porcelain factory to have employed this technique of mass production, and certainly it was used to the greatest advantage and has probably never been bettered. Printing in underglaze-blue seems to have been introduced in a somewhat hesitant manner in about 1760. Some of these designs are of great rarity and many of the more common ones are very successful. There is a tendency to decry printed pieces but as I have explained earlier, the original copper plates were engraved by talented artist-designers and such patterns are far superior to a stock design painted by some young apprentice employed painting the same basic design hour after hour, day after day. We should remember that the majority of hand-painted designs were themselves mass-produced or were stock designs produced by the hundred if not by the thousand.

The famous Dr Wall retired to Bath in 1774 where he died two years later. However, most authorities have continued the first, or Dr Wall, period up to 1783 when Thomas Flight purchased the works as a going concern, to be joined in 1793 by Martin Barr, thus giving rise to the Flight & Barr period. Henry Sandon, the curator of the Dyson Perrins Museum, has suggested in his *Illustrated Guide to Worcester Porcelain* that we should designate the 1776–93 period the Davis/Flight or middle period. William Davis had been one of the original partners or 'inventors', his name being linked with Dr John Wall's in the 1751 agreement. Davis was to continue and take the firm into the Flight period.

Within this Davis/Flight period we can fit a selection of Worcester porcelain that is of rather mediocre or commercial quality. We can perhaps excuse this slight lowering of standards when we remember the opposition that the management would have been facing at this troublesome time in Britain's history, with the loss of the American colonies. Apart from the loss of markets and hard times at home, Thomas Turner had left to establish the Caughley factory which started production in about 1775, producing in the main good but inexpensive blue and white useful wares, very often copying Worcester shapes and designs. The Derby factory was producing very fine quality decorative porcelains and the Staffordshire potters were producing not only New Hall porcelains but a huge range of good quality earthenwares that must have cut into the Worcester porcelain trade.

The Worcester factory surmounted the difficulties by concentrating to a large degree on the production of blue-printed useful wares–the staple of the industry. In many cases the patterns were traditional ones which were kept in production year after year. In these cases it is difficult to date these pieces, for the use of the standard crescent mark was continued well into the Flight period. The typical 'Dr Wall' tankard shown in Plate 58 is in fact dated 1780, four years after the Doctor's death, and some pieces bearing well-known first-period blue-printed designs bear also the post-1783 impressed mark 'FLIGHTS'.

There is, however, one very interesting new class of Worcester blue-printed porcelain. a class seemingly confined to this Davis/Flight period. Very many pieces of this type bear a fresh series of related marks–the so-called disguised numeral marks. We have the numbers 1 to 9 each used separately and disguised with Oriental-looking curves or other embellishments. Three typical examples appear on p. 90.

Up to the time of my researches published in 1969 (*Caughley and Worcester Porcelains 1775–1800*, Barrie & Jenkins, London, 1969), these marks and the whole

Plate 58 A blue-printed Worcester tankard inscribed and dated 1780. Blue shaded-crescent mark. $5\frac{4}{5}$ inches high. *Geoffrey Godden, Chinaman*

class of porcelains on which they occur were incorrectly classed as Caughley. These devices are found on a charming range of well-engraved landscape and figure patterns often featuring prominent classical ruins. Sometimes these landscapes are set in a small panel; at other times the design fills all but the edge of the piece. These European designs are quite rare, some excessively so, and the same disguised numeral marks also occur on some of the later standard prints—the floral designs and the Oriental-inspired patterns including the Worcester version of the popular 'Fisherman' or 'Pleasure Boat' print.

It would appear that the Worcester enamelled porcelains of the post-1776 Davis/Flight period were usually unmarked and in general the overglaze design became very restrained. By the 1780s the former richly coloured Worcester-style had given way to simple patterns combining underglaze-blue with overglaze gilding. The teapots and sugar basins tended to be oval rather than circular, perhaps following the Chamberlain examples. The 'cabinet-pieces' can in contrast be extremely finely decorated and such pieces often bear clear name-marks of the period.

With the exception of the one known 'Wigornia' cream-boat the early Worcester porcelains do not bear a *factory* mark. If marks occur before about 1755 they are painter's marks which are small-sized signs taking various individual forms and these normally occur on blue and white wares only, and usually only on the pre-1755 examples. The devices were often painted under the handle of a creamer or other article. The early enamelled pieces are usually unmarked.

After about 1755 or later we have the well-known factory marks. The crescent, shown below as (A), painted and unshaded on hand-painted objects, printed (B) and shaded with lines on printed designs. We also have the initial 'W' (C) in various forms painted in underglaze-blue and versions of the Dresden crossed-swords mark (D). This device sometimes has the numerals '9' or '91' placed between the blades. You will also find many slightly different versions of the 'square' or 'seal-mark' (E), a device found on many of the scale-blue ground wares. Some Oriental-type designs bear fanciful Chinese-looking character marks (F). Marks C to F will appear on Worcester porcelains of the approximate 1755–75 period. The crescent mark was continued into the Flight period, that is into the 1790s, and in the late 1770s and 1780s we have also the disguised numeral marks on blue-printed designs (p. 90).

A   B   C   D   E   F

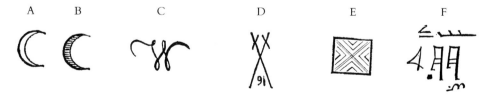

Do note that the square-mark (E) in particular can occur on hard-paste and other reproductions of Dr Wall porcelain. You should also observe that very many of the original Dr Wall-period porcelains are completely unmarked.

For the novice as yet unfamiliar with the Worcester body or glaze the best guide to identification is the shape of the object. *Close* comparison should be made with actual specimens or, where this is not possible, with pieces illustrated in the standard reference books. Apart from the forms some, but by no means all, patterns are unique to the Worcester factory. You will find the following specialist books most helpful but most general books on English ceramics give a fair coverage to this important factory: *Coloured Worcester Porcelain of the First Period* by H. Rissik Marshall (Ceramic Book Co., Newport, Mon., 1954); *Worcester Porcelain and Lund's Bristol* by F. A. Barrett (Faber, London, revised edition 1966); *Caughley and Worcester Porcelain 1775–1800* by G. Godden (Barrie & Jenkins, London, 1969); *The Illustrated Guide to Worcester Porcelain* by H. Sandon (Barrie & Jenkins, London, 1969).

A Godden tape-recorded talk on Dr Wall-period Worcester porcelains is also available with an illustrated supplement (see p. 277).

You must also–and I do mean *must*–visit the splendid collection at the Dyson Perrins Museum adjoining the Royal Worcester works in that city, and nearer home for many of us the Worcester pieces at the Victoria and Albert Museum in London are well worth many visits.

I shall return to the subject of Worcester porcelain and the nineteenth-century products in Chapter 9.

CHAPTER SIX

The hybrid hard-paste porcelains

We have in the previous chapter learnt something of the major eighteenth-century English porcelain factories, of the artificial or soft-paste porcelains and of two makes of true or hard-paste porcelains–Plymouth and Bristol. There is, however, a further type of English porcelain–a sort of hybrid hard-paste, mid-way between hard-paste and soft-paste. Many factories in the 1790–1810 period made such porcelains and they have been little researched. This is hardly surprising for so little is known about the different makers or even about the type of body employed. Most pieces are very similar in the appearance of the body. Shapes and patterns of one firm were closely followed by others and very few marked pieces exist to help our pioneer study.

I first began to be interested in these porcelains some years ago when working on my Coalport book and after excavations on the Caughley factory site. My research widened when I was asked in 1973 to read a paper at the Morley College 'Hard-Paste' Seminar. This paper was to follow David Holgate's on the New Hall porcelain, and he in turn followed learned authorities speaking on Bristol and Plymouth wares. I was to tidy up the loose ends and discuss the other hard-paste wares. Tidy up indeed, I posed more questions than I answered and certainly set myself re-thinking the whole puzzling question of this class of English porcelain.

It is strange but true that we know today far more about early British porcelains of the 1750–70 period than we do about many of the wares made at the beginning of the nineteenth century. There are two main reasons for this. First, ceramic students have concentrated on the earlier period, and second the later wares were routine useful objects–mainly teawares–which in their period excited little or no contemporary comment. They lacked the novelty of the earlier porcelains.

The study of these problem hybrid hard-paste porcelains is very closely related to the New Hall porcelains and I propose to start our discussion with these wares. There are two standard reference books on the New Hall products, the first was written by G. E. Stringer in 1949 and was simply titled *New Hall Porcelain* (Art Trade Press, London); the second is David Holgate's *New Hall and its Imitators* (Faber, London, 1971). These two authors differ on a fundamental point. Stringer denied the traditional belief that New Hall porcelain is hard-paste whereas David Holgate supports this old idea. It all depends on our definition of what is hard-paste and what is not, and this is precisely where we foundered at the Morley College Seminar. We all left this definition to others to pronounce and certainly when I prepared my talk–the last of the weekend–I assumed that such a definition would already have been given and explained.

I now find there is no generally accepted or acceptable definition of hard-paste porcelain. We have several often-repeated tests but on re-examination I find that they are unreliable. I have already mentioned that a good file will cut into most hard-pastes, certainly into New Hall. Some accepted hard-pastes show a granular fracture, a feature regarded as a characteristic of soft-paste porcelains. The degree to which enamels stand up on top of the glaze depends not so much on the underlying porcelain as on the make-up of the glaze and of the enamels and the amount of flux used and also on the firing temperature. So there go our three old tests for hard-paste porcelain, and we are left with the feel and individual experience of each collector.

One characteristic of hard-paste lies in the firing procedure. The Chinese potters apparently hardened off the biscuit porcelain at a very low heat, after which it was glazed and then subjected to the high temperature of some 1400°C, at which the body vitrified, the glaze matured and the two fused together as a whole. Most manufacturers of hard-paste porcelain followed the traditional Oriental method.

The English soft-paste porcelain manufacturers reversed the firing sequence so that the first biscuit firing was the highest and vitrified the porcelain. This was then glazed and refired at a lower temperature to mature and fix the covering skin of glaze.

The hybrid hard-paste porcelains to be discussed in this section appear to have been fired in the English soft-paste manner; they are therefore of a type of hard-paste porcelain fired in the soft-paste technique. There is a great advantage to the potter in employing this method, for once fired and vitrified the body is strong and will withstand much rougher handling than unvitrified wares. Printed designs can for example be applied, the transfer-paper pressed on in a positive manner and soaked off again, processes difficult to carry out on a lightly fired blank.

The firing temperatures to which the different mixes matured also have a bearing on the type of porcelain produced. Hard-pastes mature or vitrify at about 1400°C, some two hundred or so degrees higher than soft-paste or artificial porcelains. With the help of Henry Sandon and Paul Rado of the Worcester Royal Porcelain Company we submitted various types of porcelain to different firing temperatures, first to their standard hard-paste kiln which reaches 1435°C to 1450°C in the normal course of firing the Worcester special porcelains.

As you may expect the eighteenth-century Chinese hard-paste porcelains came through this temperature with flying colours. I was, however, surprised to find the glaze had in this range of temperatures just started to melt and flow from the porcelain. Obviously the Chinese porcelains (at least the seemingly typical pieces tested) would have failed if fired at over 1450°C. The Dresden fragments also survived the 1435–1450°C firing, as did Bristol porcelains. We have therefore

Plate 59 Foreground. Chinese hard-paste (*left*) after firing at some 1435°C, with a New Hall fragment (from the cover shown) reduced to a shapeless blob.

shown that the hard-paste Chinese, Dresden and Bristol porcelains matured in approximately the same high temperature fire. Of course, as you may have expected, the overglaze enamel decoration fired away at this temperature.

These firings led to tests on New Hall porcelain. The first piece submitted to the hard-paste kiln came out a shapeless blob (Plate 59), whereas a Chamberlain fragment kept its shape perfectly at this temperature. A further New Hall piece from the same specimen lost its shape and the glaze bubbled into a 'moon-scape' at 1250°C and a further fragment remained perfect at 1100°C. The firing temperature of the New Hall paste was probably within the 1150–1200°C range, hardly consistent with the temperature needed to mature a true hard-paste porcelain. In fact a Coalport/Caughley site waster of the 1800–10 period of the type I call 'hybrid hard-paste' stood up better to the fire at 1350°C than did New Hall at 1250°C. I must, however, point out that the New Hall partners themselves claimed to be 'Manufacturers of Real China'. Also the analysis of the body as carried out by

Herbert Eccles on a bowl of the 1795–1800 period is very similar to that of standard and accepted hard-paste porcelains. This one piece showed:

	%
Silica	73·56
Alumina	19·30
Phosphoric Acid	0·24
Lime	4·02
Soda	2·10
Potash	0·92
Oxide of Lead	0·67
Magnesia	Trace
	100·81

NEW HALL, 1781–1835

The New Hall porcelains are certainly linked historically with our two hard-paste factories of Plymouth and Bristol, which worked William Cookworthy's original patent of 1768 (which was in 1775 extended to take its coverage up to 1796). When the Bristol factory under Richard Champion failed (p. 83), Champion sought to cash in on his most valuable asset, the patent, which permitted the holder to make translucent porcelains using the vital raw materials, china-clay and china-stone. With this in mind Champion visited the Staffordshire Potteries and sought the help of his old adversary, Josiah Wedgwood. On 12 November 1780 Wedgwood reported to his partner Bentley:

> …Mr Champion of Bristol has taken me up near two days. He is come amongst us to dispose of his secret–his patent etc…. He tells me he has sunk fifteen thousand pounds in this gulf, and his idea is now to sell the whole art, mystery and patent for six and he is now trying a list of names I have given him of the most substancial and enterprising potters amongst us…

One may wonder why the leading Staffordshire pottery manufacturers should have been interested in laying out the then considerable sum of six thousand pounds to purchase Champion's patent when his own efforts to work it had been rather unsuccessful, but the manufacture of porcelain was a compelling goal. At that time Caughley, Derby and the Worcester factories were obviously prospering and practically had the market to themselves while not one potter in Staffordshire was then making porcelain, except perhaps Neale.

Wedgwood in his letter to Bentley stated that Champion was selling the 'whole art, mystery and patent'. There would seem to have been a further saleable commodity: Champion's licences to mine and take the all-important Cornish clays, and if Champion retained the licences he certainly hoped to sell the raw material and to make a profit by so doing.

It occurs to me that while Champion was producing his own hard-paste porcelain he would obviously seek to protect his patent-right to be the sole producer, but once he had ceased to make porcelain himself, and provided he had access to a supply of the raw materials, it would be in his interests to permit, by licence or otherwise, as many potters as possible to use and buy from him the materials he no longer required. This reasoning is supported by two letters written by Champion when reporting on his progress in Staffordshire. The first dated 6 August 1781 merely touches on this aspect of extending the trade: 'The present plan has a clause in it giving liberty to every potter to make the porcelain in his own works, on payment of a certain fine to the company.' A letter written on 3 September 1781 is rather more detailed and I have italicised the more interesting passages:

> ...I have now entered into an agreement with ten potters only, who if they like the manufactory on its establishment in the country are to give me a certain sum for liberty to use it in their own works, *but I have also liberty to sell to any other I please.*
>
> *In this situation I naturally look to some advantages from the sale of materials* but the high price of them compared with these of Trethewys (12 guineas a year) and Carthews equally cheap, make me have very little hopes of advantage...You will please always to carry this in your view, that the potters will buy where they please, and that there is no way of engaging them than by selling cheap.

One can, I think, deduce from this letter that Champion would have been only too glad to grant a licence to any potter that approached him and was willing to pay the price of the china-clay and china-stone. We may also hazard a guess that Champion knew that his patent rights were not all that watertight, for if they were the question of price would not arise: the potters would have to pay his price or licence fee, or not make porcelain with these ingredients.

The earliest printed account of Champion's efforts to sell his art and patent in Staffordshire is given by Simeon Shaw in his *History of the Staffordshire Potteries* (privately published, Hanley, 1829). After giving a brief account of Cookworthy's discovery and of Champion's purchase of the patent, Shaw explained that Champion:

> Sold the patent to a company in Staffordshire:–Mr Samuel Hollins–red-china potter of Shelton; Anthony Keeling, Potter of Tunstall; John Turner, Lane End; Jacob Warburton of Hot Lane; William Clowes and Charles Bagnall, Potter, Shelton.
>
> After this agreement Mr Champion directed the processes of the manufacture for the company [from November 1781] at the manufactory of Mr Anthony Keeling at Tunstall but when that gentleman [Champion] removed to London in

[April] 1782, a disagreement ensued among the partners; Mr Keeling and John Turner withdrew and they who continued together engaged as managing partner Mr John Daniel...and settled the manufactory at the New Hall, Shelton only a short time previously erected by Mr Whitehead, of the Old Hall, Hanley; on which account the Porcelain had the appellation of New Hall china and during the lifetime of the several partners, the concern has been carried forward to their great profit...

If we can believe Shaw's account, and after all he was writing at a time when the factory was still in being, we can deduce that these leading Staffordshire potters, whom we speak of as partners in the New Hall concern, did little more than put up money for the new adventure started by Champion and continued by their manager, John Daniel, while the so-called partners continued to run their own potteries where they made various types of high-grade earthenware.

We cannot now be sure if the early experimental porcelain made at the Tunstall works of Anthony Keeling in the 1781–2 period differ materially from that produced at Shelton's 'New Hall' after John Turner and Keeling had left the partnership. It should be noted that the new firm did not in the eighteenth century trade as New Hall, rather the names of the principal partners were used–'Hollins, Warburton & Co'.

The early New Hall porcelains of the 1783–6 period often go unacknowledged because in form and style of decoration they are very different from the later pieces– the silver-shape teapots and simple cottage floral designs that are to so many people typical New Hall. The early teapots were often globular in form. Many of the early designs comprised only elegant gilt borders or bands. Such early pieces are often devoid of even a pattern number, and typical examples are featured in my *British Porcelain, an illustrated guide*.

We have few original accounts relating to New Hall wares, but one for goods purchased by Josiah Wedgwood is of considerable interest. It is dated 7 September 1789 and reads:

Bt. of Hollins Warburton & Co.
Manufacturers of Real China.
Shelton, Staffordshire

1 sett cups and saucers enameld	
of 6 diffrt cups and 6 saucers	6/-
4 cups and 4 saucers blue & white	
of 4 diffrt patterns	3/6d
1 cup and saucer white & gold	2/5d

These cups and saucers of eleven different patterns for under twelve shillings were probably in the nature of samples. This brief account shows that in 1789 at least four blue and white patterns were in production but more remarkably we can see that a single gilt cup and saucer cost nearly two and a half times the price of enamelled examples. We can also see that the blue and white cups and saucers (the designs were almost certainly printed) were only marginally cheaper than the hand-painted coloured designs. By the way, these quoted prices were probably the retail ones for, from the total of 11s 11d, Wedgwoods were allowed 25 per cent discount. For my money and apparently for Wedgwood's too the tasteful gilt pieces are far superior to the simple, very repetitive enamelled designs, most of which have the appearance of having been painted by inexperienced boys rather than by trained ceramic artists.

In contrast, some rarely found New Hall porcelains were painted by talented artists, the most famous of which was Fidelle Duvivier–indeed I think he is the only proven New Hall painter known to us by name. Duvivier was born at Tournai in August 1740. He was painting for Duesbury of Derby in the 1769–73 period; he also worked at Worcester, or at least his work is known on a single signed teapot dated 1772, but this may have been an example of Duvivier's independent ceramic painting–not work carried out for the Worcester management. In the 1781–90 period Duvivier was at New Hall where he painted in a highly characteristic and pleasing style unique figure and landscape compositions. These very often include smoking kilns in the background and the distant views are wonderfully shaded off into the haze. A rare covered jug in Duvivier's typical style is shown in Plate 60. His pieces are so rare that I wonder what on earth he did with himself while he was employed at the factory! The quality of his work should have ensured that a relatively high proportion of his work was protected in cabinets and so survived more than would humble, everyday teasets. Perhaps he also painted flower subjects such as the delicately painted groups which appear on the fine presentation jugs–compositions which nearly always include a strange kidney-shaped petal (see colour plate B). Duvivier may also have been employed at Chamberlain's factory at Worcester for a short period, and his painting also occurs on a rare class of well-potted Staffordshire porcelain of the 1785–95 period–these pieces may prove to have been made by the Neale partnership. This work may be in the nature of part-time independent decoration.

On 1 November 1790 Fidelle Duvivier wrote to William Duesbury in Derby; I quote this letter in part (it appears complete in David Holgate's book):

> ...[I] take the liberty of adressing you with a few lines as mine engagement in the new Hal Porcelaine manufactory is expierd, and the propriotors do not intend to do much more in the fine line of painting, therefor [I] think of settling in New-Castle under-lime being engag'd to teech drawing in the boarding school at that place, one school I have at Stone, so as to have only three days to spare in the week for painting which time could wish to be employ'd by you preferable to eany other fabricque, because you like and understand good work...

Duvivier goes on to ask Duesbury to send him porcelain each week by wagon from Derby. Duesbury is hardly likely to have agreed to this troublesome process when

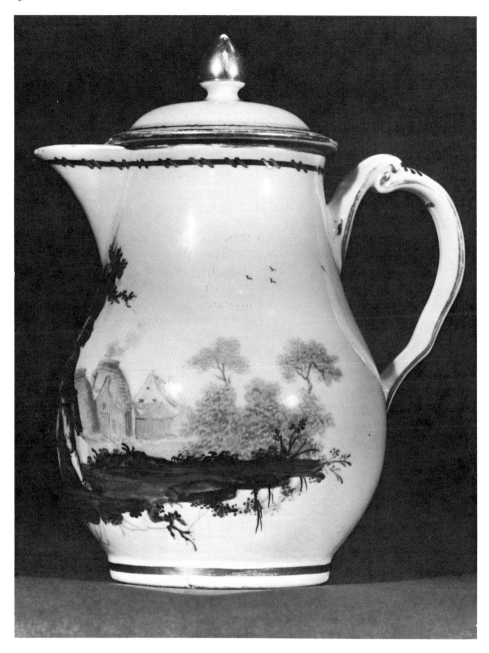

Plate 60 A New Hall covered creamer decorated in the typical style of Fidelle Duvivier, *c.* 1781–90. 5¼ inches high. *Private Collection*

he had such good ceramic artists under his own roof and under his own watchful eye. However, we can see from this letter that Duvivier was seeking part-time work and he may well have continued to paint special pieces for the New Hall management (or other local firms) for several years after 1790.

Do not think for one moment that the so-called silver-shape or turreted teapot (as in Plate 11) is typical of New Hall. It (and there are very many variations of the basic form) was only employed for a limited period, probably c. 1790–1805, and many other teapot shapes were made before and after this. Certainly over twelve totally different New Hall shapes were made. Remember also that firms other than New Hall made this basic shape of teapot.

Apart from the gilt patterns and the enamelled designs the New Hall firm also produced a range of blue and white porcelains–normally blue-printed designs having distinct Chinese influence; one pattern at least occurs also on Chinese porcelains of the period. Apart from these blue-printed pieces some very fine overglaze prints are to be found on New Hall porcelains. These are normally of the 'bat' type (see p. 66) with a delicate stippled effect. Some of these prints were dusted with gold rather than with black or other pigment. Such rare specimens are normally marked 'Warburton's Patent' in large writing letters and this mark relates to Peter Warburton's 1810 patent for printing in metallic colours.

These often charming stipple-engraved bat-prints provide a convenient link between the early hybrid hard-paste and the later New Hall bone-china, for a completely new body was introduced somewhere in the 1812–14 period. The new body was at once lighter and whiter and on some of these later bone-chinas there appears for the first time the name-mark 'New Hall', printed within a double lined circle. This name was certainly in use at an earlier period–it occurs in catalogue descriptions as early as 1802 and Duvivier used the term 'the New Hall porcelain manufactory' in his 1790 letter to Duesbury, but it was not then used as a mark.

It would seem that most writers have confused the issue of marks by illustrating written pattern numbers or describing these in words, stating that the New Hall pattern numbers were prefixed with 'No' or 'N'. This can be the case–it is often so written but by no means invariably and I could quote ten or more firms of the same period which used such standard abbreviations for the word 'number' when marking their standard designs with the relevant pattern number. Do remember that the pre-1790 New Hall porcelains seldom bore a pattern number at all. The blue and white pieces were not marked and in the case of the standard teasets only the main pieces bore a pattern number. Saucers, teabowls and coffee cups were to all intents and purposes never marked, although New Hall-type pieces from other factories are often marked.

No standard factory mark appears on the earlier hybrid hard-paste-type New Hall porcelains. A blue-printed crowned lion rampant crest-mark does very rarely occur on some blue-printed porcelains. This device has been referred to as a copy of the Frankenthal factory mark but the New Hall crest bears little resemblance to the German mark. I have already mentioned the hand-written 'Warburton's Patent' mark (with crown above) which occurs on gold printed wares of the 1810–14 period. Some painted workman's or painter's personal tally marks also occur in the 1800–20 period, of these the most frequent and characteristic being the 'F'-like device shown below. The retailer's name-mark 'E. Cotton of Edinburgh' also occurs on some teawares of the same period.

The bone-china wares can, but do not always, bear a printed name-mark as shown below and David Holgate also mentions the one-word mark 'Newhall', but this must be regarded as somewhat exceptional.

The later New Hall bone-china, produced after about 1820, had little real character and the factory was ill equipped to compete with the very many large and small firms producing the same basic body. The main partners had died; there was no drive and the works seem to have gradually declined until in March 1831 the factory, mill and land were offered for sale by auction. They were not then sold but were advertised to be let in August and September 1832. In October 1835 the stock of the 'Valuable & Extensive stock of burnished gold china' was offered for sale, the auction notice then stating 'The New Hall Company are declining business and have let the premises, which they now occupy, with immediate possession...' Some six years later John Boyle, Herbert Minton's former partner, entered the following observations in his diary under the date 27 July 1841: 'Looked over the New Hall manuf. and found all the places in bad repair to such an extent indeed that I do not consider it tenantable in its present state. The ovens also are too large for the Hovels and all the sagger houses are small and inconvenient...'

Nevertheless the name New Hall was continued up to 1956 by various firms situated on the original site, the last being the New Hall Pottery Co. Ltd, in the 1899–1956 period, and some of these later firms legitimately used the description 'New Hall' on their products.

The standard book on the New Hall wares is undoubtedly David Holgate's *New Hall & its Imitators*. G. Grey's New Hall chapter in *English Porcelain 1745–1850*, edited by R. J. Charleston, is a most useful contribution as is also the same authority's paper published in the *Transactions of the English Ceramic Circle* (vol. 8, part 1, 1971). The *Collectors Guide* of April 1971 contains articles by Mrs Holgate and myself under the general heading 'The Total Look of New Hall' and of course Dr

Watney's *Blue and White* book deals with this section of the New Hall products.

Note that not all simple floral sprig designs are of New Hall origin–the so-called New Hall patterns were popular, inexpensive ones of the period and as such featured in the pattern book of nearly every factory.

CHAMBERLAINS, *c.* 1788–1852

Leaving Staffordshire for the time being I want to follow our trail of hard-paste-type porcelains to the city of Worcester, to the works of Robert Chamberlain. I have explained (p. 91) how in 1788 Chamberlain left the main Worcester factory to set himself up as a decorator and retailer and how at first he was content to decorate blanks made at the Caughley factory. But at an unknown date between 1789 and December 1793 Chamberlain commenced the manufacture of his own porcelains.

A sample of this Chamberlain porcelain (a cup of pattern 55) was analysed for me at the North Staffordshire College of Technology with the following result:

	%
Silica	68·61
Alumina	23·52
Potash	3·61
Soda	1·27
Lime	1·14
Ferric Oxide	0·34
Magnesia	0·16
Loss (calcined at 950°C)	0·34

This is remarkably similar in the main constituents to a Bristol analysis and to a New Hall one published by G. E. Stringer. A piece was also tested at the British Museum Research Laboratory by X-ray defraction analysis and reported as being a hard-paste porcelain.

Regarding the heat-test we submitted a fragment of a hunting pattern teaset (Plate 61) of about 1795 to the Worcester hard-paste kiln which reaches some 1435°C (cone 15), at which temperature you may remember a New Hall fragment melted into a shapeless mass. Of the Chamberlain pieces, Henry Sandon commented: 'The Chamberlain piece was a great surprise–it certainly looks to be a hard or near hard-paste body but which was never fired up as high as its potential. At our 1435°C temperature the body held well and even became more translucent…'

Although the thin fragment retained its shape in the hard-paste kiln, it was probably originally fired at about 1300°C, still a somewhat high temperature. The glost-firing was, as might be expected, lower and in this case the glaze bubbled and blistered in a kiln reaching 1220°C.

On all counts we can regard the early Chamberlain body as a hybrid hard-paste and it was certainly able to stand a hard-firing very much better than the New Hall body.

As to the introduction of the Chamberlain porcelain, entries in the Chamberlain account books suggest that he was making, or about to make, his own wares in 1791, and monies paid to modellers and throwers in the later part of this year confirm our impression. The production of Chamberlain's earliest porcelain was probably rather limited and he certainly continued to decorate some Caughley blanks for several years after he was making his own porcelains. By January 1796 when the following letter was sent from the factory, the output would seem to have increased:

Sir,

By a late material improvement of our kilns we have been enabled to make much larger quantity of china, in consequence of which Messrs Chamberlain will be now happy in the favour of your orders...On every painted teapot we write *warranted* which never having in one instance failed...

The early Chamberlain hard-paste-type porcelains made between 1791 and 1796 were seldom marked and even pattern-numbers were not used before about 1794, although at least thirty-two numbered designs were in production by February 1794. The early unmarked examples are rare and little known, in fact as far as I know examples have not been illustrated in any of the standard reference books, most of which–including my own *British Porcelain, an illustrated guide*–start with the standard oval-bodied teapots with various flutings. These standard shapes are described in the January 1796 inventory as 'Bell fluted' or as 'shanked' and 'new fluted'. In fact, 'shanked and fluted' teapots, creamers and other tewares were included in a stock-taking list of December 1793 and they were in the 'biscuit', or unglazed, state so they were of Chamberlain's own make not Caughley blanks. This December 1793 list includes:

40 teapots, sorted in biscuit	valued at	6/8d
50 teapot stands and spoon trays in biscuit	,, ,,	8/4d
70 dozen ewers, sorted	,, ,,	£7/0/0d
160 sugar boxes	,, ,,	£1/6/8d
230 dozen pressed and plain coffee cups	,, ,,	£23/0/0d
7 dozen tea and coffee pots, toys	,, ,,	£7/0/0d

The low value put on undecorated stock is remarkable. Teapots at two old pence each, twenty cream ewers to the pound, etc, show, if the figures were realistic, the basic low cost of the initial manufacturing process.

Let us take the first entry '40 teapots, sorted'. I think 'sorted' must mean that more than one shape was included in the count. It can hardly refer to the pattern because the pots were not yet glazed. I feel sure that one of these Chamberlain teapot shapes was very similar to the contemporary New Hall turreted teapot of the 'silver shape'. I have shown you in Plate 35 such an early Chamberlain example,

Plate 61 An early Chamberlain-Worcester creamer of the hybrid hard-paste body, *c.* 1795, 4¼ inches high. *Geoffrey Godden, Chinaman*

of a very hard-looking paste. The Chinese-style floral design, pattern number '2', appears on other early Chamberlain porcelains of characteristic form and I have a similar shaped but rather later teapot which is plainly marked 'Chamberlains Worcester. Warranted'. The word 'warranted' as used here, and in the 1796 letter just quoted, probably means that the teapots were warranted to stand the shock of hot water without cracking. Teasets of the same early period included spoon-trays–a component soon discontinued–and sometimes low 'Chelsea-ewers' of the type made at Caughley, Derby, Lowestoft and at the New Hall works.

Many of the early patterns were simple Chinese figure designs often rather naively painted. The little creamer shown in Plate 61 is a good example. The shape is very much in the New Hall style, but then several manufacturers made rather similar shapes. The painted pattern also occurs on New Hall porcelain and on Dr Wall Worcester wares and it occurs again in the Chamberlain list as number 9 'Hunting pattern in compartments'. Here we have a little known early Chamberlain pattern on a rare jug form of about 1795.

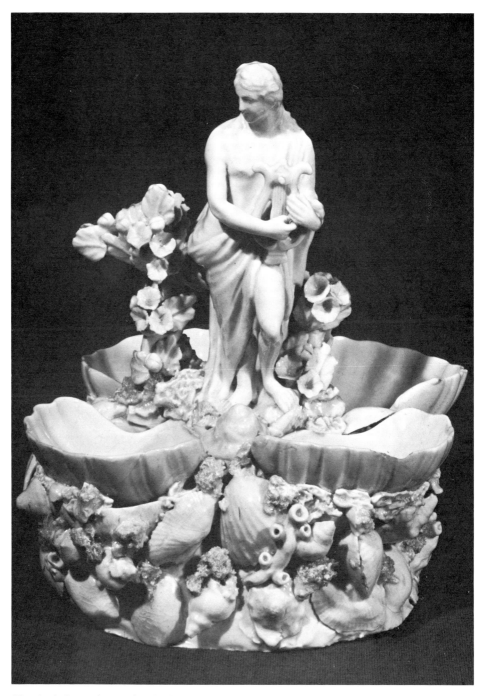

Plate 62 A fine and rare Chamberlain-Worcester 'pickle-stand', a model included in the Christmas 1795 factory stock-taking list. $9\frac{1}{4}$ inches high. *Author's Collection*

I will not dwell too long on these Chamberlain useful wares for the subject is vast. (I have been working on my Chamberlain book for over seven years now.) But I must just show that at a quite early date Chamberlain was making ornamental wares or at least quite complicated and imposing centre-pieces for the table. The January 1796 inventory lists in the biscuit-room a figure of Apollo and in the Christmas 1795 stock-taking list we find listed 'I pickle-stand, Apollo, glazed 10/6d'. Such a completed piece was sold to Michael Loveley of Honiton in November 1797; the sales entry then read 'I rich 4-shell pickle-stand with figure of Apollo, £3/3/od'.

Such a piece is illustrated in Plate 62 and in body and glaze is quite typical of these early Chamberlain-Worcester hybrid hard-paste wares. Having seen this fine piece you may not be surprised to learn that this firm also made animal and bird models, and this figure of Apollo was also adapted to form a fine watch-stand or mantel-clock!

In the late 1790s Chamberlains produced an amazing array of finely and often richly decorated porcelains–ranging from magnificent dinner-services to thimbles. It would seem, however, that Chamberlains did not seek to compete with Thomas Turner of Caughley in the production of blue and white wares, except in the traditional Worcester 'Royal Lily' or 'Queen Charlotte' pattern (a very formal compartmented floral design). I shall return to complete the story of this factory in Chapter 8 where I will relate how the present Royal Worcester company came to be formed and how it related to the Chamberlain firm. In the meantime you would be well advised to keep a good look-out for examples of this early Chamberlain-Worcester porcelain, which is the subject of one of my tape-recorded talks (see p. 277).

GRAINGER, c. 1801–1887

Just as in 1788 Chamberlain had left the main Worcester company and set up on his own account, so in turn did Thomas Grainger leave Chamberlain. The early Grainger porcelains are seldom marked, and in shape and in the added patterns they are very similar to the Chamberlain pieces of the same period. I will give more details of this factory in Chapter 8 but I should mention here that his early porcelains are of the class of hybrid hard-paste. Some of the teawares are featured in my *British Porcelain, an illustrated guide.*

CAUGHLEY, c. 1775–1799

I have already given a general account of the Salopian or Caughley porcelains in Chapter 5 where I explained that the body was a soapstone one similar to that employed at the Dr Wall factory at Worcester. This is so for the major part of the factory's existence under Thomas Turner, from c. 1775 to 1799.

There are, however, some pieces which appear to be of Turner's period which are of a totally different body–having only a trace of magnesia and therefore soapstone and having a cold, hard appearance: it is in fact a type of hard-paste porcelain. The great difficulty is to determine if these pieces are pre-1799 true Caughley porcelains made under Turner's management or if they were made after the Coalport partners had acquired the works. The trouble is that the new owners worked the same site and used the old moulds and the Turner copper-plates.

We need to find an impressed 'Salopian' example of this hard-paste type, or a piece bearing a date prior to October 1799. There are some pieces of this Shropshire hard-paste bearing an impressed Royal Arms device, a mark found on several wasters at the Caughley factory site. The significance of this mark is unknown but it may be relevant that in the closing-down sale of Turner's stock he advertised it as the stock 'of the Royal Salopian porcelain manufactory'. The Coalport partners did not as far as I am aware claim any royal association and this Royal Arms mark was probably used by Turner before his retirement.

I show in Plate 63 an oval covered sugar-basin bearing this mark. In general style it is very different from our picture of the normal Caughley porcelains but it does have near parallels in Chamberlain-Worcester, New Hall, Coalport and other porcelains. The porcelain itself is well worth study. It is a very cold, hard-looking body, but it is very poorly potted with prominent firing cracks and other faults. This is in sharp contrast to the standard Caughley soapstone body which like that used at Worcester seems to have given few manufacturing problems. On the evidence of this one piece the introduction of the new body was a retrograde step. The reason for the change is not certain, perhaps Turner was trying to emulate the Chamberlain body or the one employed by his competitors just up river at Coalport. The New Hall company was also capturing much of the market and this firm's patent for a hard-paste porcelain had lapsed in 1796.

When a factory such as Caughley suddenly changes from its well proven and highly successful soapstone body to a completely different hybrid hard-paste porcelain, we can judge there was some good reason–even if it was a case of following the fashion.

COALPORT (Rose & Co.), c. 1791 to present day

We cannot at present be sure when the main Coalport porcelain factory commenced production. The early writers had access to some documents which maintained that the first works were on the Jackfield side of the River Severn, opposite Coalport. These works carried on by 'Mr Rose, in conjunction with a Mr Blakeway' were soon transferred across to Coalport. The Chamberlain factory records contain a reference to a letter sent on 13 June to 'Mr Rose,

Plate 63 An oval Caughley/Coalport covered sugar-basin on the hard-paste body. Moulded Royal Arms mark, *c.* 1800. *Geoffrey Godden, Chinaman*

manufactory, Salop' but this could have been intended for Rose while employed at the Caughley factory not at Coalport. However, early in 1793 there were obviously two separate factories in the locality, Turner's (at Caughley) and Blakeway's (presumably at Coalport), for we have a letter dated 16 February 1793 which reads in part: '...I could not get any oval trifle dishes at the price you mention, nor any round ones from Blakeways...the cream ewers I had off Turner are cheaper than Blakeways'.

Unfortunately we do not know if the Blakeway (and Rose) factory was then situated at Jackfield or if it was then at Coalport. We do, however, have a diary entry made on 1 June 1796 which clearly states that it was then at Coalport near the famous tar springs: 'about 100 yards from this...is a porcelain manufactory lately established'.

The *Shropshire Journal* of 24 August 1796 reported that the Prince and Princess of Orange visited the Coalbrookdale Ironworks, the cannon foundry, the tar springs and then proceeded to the Coalport china factory 'where His Highness bought some pieces of Mr Rose'. This report serves to remind us that the factory was in the heart of the Industrial Revolution country, a district steeped in history and with many popular sights for the traveller. The locality is now an interesting and thriving open-air museum. This 1796 report also tells us that Mr Rose was probably the dominant partner, having superseded Edward Blakeway. The Coalport firm now traded as 'Rose & Co' or rarely as 'Rose Blakeway & Co'. There were in fact three partners in the eighteenth century–John Rose, Richard Rose and Edward Blakeway but it was John Rose's name that was forever to be associated with the name of Coalport porcelain.

Joseph Plymley's *General View of the Agriculture of Shropshire of 1803* tells us that: 'At Coalport coloured china of all sorts and of exquisite taste and beauty is made...and in which...including its dependencies, the most china is manufactured of any works of that sort in Great Britain, there are employed about 250 persons.' The 'dependencies' no doubt included the Caughley factory which had been purchased by the Coalport partners in October 1799 and which was continued by them until about 1814. This early-nineteenth-century claim, that Rose & Co. produced at Caughley and Coalport more porcelain than any other manufacturer, was probably true.

Our present-day knowledge of the early wares is somewhat restricted. We do not know about the very earliest pieces made on the Jackfield side of the river and we have little knowledge of the earliest true Coalport pieces. In contrast, however, we do have a very good idea of the post-1799 porcelains made by the Coalport partners at their newly acquired Caughley factory, for the site has yielded thousands of interesting wasters. These Caughley wasters were of a very hard-paste, which when submitted to the Worcester kilns stood up to a temperature of 1350°C, far better than a piece of New Hall of the hard-paste period.

I had a John Rose & Co. example analysed at the North Staffordshire College of Technology and this gave the following result:

	%
Silica	75·94
Alumina	18·95
Potash	2·12
Soda	1·21
Lime	0·78
Ferric Oxide	0·34
Magnesia	0·17
Titanic Oxide	0·02
Loss, calcined at 950°C	0·33
	99·86

I think most authorities will acknowledge that such a body is of the hard-paste type. Certainly it looks it. It would be difficult to find a more compact and heavy body, and a fracture appears more conchoidal or glass-like than Bristol hard-paste porcelain.

Now these hybrid hard-paste Rose & Co. porcelains of the type found on the Caughley site would post-date October 1799 and the problem remains: what porcelain did the Coalport partners produce before this? There is some reason for accepting that in the mid-1790s this body was of the soapstone-type similar to that made at Worcester and at Caughley. This is the most likely theory and one supported by Charles Hatchett's diary. On Saturday 28 May 1796 this very knowledgeable writer visited Worcester where he 'went to see the porcelain manufactory belonging to Messrs Flight and Barr. I have observed [he noted] that the Steatites of Cornwall is used as an ingredient...' This would be the Cornish soapstone which, as we already know, formed a vital part of the Worcester mix. When Hatchett visited the Coalport factory four days later he observed: 'The ware is like that of Worcester and the materials are the same.' (*The Hatchett Diary*, edited by Arthur Raistrick; D. Bradford Barton Ltd, Truro, 1967.) If we can believe this contemporary account, the Coalport porcelain of the 1796 period was of the soapstone type—yet the post-1799 Rose & Co. Caughley fragments are of a completely different body with only a trace (0·17 per cent) of Magnesia.

As the New Hall hard-paste patent ran out in 1796 other manufacturers would then have been free to experiment with and use (if they so wished) the china-clay and china-stone to make a translucent hard-paste-type porcelain. At some time between June 1796 and 1800, the Coalport partners switched to a hard-body. We can narrow the period to the two years 1796–8, when we consider the blue-printed jug shown in Plate 64. This, as you can see, is dated 1798 and it is of the hard-paste-type body. The Chinese-style landscape design is one of many related ones found on a large range of these early Rose & Co. porcelains.

Plate 65 shows a selection of Rose & Co.'s post-1799 porcelains decorated in underglaze-blue. These pieces link with finds on the Caughley site and illustrate the later re-use of Thomas Turner's eighteenth-century Caughley engraved designs. In general the Rose & Co. pieces are thicker in the potting and heavier in weight than the earlier Caughley examples and of course the body itself, or rather the thickly applied glaze, looks and feels harder. The blue too is a lighter and brighter tone.

Moving away from the blue and white porcelains, which in general terms emulate the Caughley shapes and designs, we must mention the overglaze simple floral designs in the New Hall manner. Much teaware was decorated in this popular style and (helpfully to us now) the shapes were quite different from those employed by the Staffordshire New Hall company. I show a few sample fragments from the Shropshire site in Plate 66, together with a rare, dated, two-handled tankard decorated with one of these standard patterns (Plate 68). The basic and characteristic Rose & Co. shapes are featured in my book *Coalport and Coalbrookdale Porcelains* (Barrie & Jenkins, London, 1970).

Plate 64 An early Coalport hard-paste porcelain presentation jug dated 1798. Underglaze-blue printed designs. $8\frac{1}{4}$ inches high. *Geoffrey Godden, Chinaman*

Plate 65 A selection of Coalport hard-paste porcelains of the 1800–1805 period. The bird prints show the re-use of Caughley copper plates. Ironbridge jug $8\frac{1}{2}$ inches high. *Geoffrey Godden, Chinaman*

Plate 66 A selection of New Hall-type enamelled designs on 'wasters' from the John Rose Caughley site, *c.* 1800–1805. *Author's Collection*

Surveying our quite large collection of Coalport porcelain of the 1800–15 period, one is impressed by the richness of the decoration. Of course many pieces are but modestly decorated and some have only a very slight pattern in gold but the so-called 'Japan' patterns really stand out, with their areas of a deep underglaze-blue with overglaze red, green and gilt embellishments. Such Japan patterns are normally associated with the Derby factory but they were common to most ceramic manufacturers. They were cheap to produce, being repetitive broad designs that could be painted by apprentices, and yet to the buying public they looked rich and a 'good buy'. The John Rose company produced a great many such patterns and probably they made more of this class than the Derby factory. I show in Plate 67 a typical plate of what I term the 'flower pot' design–a pattern, by the way, very popular in the late seventeenth and early eighteenth centuries when it appeared on the imported Japanese porcelains. To the right of this completed plate you will see some factory wasters from a similar plate but bearing only the underglaze-blue portions–a plate that obviously was discarded for some reason before it passed to the enamelling department.

I can mention here only the blue and white pieces, the New Hall-type designs and the Japan patterns as representing the main types of Rose's early Coalport hard-paste porcelains. Other designs are featured in my Coalport book and further New

Plate 67 A Coalport lobed edged plate of a popular so-called 'Japan' pattern, shown with factory 'waster' bearing the underglaze-blue portions, *c.* 1805. *Author's Collection*

Hall-type designs and some characteristic John Rose Coalport shapes are illustrated in David Holgate's paper 'Polychrome and Hard-Paste Caughley Porcelain', published in the *Transactions of the English Ceramic Circle* (vol. 7, part 1, 1968). The later post-1815 John Rose porcelains will be discussed in Chapter 8.

REYNOLDS, HORTON & ROSE; ANSTICE, HORTON & ROSE, 1800–1814

I have in the previous section deliberately mentioned on many occasions 'Rose & Co.' rather than refer in a general way to Coalport as one factory. The reason is simply that there were at Coalport, in this hard-paste period, two separate thriving factories, a mere stone's throw apart.

The rival factory was established in June 1800, the first partners being William Reynolds, William Horton and Thomas Rose, but three years later, on Reynolds's death, Robert Anstice joined the two remaining partners and they traded as Messrs Anstice, Horton & Rose, or as Anstice, Horton & Co. The factory was sold to the

Plate 68 A Coalport hard-paste double-handled mug dated 1802, again showing a New Hall-type design. 7½ inches high. *Messrs Phillips*

John Rose company in 1814, after the partnership had been dissolved, on 7 February of that year. For the whole life of the factory, from 1800 to 1814, only this hybrid hard-paste porcelain was produced. In the main, useful table-wares were produced decorated with at least 1419 different patterns plus the unnumbered blue and white designs. A sale advertisement published in *The Times* in January 1814 most probably relates to the auction of the stock belonging to the Anstice partnership. The advertisement, here quoted in part, suggests a large and varied output including very colourful patterns:

> ...on account of the manufactures and in consequence of a dissolution of partnership.
>
> The genuine and extensive stock, consisting of several superb and costly dinner and dessert services, in imitation of fine old Dresden and rich Japan [pattern] déjeuné services and supper sets, cabinet and ornamental vases, cups and cans, tea and coffee equipages and bowls, pencilled [a contemporary name for painted] in landscape, birds, fruit and flowers, figures and various designs and painted in rich colours, and superbly gilt; an assortment of blue and white of every description and a profusion of white china...

The Anstice, Horton & Rose shapes are very close copies of the standard John Rose forms, although there are always slight differences when the two versions are placed side by side. Such comparisons are featured in my *Coalport and Coalbrookdale Porcelains*. Apart from the key-shapes shown in my specialist book and in specimens included in my reference collection, we have a further source of information on these little known wares. Strangely this source is the pattern book of the rival John Rose company where there are included various references to the Anstice, Horton & Rose numbers, for some designs were made by both firms. For example, in the John Rose pattern book we see drawn and coloured the design on the punch-bowl shown in Plate 69. The John Rose number for this pattern is '319' but there also appears the notation that it was the rival partnership's design number '696'. The higher number appears on the bowl in Plate 69, a splendid and richly gilt example of Anstice, Horton & Rose's hybrid hard-paste porcelain.

An array of these always unmarked Anstice porcelains will startle most collectors for the diversity and decorative merits of the wares. It was a short-lived factory almost unknown to most ceramic students, but the porcelains must surely repay close study and attention.

Plate 69 A colourful Anstice, Horton & Rose, Coalport punch-bowl of pattern 696. Diameter 11 inches. *Geoffrey Godden, Chinaman*

DAVENPORT, c. 1793–1887

The name Davenport is a family one, not a place-name. The Davenport factories (there were four of them) were situated at Longport in the Staffordshire Potteries. At first only earthenwares were made, but from an unknown period, about 1800, some good quality porcelains were also produced. The early pieces made before say 1810 were of the compact semi-hard-paste type but later the then standard bone-china was adopted.

As yet we have not identified the earliest Davenport teawares, probably they were rather similar to the New Hall porcelains. We have some very attractive and well potted dessert wares, some of which bear the standard impressed DAVENPORT name mark in conjunction with the anchor device. A small sugar tureen from such a dessert service is shown in Plate 70. Other typical forms are shown in my *British Porcelain, an illustrated guide*. We will be discussing the later Davenport bone-china on p. 198.

ISLINGTON CHINA MANUFACTORY, LIVERPOOL.
(THOMAS WOLFE & CO.), c. 1796–1800

In 1796 Thomas Wolfe who had occupied and worked the Islington China Manufactory in Folly Lane, Liverpool, from February 1790, took two further partners. These were John Lucock (or Luckcock) and Miles Mason, and the three traded there as Thomas Wolfe & Co. Miles Mason, of whom we shall hear more a little later, was a leading 'chinaman' in London and had been a great purchaser of the imported Chinese porcelains. When the East India Company decided to cease their large-scale importations of this commodity in the early 1790s Mason must have looked round for an alternative source of supply and then to this partnership with Thomas Wolfe the Liverpool potter. Porcelain of our hybrid hard-paste type was made by this partnership working Pennington's old works. At the same time Mason was in partnership with George Wolfe at Lane Delph in the Staffordshire Potteries but this partnership was seemingly for the manufacture of earthenwares, not porcelains.

Miles Mason had married money and he may have provided the financial backing for these two enterprises. He would also have provided a valuable retail outlet for their products in London for he was there firmly established as one of the leading dealers of the period.

We owe our present knowledge of the porcelains produced by Wolfe & Co. at Liverpool in the closing years of the eighteenth century to the excavations of Alan Smith. His finds in the form of site wasters are featured in the *Transactions of the English Ceramic Circle* (vol. 8, part 2, 1972). These shards include simple New Hall-type floral patterns and, as you might expect from a factory partly owned by a London 'chinaman', some blue-printed teawares bearing Chinese-style designs.

Plate 70 An early Davenport porcelain dessert tureen. Impressed name and anchor mark, *c.* 1810. 6¾ inches high. *Geoffrey Godden, Chinaman*

Plate 71 shows some of these site wasters and in the illustrated supplement to my Mason tape-recorded talk, I show a range of related wares (see p. 277). I have very recently located some of the enamelled patterns in the style of New Hall and Chinese export-market teawares and one day the other articles made at the Islington China Manufactory will no doubt be identified and show the whole range of these Liverpool hybrid hard-paste porcelains of the 1796–1800 period.

The *London Gazette* of 5 July 1800 records the dissolution of this Liverpool partnership as from 7 June. The Staffordshire partnership had been dissolved two days earlier and we next hear of Miles Mason setting up on his own account in the Staffordshire Potteries.

The Liverpool-made Wolfe & Co. porcelains do not bear a factory mark nor even a pattern number.

MILES MASON (b. 1752), *c.* 1804–1813

As I have noted, Miles Mason, the London china dealer, had in the late 1790s been in two manufacturing partnerships–one at Liverpool for the production of porcelain

Plate 71 Four unglazed 'wasters' from the Wolfe-Mason Liverpool factory site, showing typical blue-printed designs, *c.* 1795–1800. *City of Liverpool Museums*

and one at Lane Delph in Staffordshire for the manufacture of earthenwares. These two partnerships were dissolved in June 1800.

The Lane Delph Pottery would seem to have been subsequently worked by Miles Mason as a 'china manufactory' and had been so occupied 'for some years past' to quote from a November 1805 sale advertisement. We cannot, however, be sure when this was opened as a porcelain works, for Miles Mason's famous and oft quoted advertisement of October 1804 gives the impression that the Mason porcelains were a recent innovation and Mason appears to have been directly engaged with his London business until 1802: '...Miles Mason, late of Fenchurch Street, London...has established a manufactory at Lane Delph...upon the principle of the Indian [meaning Chinese] and Sève [Sèvres] china...' (The advertisement from the *Morning Herald* is quoted in full in my *Illustrated Guide to Mason's Patent Ironstone China*.)

Miles Mason moved from Lane Delph to Fenton in 1807 and a second factory was opened there in 1811. By this period he had built up a good reputation, as is shown by the following report written by the manager of Wedgwood's London retail showroom: 'Mr Mason of Lane Delft is in town and he called upon me and in the course of conversation said that we should sell immense quantities of china here,

Plate 72 An attractively simple Miles Mason porcelain teapot. Pattern number 2, *c.* 1805. 10¾ inches long. *Geoffrey Godden, Chinaman*

if we had it and that he should be very happy to make it for you. His china is I believe very good and he has great orders for it...'

In general the early Miles Mason porcelains are in decoration similar to that made earlier at Liverpool. Many simple floral designs in the New Hall tradition occur. The teapot shown in Plate 72 is impress-marked M. MASON and also has the painted pattern number 2; it is typical of a whole class of Mason porcelain. Other teawares bear coloured prints of Chinese figure-subjects and a very large selection of early wares bear blue-printed Chinese-style landscape designs–the Pagoda or Broseley pattern–rather similar to the later willow pattern. These underglaze-blue prints link with the earlier Liverpool porcelains and it is often impossible to tell in which city the unmarked Mason porcelains were made, though the shapes can be a good guide.

The later, post-1807 porcelains became more decorative. Finely painted vases were made, as were dessert and dinner services, but the teawares predominate and are often just as fine as the Spode or Flight, Barr & Barr porcelains. Some of the Mason stipple-engraved or etched printed designs are of the highest order and quite individual. The Mason porcelains are of the hybrid hard-paste type, at least the examples made before about 1810 are, after which the paste appears to have been changed to the bone-china body.

A fragment of a mandarine pattern oval teapot-stand of the 1805–10 period was analysed for me by Mr M. Worcester with the following result:

	%
Silica	63·460
Alumina	26·760
Potash	3·253
Soda	1·792
Magnesia	1·762
Lime	1·288
Ferric Oxide	0·046
Not determined	1·640

This result is very near the hybrid hard-paste Chamberlain body although this Mason analysis may be affected slightly by glaze on the sample submitted.

In the firing tests the Mason fragments stood up well to high temperatures–nearing 1400°C and, using this method, the body seems very much harder than New Hall. The translucency of some Mason pieces can, however, be rather poor and in general the pieces are thickly potted.

In 1813 the famous Mason's Patent Ironstone China–a hard durable earthenware–was introduced. The patent had been taken out in the name of Charles James Mason, who was Miles Mason's third son. I believe that by this period Miles had all but retired. Certainly the new ironstone body proved extremely popular and I think his sons would have been more interested in developing and producing their new body than in producing porcelains in keen competition with many other manufacturers. For all practical purposes I think that the manufacture of Mason's porcelain ceased in 1813 after being in production for only about ten years. I must state that other authorities believe that production continued into the 1820s, and some rare later porcelain examples certainly exist. Miles Mason died in April 1822.

The Mason porcelains sometimes bear the impressed name-mark M. MASON but this normally occurs only on the more important pieces such as teapots and by no means on all such pieces. Some blue-printed designs have a mock Chinese seal-mark with MILES above and MASON below. You should note that many other manufacturers used the basic Oriental seal-device in various forms (without the name) and you should not assume that all such seal-marks indicate a Mason origin.

Much research remains to be carried out on these interesting porcelains. Reginald Haggar has given us very good foundations to build upon and I refer you to his book *The Masons of Lane Delph* (Lund Humphries & Co. Ltd, 1952), to his excellent paper 'Miles Mason' in the *Transactions of the English Ceramic Circle* (vol. 8, part 2, 1972), and importantly to his recent joint work with Elizabeth Adams, *Mason Porcelain and Ironstone 1796–1853* (Faber, London, 1977). Mason patterns and characteristic forms are also featured in my two large general works on British porcelains and in the illustrated supplement to my tape-recorded talks on Mason productions (see p. 277).

TURNER, c. 1759–1806

We are concerned here with a famous earthenware potter, or rather a family of potters, who on occasions turned their attention to the manufacture of porcelain. The standard mark on their varied but always fine quality wares is the impressed name-mark TURNER. The founder of the firm was John Turner, 1738–87. His pottery was continued by his sons William (1762–1835) and John (1766–1824). John Turner was apprenticed in 1753 to Daniel Bird, a famous potter, and he seems to have been established on his own account at Lane End in 1759. I do not propose to discuss the various excellent Turner earthenwares for you can readily turn to the standard book *The Turners of Lane End* by Bevis Hillier (Cory, Adams & Mackay, London, 1965) or see typical pieces featured in my *British Pottery, an illustrated guide*.

Turning to the very rare Turner porcelains, it seems likely that John Turner made some experiments in this field in the 1780s just before his death in 1787. There is an impress-marked TURNER small mug or tankard in the Stoke Museum which would relate to this period, and I have an early unmarked flower-painted teapot which I attribute to Turner. There is also the documentary beaker inscribed 'Lane End, July 1787', showing the interior of a pottery. This piece is linked with the much travelled Louis-Victor Gerverot, who reputedly agreed to teach Turner the secrets of porcelain manufacture and to build his kilns in the 1786–7 period. This beaker is signed by the former New Hall artist Fidelle Duvivier (see p. 149) and you may remember that Turner had been one of the original partners in the New Hall concern.

It would appear that the young Turners, when they succeeded their father in 1787, ceased to manufacture porcelain for a period of years, but it seems on the evidence of some rare marked examples that they returned to this branch of the trade in about 1800. Some simple oval teapots and covered sugar-bowls exist with the standard impressed name-mark TURNER. One such example is shown in Plate 73, made in our hybrid hard-paste-type body. This piece and other unmarked examples that link with it are remarkable for the very fine, trim, crisp potting. The Turner porcelains are extremely fine–perhaps too good and costly for the market. It is true to say that at present we know of more examples of 'Girl in the Swing' porcelains or of triangle-marked Chelsea porcelains of the mid-1740s than we do of marked Turner porcelains of the 1795–1805 period. As with other classes of English porcelain, the Turner wares offer great scope for the keen collector, student or researcher and no doubt in time we will be able to attribute with more certainty more porcelains to this famous family.

In 1803 the two Turners took as partners John Glover and Charles Simpson but in November John Turner retired from the partnership to join Minton as manager, and on 27 March 1806 the partnership was dissolved. The works were advertised and the wording is of some importance to our consideration of the porcelains: 'An old established…manufactory, lately occupied by Messrs Turner & Co. at Lane End, in the Staffordshire Potteries; where the making of porcelain and

Plate 73 A rare and well potted Turner porcelain covered sugar-basin, *c.* 1800. 5½ inches high. *Geoffrey Godden, Chinaman*

earthenware, in all its branches, has been carried on to a great extent, for a great number of years...'

Any Turner porcelain must pre-date 1806 and in July of that year the two brothers were declared bankrupt.

ENOCH WOOD, Early Nineteenth Century

Enoch Wood was a very famous potter who worked the Fountain Place Pottery at Burslem under various titles from *c.* 1784 to 1840. We have a class of earthenware and porcelain obviously the product of a leading manufacturer but bearing the inconclusive or puzzling impressed mark 'W(xxx)'. This mark could well fit the name Wood and I suggest that Enoch Wood used this form of mark as he is seemingly the only potter of this name who produced such a wide range of quality products.

These porcelains are of our hybrid hard-paste type. Apart from teawares, some very fine bulb and flower pots for the mantelshelf were made (see colour plate C). Some of this 'W(xxx)' marked porcelain would seem to have been purchased in the white by the independent decorator William Billingsley and painted and gilt at his Mansfield workshop in the 1799–1802 period. Some of these Enoch Wood-type porcelains are marked 'Billingsley-Mansfield' (in various written forms), see Plate 50 of my *Illustrated Encyclopaedia of British Pottery and Porcelain*, which shows such a Billingsley marked bulb-pot of a typical Enoch Wood form.

I show in Plate 74 a rare 'W(xxx)' marked teapot from a teaset that was also probably decorated in Billingsley's Mansfield studio. Much research remains to be carried out on this most tantalising class of porcelain–typical examples of which are included in my reference collection at Worthing.

Plate 74 A rare Enoch Wood porcelain teapot probably decorated in Billingsley's Mansfield studios, *c.* 1800. 6 inches high. *Major G. N. Dawnay*

THE PROBLEM PIECES

I have set out basic details about some of the known manufacturers of this class of hard-looking porcelains, of those makers who sometimes at least marked their products. We are, however, left with a large number of pieces, very often of New Hall type, which do not seem to link with the known makes or makers.

The trouble is that we have more types of porcelain than known manufacturers!

If we accept that the majority of these porcelains–of which the teapot and creamer shown in Plate 75 are but samples–were made in the 1785–1810 period and if we then search the Directories and other records of the period we get very little closer to solving the problem.

Taking first William Tunnicliff's *Directory of Staffordshire* of c. 1786, the only potters listed as making porcelain were: (a) Heath, Warburton & Co.–that is the New Hall partners; and (b) Hugh Booth of Cliff Bank, Stoke.

Hugh Booth's working period at Cliff Bank would appear to be c. 1781–9; he died in 1789. However, that is not the end of the story for the works were subsequently continued by his brother Ephraim and in the 1791–1802 period the trading style was Ephraim Booth & Sons, and from 1802 to 1808 these sons, Hugh and Joseph, continued the pottery which was later taken over by Adams. The various Booths working at Stoke therefore cover the years 1781–1808, a period vital to our present researches. They were evidently of some standing as they are mentioned in contemporary Derby, Minton and Wedgwood accounts, and yet I do not know of any marked examples of their products–but then the New Hall porcelains of the same period are unmarked, except for one special teapot in the Victoria and Albert Museum.

I think we should seriously consider the Booths as probable manufacturers of the very, very close copies of New Hall tearwares, the types like this teapot which so many collectors regard as of New Hall make. We must remember, however, that I have assumed that all these Booths working the Cliff Bank Pottery produced china or porcelain on the evidence of a single entry in Tunnicliff's *Directory* published in 1787. Hugh Booth's entry reads: 'Booth Hugh, manufacturer of china, china glaze and Queens ware in all its various branches.' The majority of the potters had the simplest of descriptions against their name–even Josiah Spode and John Turner had the one word–'Potter'. Here lies one of our little problems: the brevity of the contemporary Directory entries.

In the early 1800s there were several new firms listed in one or more Directories as making porcelain, but of course not all these would have made the hybrid hard-paste wares we are now discussing. There was William Adams of Cobridge and Stoke–but one would have expected some at least of his porcelains to have been marked. I know nothing of the potter John Blackwell of Cobridge, except that his working period was c. 1784–1814. John Davenport of Longport worked from c. 1794 onwards. As I have previously stated, the marked Davenport dessert wares seem to post-date 1800 and we do not know if slightly earlier unmarked tearwares were made. There was the little-known Neale & Bailey partnership of c. 1790–1814. John and George Rogers of Longport (1784–1814) are also recorded as making porcelain, as are Wolfe & Hamilton of Stoke (1800–1811) and John Yates of Shelton (1784–1835).

(E) A superb quality Bloor-Derby bone-china plate with rich tooled-gilding showing that Derby porcelain of this rather unfashionable period could rival any make. Printed 'Bloor-Derby' name mark. Diameter $8\frac{3}{4}$ inches, *c.* 1803–1805.

See p. 201.

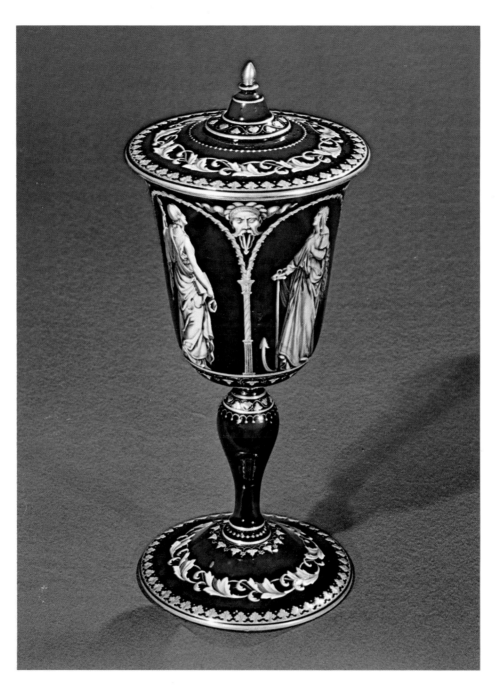

(F) A superb quality Kerr & Binns period Worcester chalice decorated by Thomas Bott in the style of Limoges enamels. Printed shield mark incorporating the artist's monogram and the date 1855. 10½ inches high.

See p. 213.

Plate 75 A New Hall-type turreted teapot and creamer of the hybrid hard-paste body, *c.* 1795. Creamer 4¼ inches high. *Messrs Christies*

These problem hybrid hard-paste porcelains, which are nearly always teawares, offer a great challenge to the collector. No doubt we shall, with co-operation among collectors and students in the reporting of slender clues, of dated or marked pieces, gradually solve the puzzle–as did Dr Watney with the difficult and unmarked Liverpool porcelains–but at the moment there are few more formidable tasks in our porcelain adventure than segregating these teawares of the 1785–1810 period. A word of caution over dating these simple New Hall-type porcelains for they are, I believe, rather later than most people think. I once owned a standard New Hall helmet-shaped creamer dated 1804, of the type almost always attributed to the 1790s.

We are still far from certain about the basic body, a rather grey material, which I have termed a hybrid hard-paste. As a class it was an important one, related to the New Hall body and linking our early soft-paste porcelains with the later bone-china which was destined to become the standard British ceramic body, as famous today in the world markets as the Dresden (or Meissen) porcelains were two hundred and fifty years ago.

Before we leave the subject of hard-paste porcelain let us briefly review the supply of porcelains available to the housewife seeking a tea or dessert service in the 1780s or 1790s.

In my talk at Morley College in 1973 I startled many of the audience by stating: 'I contend that by the 1790s hard-paste tea-services probably out-numbered all other types in use in the British Isles...'

This is not only a matter of balancing the few British makers of soft-paste porcelains, Caughley, Derby, Lowestoft, etc, against New Hall, Coalport, Chamberlain and the other makers of our hybrid hard-paste porcelains. We have to take into account the porcelains imported into England, imports which were on a very large scale. First we have the mass imports of the forerunner of all hard-paste porcelains–the Chinese wares. These had been flooding into the country for well over a century. They were quite inexpensive and, until the ever-rising import duties more than doubled the cost, they undersold British products. Every eighteenth-century British 'chinaman' stocked such standard wares, which in the main comprised underglaze-blue willow-type Oriental landscape patterns and simple overglaze-enamelled designs rather similar to many of the standard New Hall patterns. Some of these blue and white Chinese porcelains were further embellished in England with gilt borders, etc, giving rise to some novel but saleable Anglo-Chinese productions.

Apart from the Chinese hard-paste porcelains there was a minor but fashionable flood of French porcelains. Under the January 1787 Treaty of Commerce and Navigation these porcelains were imported at the reduced duty of 12 per cent as opposed to the old 80 per cent tax. Flight, of the main Worcester porcelain factory, stocked his London showroom with French porcelains which he had journeyed across the Channel to purchase. Thomas Turner of Caughley also visited France and on the evidence of some of his own products he found the French wares well worth emulating (see Plate 33). English china-painters also found the French hard-paste blanks a good 'canvas' for their craft. The French porcelains were often of new shapes which found favour with the public and, more importantly, the china itself was of a refreshingly white colour contrasting with some of the English soft-paste and with the greyish toned New Hall-type hybrid hard-paste porcelains.

Of course the importation of French porcelains was often interrupted by the wars of the period but the French products had a great influence on English porcelains, on English ceramic forms and patterns.

CHAPTER SEVEN

English bone-china and felspar porcelain

The respected Staffordshire ceramic historian Reginald Haggar has defined bone-china as 'The standard English porcelain since 1800. It is basically hard-paste, modified by the addition of bone-ash which may be as much as 40 per cent of the ingredients of the bone-china body...'

The introduction of bone-ash into a ceramic mix, in the form of calcined animal bones, was no new invention. More than forty per cent bone-ash has been detected in Bow porcelains of the 1750s. An equally large percentage was included in the Lowestoft mix. Bone-ash was also present in gold-anchor period Chelsea porcelains, in Derby and other makes of British porcelain.

SPODE (porcelain *c.* 1797–1833)

We have very few if any firm facts relating to the introduction of bone-china, the standard nineteenth-century and present-day English porcelain body. Credit is normally given to Josiah Spode II. Yet the very sound ceramic chemist and practical potter William Burton in his excellent book *A History and Description of English Porcelain* (Cassell & Co., London, 1902) states: 'The idea that Spode first introduced bone-ash into the body of English china about the year 1800 is absolutely untenable; but it is extremely probable that the tradition arose because he first abandoned the practice of calcining or fritting the bone-ash with some of the other ingredients and used the simple mixture of bone-ash, petuntse, and china clay, which, since his day, has formed the typical body of English porcelain...' Be this as it may, the Spode factory must be regarded as the birthplace of bone-china as we understand the term today. For the commercial production and for the purity of body and trimness of manufacture and excellence of decoration Josiah Spode led the way. He had come fresh from the London retail-shop to manage the considerable earthenware factory at Stoke and he must have been in a position to know just what the public wanted in the way of rich-looking useful porcelains. He set about meeting this demand.

The resulting bone-china was a marriage, a happy marriage, of the basic hard-paste materials, china-stone and china-clay, with ground animal-bones which had been previously used by several of the soft-paste manufacturers. The result briefly was a fine white body, very workable and capable of being formed and turned to a thin gauge and yet retain its shape in the kiln. As well as being pleasing to the eye, it is strong and compact and reasonably light in weight and not as cold to the touch or as brittle as the Continental hard-paste porcelains. It is as near perfection as a ceramic body can be–in fact to some eyes attuned to the beauties of early soft-paste porcelain it is too perfect and regular!

Leonard Whiter, the modern historian of the Spode firm and its products and also the author of that magnificent book *Spode* (Barrie & Jenkins, London, 1970), makes the valid point that there is no one bone-china recipe and, further, that the larger firms would have employed differing formulae at any one time for different types of ware or for different qualities of objects. The 'best-body' would not have been used for chamber pots!

Mr Whiter gives three Spode recipes, the first of which reads:

	%
Bone	35·5
China-clay	23·5
China-stone	17·6
Blue clay	11·7
Flint	11·7
	100·0

He also mentions that all such bodies would have contained a very minute quantity of blue stain to improve the whiteness of the body.

I must not dwell on the superb Spode porcelains: you can do no better than consult Leonard Whiter's very detailed and well illustrated book. You will find that some ninety-five per cent of these post-1800 Spode porcelains bear one of several helpful name-marks. These marks were used up to 1833 when the new Copeland & Garrett partnership came into being (see p. 225). I will also mention the fine Spode porcelains when discussing the felspar porcelain body (p. 188).

MINTON, 1793 to the present day

Josiah Spode's greatest commercial rival was Thomas Minton (1765–1836), a one-time apprentice engraver to Thomas Turner at Caughley who later engraved some of Spode's own blue-printed patterns while he (Minton) was practising his craft as an independent designer and engraver of copper-plates. I have suggested in my book *Minton Pottery and Porcelain of the First Period 1793–1850* (Barrie & Jenkins, London, 1968) that it was probably Spode's demand for more and more engraved copper-plates that suggested to Minton that if he was to make his mark in the world he must establish his own manufactory and not be content to engrave for others. Make his mark he most certainly did.

Thomas Minton purchased land at Stoke for his factory in 1793, but it was not until May 1796 that it was in production. The first modest receipts cover the period 23 May to 3 June: the magnificent sum of £33.10.10½d was received for goods sold during this ten-day period. His first productions were purely earthenwares and it was not until December 1797 that we find in the records a mention of china or porcelain; the year 1798 would therefore be a more reasonable one to mark the entry of Minton into the field of porcelain to compete with Spode, Derby, Chamberlain and Flight of Worcester. Minton's early porcelains mainly comprise tea-services, this delicate body being eminently suited to this staple article of trade-while the dessert and dinner services were normally made in earthenware. The teaware designs were at first very simple-one feels that Minton was endeavouring to capture the market with inexpensive sets. Their simple patterns are charming and have a fresh clean appearance. Several of the early designs in the Minton pattern book link with popular New Hall designs, for example Minton pattern 7 is New Hall design 195-one of the most common New Hall floral-spray designs. Other Minton patterns are very similar to Pinxton patterns and several are paralleled in the Spode pattern books.

Plate 76 A Spode (*left*) oval sugar basin of the 1800–1805 period and a Minton example of very similar form. 4¾ and 5¼ inches high. *Geoffrey Godden, Chinaman*

I have yet to find a Minton teapot bearing one of the really early designs below say number 20. Such pots of the 1798–9 period may well be similar to the New Hall-type turret teapots. The Minton teapots and sugar-boxes bearing patterns from about number 50 are very similar to the Spode forms of the same period, about 1800. From this period onwards we find a very close similarity between the teaware forms of the two great rival factories. Look at the sugar-boxes shown in Plate 76.

Quite apart from the shapes, the bone-china body is also similar although the Minton version is somewhat more open and the glaze does tend to craze slightly. Nevertheless we must regard Minton as one of the great early bone-china potters, probably closely following Spode's lead.

The post-1805 Minton teaware shapes closely followed the Spode forms and of course those of the other firms that were producing bone-china. The Minton patterns became more pretentious and expensive once the Minton porcelains had become firmly established. The firm also extended its range of products, making dessert-services in porcelain as well as ornamental pieces such as vases, often very gaily embellished.

However, in or about 1816, Minton discontinued the manufacture of porcelains although the factory continued to produce various earthenwares on a large scale. After a lapse of eight years Messrs Minton returned to the porcelain market. These new Minton porcelains are quite different from those made in the 1798–1816 period and I will discuss these later wares when we examine the major late-nineteenth-century factories in Chapter 9.

The early Minton pieces did not bear a factory mark before about 1805. They did, however, often bear a neatly written pattern number, sometimes prefixed 'N' or 'No'. The occurrence of such pattern numbers is of little help for such markings will be found on most English porcelains of the period, but we can check the Minton numbers against the factory pattern book and from this cross-checking build up a record of the basic Minton forms. This information permits us to identify at least some of the unmarked specimens. These basic shapes are featured in my specialist book on Minton.

After about 1805 the Minton porcelain often, but not invariably, bore a hand-painted device rather similar to the Sèvres crossed L's mark. This Minton mark was normally painted in blue enamel and in most cases the relevant pattern number was added below the main device. This mark was used from c. 1805 to the end of the first porcelain period in 1816. It was not used in the next period and a pattern number above 500 would post-date 1810.

539

J. & W. RIDGWAY, *c.* 1808–1830

I have included this section in my coverage of bone-china manufacturers to show that some quite large and important firms are not at all well known, yet their productions closely rival the popular Spode and Minton wares.

The brothers John and William Ridgway joined their father (Job) in 1808. In this same year the production of bone-china was added to that of earthenwares at the firm's Cauldon Place works at Shelton in the Staffordshire Potteries.

In general terms these new Ridgway porcelains were in the Spode style, with quality scenic bat-prints embellishing some teawares. Other colourful designs were added to the popular 'London' shape teawares of the 1810–15 period and some superb dessert-services were made.

Unfortunately very, very few pieces bore a factory mark and our present knowledge of the wares is based on the existence of all too few name-marked pieces and the discovery of some of the original pattern books. The standard reference book is my own specialist work *The Illustrated Guide to Ridgway Porcelains* (Barrie & Jenkins, London, 1972) but much research remains to be carried out on these little-understood Ridgway wares.

In 1830 the two brothers separated, John continued the Cauldon Place works and was later appointed Potter to Queen Victoria, making, especially in the 1840s and early 1850s, some magnificent porcelains. William Ridgway concentrated on the production of earthenwares rather than porcelains. The name Ridgway, after changes of trading style (see p. 223) has continued down to the present-time.

CHARLES BOURNE, *c.* 1807–1830

I have included Charles Bourne in this section on bone-china to give a contrast between the big manufacturers, such as Minton and Spode, and the host of smaller firms who were producing good quality porcelains in the same period. In the main these smaller firms did not use a mark and their products tend to be attributed to one of the commercially desirable factories!

Charles Bourne, however, was an exception to this general rule. We can correctly designate his pieces as he employed a simple method of identification. The pattern number was placed below his initials 'CB' in fractional form.

Plate 77 A small selection of Charles Bourne's Staffordshire porcelains of the 1815–25 period, each marked with the initials 'C.C.' above the pattern number. *Geoffrey Godden, Chinaman*

Charles Bourne was potting at the Foley Potteries, Lane End, in the Staffordshire Potteries from at least 1807, but his porcelain would seem to date from about 1815. His bone-china porcelain was compact and of a good white tone; the covering glaze was thin, clear and craze-free. In quality and often in form the Charles Bourne porcelains are very similar to the Spode wares.

This porcelain manufacturer retired 'on account of ill health', to quote from the sale announcement, towards the close of 1830. His china and earthenware manufactory then contained three biscuit-kilns and three glost-kilns, with hardening and enamelling kilns too, and it stood in five acres of land.

The now rare Bourne porcelains are often very colourful and the gilding is of a high order. The standard products comprise teawares, dessert wares, small vases and some very rare animal models. Some of these are shown in Plate 77, which illustrates a little display I had in February 1975–the first of my monthly exhibitions of English porcelains. Most of these pieces are now in the City Museum and Art Gallery at Stoke-on-Trent. Arnold Mountford, MA, FSA, FMA, took the opportunity to journey south to capture the largest collection of these rare and attractive porcelains then on the market. He and his museum had a very good buy–a unique opportunity–while, I regret to say, other curators nearly on my doorstep, failed even to call to see the exhibition.

DANIEL, c. 1823–1845

In the last section I likened Charles Bourne's products to the Spode porcelains. We now consider a class of porcelain which is directly related to the Spode wares, for Henry Daniel with a talented team of enamellers and gilders was responsible for decorating all the Spode porcelains. He in effect had a separate decorating studio within the Spode factory. This novel, if not unique, arrangement was terminated by mutual consent in August 1822.

By the following July, Henry Daniel had taken over Joseph Poulson's Stoke factory and in March 1827 additional premises were acquired at Shelton. Henry had been joined by his elder son Richard and until 1826 they traded as 'Daniel & Son', subsequently as 'Henry & Richard Daniel' using marks such as 'H & R Daniel. Stoke-upon-Trent. Staffordshire'. In 1827 the Daniels produced some truly magnificent dessert and dinner services for the Earl of Shrewsbury. As Simeon Shaw noted in 1829, these sets were 'of the most brilliant and costly kind ever manufactured in the district'. You will see from Plate 78 that this contemporary ceramic historian was right. I have in my reference collection some of these superbly painted and richly gilt wares; other typical pieces are shown in my *British Porcelain, an illustrated guide*.

The Daniel decoration, especially the ground colours and the gilding, cannot be faulted for quality although they may be rather too rich for some tastes. The Daniels were, we must admit, decorators rather than potters and although the shapes are

Plate 78 A superb quality Daniel porcelain plate bearing the Earl of Shrewsbury's armorial bearings, *c.* 1827. *Geoffrey Godden, Chinaman*

novel and characteristic, the porcelain and the glaze can on many pieces be below standard. The body is somewhat open and tends to contract, causing open cracks, and the glaze crazes easily. Not all pieces can be so faulted but the body is by no means as stable as it should have been. (Davenport porcelains of the 1830–50 period also have a tendency to crack.) Yet on seeing a selection of these scarce wares, you will surely be astounded by their magnificent decoration.

Some few pieces bear written or printed name-marks but the majority of specimens are unmarked, except for neatly written pattern numbers. These numbers are normally of four figures and range up to about 9000.

Henry Daniel died in April 1841 and his son Richard continued the factory at Stoke to at least 1845. These Staffordshire-made porcelains should not be confused with the later wares sold by the London retailers Messrs Daniell (with a double 'l') and which often bear this retailer's name-mark.

HERCULANEUM-LIVERPOOL, *c.* 1796–1840

Messrs Samuel Worthington & Co. established the 'Herculaneum' factory at Liverpool in 1796. This firm had a large trade in various types of pottery and for a period from about 1800 some now rare bone-china wares were made. These pieces were very seldom marked and the identification of these early-nineteenth-century Liverpool porcelains is in its infancy.

The few impress-marked HERCULANEUM pieces known to us show the body to be white and pure, covered with a good glaze somewhat prone to very fine crazing. The glazed-body has a strange soft, warm, almost oily feeling. Some fine bat-printing occurs, also some superb landscape painting as well as a range of Spode-type designs. As yet we have only identified the teawares such as the teapot shown in Plate 79 (also a jardinière and a vase form), but as we are able to piece together the porcelains made at this Liverpool factory we may well have other objects to add to the list of products—including, I believe, a class of scenic designs painted in silver or platinum lustre.

The whole range of nineteenth-century Liverpool ceramics are discussed and illustrated in Alan Smith's *Illustrated Guide to Liverpool Herculaneum Pottery* (Barrie & Jenkins, London, 1970).

Plate 79 A rare impressed marked 'Herculaneum' Liverpool porcelain teapot, showing characteristic handle and knob, *c.* 1805–10. 10 inches long. *City of Liverpool Museums*

WEDGWOOD, *c.* 1812–1822

The famous firm founded by Josiah Wedgwood is of course well known for its various excellent earthenwares, and one might think that a company with such a high reputation for pottery would not need to enter the porcelain market. Messrs Wedgwood did, however, produce excellent bone-china tea-services and other items for a mere ten-year period from about 1812 (see colour plate D).

The porcelain was of a good white body covered with a clear close-fitting craze-free glaze. The teawares are trimly potted and are normally decorated with restraint. The dessert wares are not so successful, and other Wedgwood porcelain objects are very rarely found today. These early-nineteenth-century pieces often but not always bear the simple red-printed name-mark WEDGWOOD. Typical specimens are shown in my *British Porcelain, an illustrated guide*.

In 1878 the Wedgwood firm returned to the porcelain market and from then onwards this body has formed a larger and larger percentage of the Company's total production. These later Wedgwood bone-china wares are of course quite different from the earlier designs and shapes.

IN GENERAL

I have selected for discussion in this bone-china chapter a few manufacturers: two large concerns, Spode and Minton; three relatively small and little-known manufacturers, Ridgway, Bourne and Daniel; plus the Herculaneum-Liverpool and the Wedgwood porcelains. To cover fully the producers of bone-china would mean that this section would extend beyond the confines of this work, for almost all nineteenth- and twentieth-century English porcelain manufacturers concentrated on this now standard ceramic body.

I have said 'almost all'; there were exceptions but these were quite short lived. The New Hall partners in Staffordshire continued to produce their hard-paste-type porcelain until the 1812–14 period, after which they gave way to the whiter bone-china body (see p. 152). The Coalport company likewise changed from a hard-paste to a bone-china body at about the same time. At least one of the Swansea porcelain bodies of the 1814–17 period is a soapstone rather than a bone porcelain. Perhaps not surprisingly the Worcester firm kept to their well-tried and very successful soapstone-type porcelains at least into the 1820s or 1830s but except in this city the bone-china was accepted as standard in all English ceramic centres. I state 'standard', but of course the various firms favoured slightly different mixes and for the less costly lines the body would be accordingly amended.

FELSPAR PORCELAIN

One of the major subdivisions of bone-china was termed by Josiah Spode II 'Felspar Porcelain'. A British source of felspar was discovered by Thomas Ryan on the Wales–Shropshire border in February 1819. Leonard Whiter in his book *Spode* gives a most interesting account of the introduction of felspar into ceramic bodies and glazes. This authority makes the point that felspar porcelain is bone-china; the felspar merely replaces the Cornish stone which itself contains felspar. Felspar is the 'petuntse' of the Chinese true porcelains. Mr Whiter relates how the newly discovered British felspar was submitted to John Rose of the Coalport works and how it was at first rejected by him. But after much prompting Rose introduced his famous lead-free felspar glaze, a material that won for Rose the Society of Arts' Isis gold medal. This award, although only for the glaze, was used to great advantage by the Coalport company when a series of prominent printed marks were placed on their porcelains from June 1820. One of these marks is reproduced below and you will see that Rose favoured the spelling 'Felt Spar'.

Having found a customer in John Rose, Thomas Ryan turned his attention to selling his felspar to the Staffordshire manufacturers, a task no doubt helped by the special Coalport mark and the Society of Arts' medal. Other manufacturers would obviously want to produce the well publicised new felspar porcelain. The Wedgwood archives contain a written account by Ryan of his endeavours to sell this raw material. Here we learn that 'Mr Spode gave an order for fifty tons at £15 per ton; the quantity on the wharfs was instantly removed to Stoke and the order was completed in a short time. The cheaper sort of felspar was purchased in large quantity by E. Mayer & Son, T. Minton, Messrs Ridgway and others.'

Spodes can have lost little in placing their new felspar porcelain on the market for they too emulated the large Coalport painted marks and used their own, one version of which incorporates the date 1821. This Spode mark is shown below and it can be noted that such special marks normally occur only on the finest pieces. The Spode felspar body, being regarded as superior to the standard bone-china, contained some 15 per cent felspar and about 45 per cent bone. We must remember also that a felspar body would have a felspar glaze. This covering and ground for the enamelled and gilt decoration was (to quote again from Mr Whiter's book) 'of a quality never bettered since…the word "luscious" has been aptly used to describe it'. A part of a Spode felspar porcelain dessert-service is shown in Plate 80.

Plate 80 Part of a Spode felspar-porcelain dessert-service, hand-painted within pale pink borders. Pattern 4485, *c.* 1820. *Messrs Christies*

Minton also produced a felspar body and had engraved special elaborate marks to be placed on such wares. The term 'Felspar Porcelain' was all the rage and I would make the point again that our twentieth-century description 'bone-china' was not used at all in the nineteenth century.

Messrs John and William Ridgway also produced a fine compact and white felspar porcelain from the early 1820s onwards but their examples were not marked before the 1840s (see p. 183). Ryan mentioned E. Mayer & Son as being purchasers of his felspar. If this was used in a porcelain body as it probably was, then we have another firm producing unmarked bone-china and felspar porcelain. Elijah Mayer had potted at the Cobden Works, High Street, Hanley, from the 1780s to *c.* 1804. From *c.* 1805 to 1834 the works were continued by Elijah Mayer & Son, and Directory entries list this firm as china and earthenware manufacturers. Simeon Shaw in his *History of the Staffordshire Potteries*, after mentioning Mayer's earthenwares, noted that the works were 'now notable for a species of porcelain manufactured only here...' Research may in time show that the Mayer firm made a good range of porcelains in addition to the quality earthenwares which are sometimes marked.

We also have scant information on another manufacturer of felspar porcelain, Messrs James & William Handley, who principally potted at the Kilncroft Works, Chapel Street, Burslem, in the 1822–30 period, but were formerly of High Street, Shelton (1822–3). I do not know of any marked pieces from this firm but Simeon Shaw noted: 'Messrs James & W. Handley, then of Shelton...introduced a Porcelain from feldspar chiefly, of very excellent quality; and of this they made several vases, much larger in size and truly elegant and original in design than any before produced...' Shaw then indicates that production was discontinued but no doubt porcelain useful wares were made by the firm in the early 1820s. These products represent yet another void in our study of the so complicated early-nineteenth-century porcelains. While I do not wish to run away from problems, we must press on to discuss the many major nineteenth-century manufacturers that we do have knowledge of.

The following two chapters will therefore include notices of the more important post-1810 porcelain manufacturers.

CHAPTER EIGHT

The major nineteenth-century factories

My coverage of the major nineteenth-century British porcelain factories is divided into two sections. Here we are dealing in the main with the factories best known for their products made before 1850, although in some cases the firms continued long after this period. In the next chapter we can consider the firms that came to prominence in the second half of the century.

SAMUEL ALCOCK & CO., *c.* 1828–1859

If instead of major factories I had headed this chapter 'The Well-Known Nineteenth-Century Factories', we would not have been able to include this very important firm, for Alcock was a major producer but by no means a well-known one. Samuel Alcock owned the famous Hill Pottery at Burslem as well as a separate factory at Cobridge. In 1833, some five years after Alcock set up as a potter, a Government Inspector reported that Samuel Alcock's 'Porcelain and China Works' employed four hundred persons. He also noted that forty-two painters were employed (one-third of them adult males), 'a greater number than I had before observed in one apartment'. About five years later John Ward in his *The Borough of Stoke-upon-Trent* (W. Lewis & Son, London, 1843) wrote in high praise of the contemporary Alcock porcelains:

> The productions of Messrs Alcock & Co., in ornamental china, are of a first rate description, consisting of table and tea services, enriched with exquisite landscape paintings and other devices; of vases, fancy bouquettes, articles of toilette and elaborately modelled subjects from history and romance in biscuit china...

Apart from some fine portrait-busts and other models made in the unglazed white 'biscuit china', most of the Alcock porcelains of the 1830s and 1840s appear to be unmarked. Here lies the reason why the firm is so little known and why many of Alcock's productions have in the past been classified as Rockingham, Coalport or as other fashionable makes. The quality is there but not the name of the maker.

The Alcock bone-china body is of good quality; it is well potted and often very richly decorated–even with encrusted flowers in the Coalbrookdale (Coalport)

Plate 81 A floral encrusted Samuel Alcock porcelain vase, a basic form registered at the Patent Office in February 1844. 10 inches high. *Geoffrey Godden, Chinaman*

manner (Plate 81). Rococo Rockingham-style shapes were favoured, especially for the teawares which included low, wide teacups in which the tea cools all too quickly!

Samuel Alcock & Co.'s display at the 1851 Exhibition included porcelain dessert-services, teasets, dinner-services (also 'white granite' ironstone-type services), centre-pieces, individual plates, ornamental pen-holders, spill vases, elaborate vases and relief-moulded jugs as well as groups. At this period the Burslem Works gave employment to no less than 687 persons and was run by Samuel's widow with Samuel Alcock junior, then aged twenty-five, acting as manager assisted by his younger brother Thomas. The founder of the firm, Samuel Alcock, had died in 1849.

Apart from the glazed porcelain pieces–the teasets, the dessert-services, the vases, baskets etc, the Alcock firm also produced a great quantity of relief-moulded parian jugs from the 1840s into the 1850s. Many of these are of excellent quality. Other jugs, vases and other pieces were printed with classical figure subjects, and a good selection of useful earthenwares were also made. Some characteristic pieces are featured in my *British Porcelain, an illustrated guide* and it is easy to predict that the

(G) A Minton tinted parian tray made for the Paris Exhibition of 1878 and decorated by M. L. Solon in the pâte-sur-pâte technique. Signed 'L Solon 78'. Printed globe mark in gold with year mark for 1878. 18 inches long.

See p. 221.

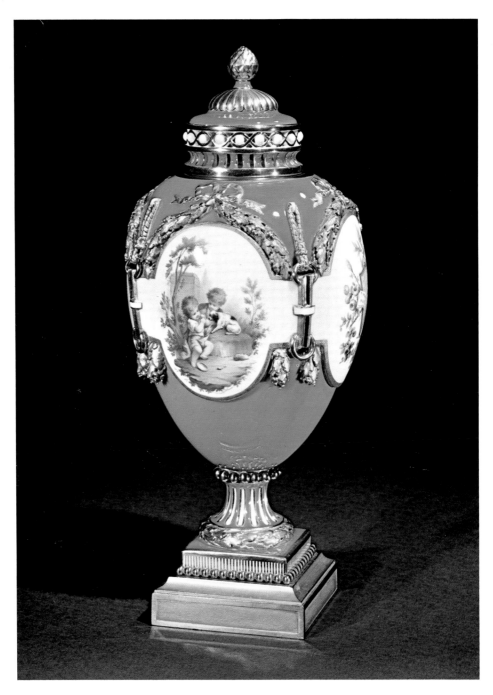

(H) A Minton bone-china covered vase in the Sèvres-style illustrating not only the excellence of the Minton turquoise ground colour but also the general superb quality of the gilding and the painting. See p. 229.

Alcock wares will in future rightly command the collector's respect and attention.

The identification of these porcelains mainly depends on a study of certain key-shapes as shown in my *British Porcelain*, forms that were in several cases registered at the Design Registry in Samuel Alcock's name. Few pieces bear a factory mark—except, that is, the parian and other jugs. When marks do occur they incorporate the firm's name in full or the initials 'SA' or 'S A & Co', sometimes with the Royal Arms device. The pattern number sequence is very high—normally well above five thousand or the number maybe a fractional form such as

$$\frac{2}{5777}$$

In 1860 Messrs Sir James Duke & Nephews succeeded Samuel Alcock & Co. at the Hill Pottery, Burslem. This new firm also produced good quality porcelains which were nearly always unmarked, although an impressed hand-device was sometimes used.

CHAMBERLAINS, *c.* 1788–1852

I have already covered the early history of Robert Chamberlain's Worcester porcelain company pp. 91 and 153. I can now proceed to outline the post-1800 developments at this very important Worcester porcelain factory.

In August 1802 when Lord Nelson visited Worcester he inspected the Chamberlain factory and retail shop but apparently disregarded the rival Flight & Barr establishments. Lord Nelson also ordered several superb Chamberlain services, the teapot shown in Plate 82 being one component.

In September 1807 the Prince of Wales visited the Chamberlain works and granted Chamberlains the honour and style of 'Porcelain manufacturers to His Royal Highness the Prince of Wales', a fact recorded in several post-1807 marks, and later amended to read the 'Prince Regent'. The Prince's patronage was also reflected in the name of a superior and costly new body termed 'Regent China' which was introduced in 1811.

Apart from Royal orders, the Chamberlain company produced some truly magnificent porcelains and, not surprisingly, in 1813 it was decided to open a retail establishment in London. This was situated at 63 Piccadilly, and in July 1816 new premises at 155 New Bond Street were taken; in 1840 further premises at 1 Coventry Street were acquired. The addresses of these retail shops are often incorporated in the relevant Chamberlain marks and are helpful in dating an example (see p. 196). The range and general style of the Chamberlain wares of the 1813 period can be gauged if I quote you some of the contemporary descriptions of pieces sent to stock the Piccadilly shop. In 1813 thirty-nine cases of porcelain valued at £3279.2s.3d were forwarded from the Worcester factory. Apart from tea, dessert and dinner services we find listed in the contemporary records items such as:

Plate 82 A superb Chamberlain-Worcester teapot, part of a service made for Lord Nelson in the 1802–1805 period. 10 inches long. *Messrs Christies*

A rich full size Regent vase, painted by Humphrey Chamberlain with the Triumph of Mercy

Valued then at £31-10-0d

2 Regent vases painted by Walter Chamberlain with King John and the Taming of the Shrew

Valued then at £8-8-0d each

3 large mugs pattern '403' painted with dead game

Valued then at £5-5-0d each

Bowls in various rich patterns

Various types of candlesticks

Very many ornamental inkpots, inkstands and pentrays

Jugs such as–Quart jug painted with dogs £4-4-0d

Baskets, spill-vases

Costly specimen plates such as '1 plate Coriolanus at £31-10-0d'

Richly decorated cups and saucers such as '2 cabinet cups and stands, figures and gold at £5-5-0d'

There were also house-shaped pastile burners, figures and small animals, such as cats, greyhounds, pug dogs, spaniels and griffins. Among the smallest articles were porcelain thimbles valued at 1/6d each.

Many of the sumptuous ornaments or specimen plates were painted by Humphrey Chamberlain junior, an artist or miniature painter who died in 1824 at the early age of thirty-three. His brother, Walter, also painted on Chamberlain porcelains; they both excelled in figure subjects. Other fine quality figure designs were painted by the justly celebrated and much travelled Thomas Baxter. Baxter had been born in Worcester and after working in his father's London porcelain decorating studio, Thomas Baxter painted for Flight, Barr & Barr of Worcester (c. 1814–16), than at Swansea (c. 1816–18), but his last years were spent at Chamberlains in whose employment he died in April 1821. Apart from the figure subject artists, there were talented flower painters such as Samuel Astles, James Taylor or John Webster and George Davis the celebrated bird painter, who was also a fine flower painter. There were also talented landscape painters such as Doe, Muchall and John Wood.

The Chamberlain porcelains of the 1810–30 period are really superb, rivalling any manufacturer of the period. In quantity the output seemingly exceeded that of the Flight, Barr & Barr partnership at the old Dr Wall Worcester factory, and in body and decoration the Chamberlain wares were far superior to the contemporary Derby productions. However, in the 1830s one senses that there was something of a decline, with the major Staffordshire firms such as Minton and Spode (Copeland & Garrett after 1833) taking much of the trade. Chamberlains followed the fashion in changing to a standard bone-china paste at a date probably in the early 1840s. In 1840, no doubt in an effort to pool resources and strengthen the trading position, the two hitherto rival firms of Flight, Barr & Barr and Chamberlain were combined. In effect, the firm established by a mere apprentice had taken over and absorbed the former great Worcester porcelain factory which had been founded ninety years earlier. The take-over, or 'marriage', of the two firms cannot now be counted as a great success. Perhaps the loss of the old rivalry was to blame? Various new lines were tried, such as the mass-production of buttons and the manufacture of door-furniture, but these endeavours could not stem the general decline. Perhaps the times were against them, for in 1848 the famous Derby factory had been forced to close after a lingering death. Messrs Chamberlains remained to display their wares at the 1851 Exhibition but here the Chamberlain pieces must have shown up badly against the products of the other great ceramic enterprises.

In 1851 also, the last of the Chamberlains, Walter, left the partnership, leaving W. H. Kerr in sole command. He was to turn to R. W. Binns to join him in an effort 'to exalt the name and to enhance the reputation of Worcester porcelain'. This they succeeded in doing under the trade-name of 'W H Kerr & Co.' or alternatively 'Kerr & Binns', a happy partnership of the 1852–62 period that led to the foundation of the now internationally renowned 'Royal Worcester' company (see pp. 234–7). We must not, however, consider the Chamberlain period as a mere bridge between the great Dr Wall factory and the present Royal Worcester combine. Messrs Chamberlains has a long and noble history of its own and within the sixty-four-year life of this factory some of England's most magnificent porcelains were produced, pieces that graced palaces and brightened many a more humble home.

The post-1810 Chamberlain marks normally comprise or include this name, with various addresses or trade styles as set out below:

Chamberlain's
Worcester,
& 155,
New Bond Street,
London.
Royal Porcelain Manufactory.

Written or printed mark, *c.* 1811–40. Note the addition of a crown and the word 'Royal'.

H. Chamberlain & Sons

Rare form of mark sometimes found incised, *c.* 1811–27.

Chamberlain's
Worcester,
& 63, Piccadilly,
London.

Written or printed mark, *c.* 1813–16. Note the Piccadilly address.

Chamberlain's
Regent China,
Worcester,
& 155,
New Bond Street,
London.

Printed mark used on 'Regent' body, *c.* 1811–20. This mark is mainly found on services made from this special and expensive body.

Several variations of the above basic marks may be found. The addresses are an important guide to dating. Some marks incorporate the words 'Porcelain Manufacturers to H.R.H. the Prince Regent'.

CHAMBERLAIN & CO.
WORCESTER
155 NEW BOND ST.
& No. 1
COVENTRY ST.
LONDON.

Printed mark, *c.* 1840–5. Note addition of '& Co.' (and Coventry St. address). The first three lines of this mark were also used at this period mainly on small examples.

CHAMBERLAIN & CO. WORCESTER

Written or printed mark in various forms *c.* 1846–50 with or without crown above.

CHAMBERLAINS

Impressed or printed mark, with or without 'Worcester' below, *c.* 1847–50.

Printed mark, *c.* 1850–2.

Plate 83 A floral encrusted Coalport porcelain vase of the type known as 'Coalbrookdale', 1830. 12 inches high. *Geoffrey Godden, Chinaman*

Typical and representative Chamberlain porcelains are featured in my two big general books, and I am preparing a new specialist work provisionally titled *Chamberlain-Worcester Porcelains*, which will give a mass of information on these wares and illustrate a wide range of shapes and patterns. In the meantime, I have prepared a tape-recorded talk with illustrated supplement featuring these Chamberlain wares (see p. 277).

COALPORT, *c.* 1791 to the present day

I have already given in Chapter 6 an account of the early John Rose porcelains and also details of the other porcelain manufacturers at Coalport, Messrs Anstice, Horton & Rose. The porcelains made by these two firms were first of the hybrid hard-paste variety. The Anstice works were taken over by the John Rose company in 1814 and the two factories, separated only by a narrow canal, were rebuilt and amalgamated. The body too, at about this period, was changed to a bone-type porcelain, rather softer than most of that period and the wares were in general rather thickly potted. As mentioned on p. 188 John Rose had been awarded a Society of Arts' gold medal in 1820 for his lead-free felspar-glaze.

Magnificent dessert-services (also teasets and dinner-services) were made with relief-moulded borders in the style so often associated with the Welsh factories, and the flower painting can equal some of the Swansea porcelains; indeed the talented china-painters in London used Coalport as well as Swansea and Nantgarw blanks.

Other very decorative Coalport porcelains were embellished with relief-moulded and coloured flowers (Plate 83). Pieces of this class are often termed 'Coalbrookdale' and some pieces bear abbreviated marks such as 'CDale' or 'CD' although other pieces bear the standard name 'Coalport'. You must remember that most factories of the 1820–40 period made some floral encrusted wares but Coalport and Minton led the field in this class of Dresden-inspired porcelain.

Of the more useful wares the Coalport company, which traded as John Rose & Co., produced a fine selection of teawares often very richly decorated and often mistaken for Rockingham as the shapes tend to be rather rococo. Dessert-services were another great stand-by of the factory. Most were finely painted with flowers, but other examples can be in the Sèvres-style with coloured borders, with birds in landscape depicted in the centre of the plates and dishes.

Apart from the Society of Arts' mark, very little Coalport porcelain of the 1815–50 period is marked. However, the table-wares at least normally bear a pattern number and as some of the original pattern books have been preserved we can build up a series of standard forms and so gain a good idea of the Coalport productions. Many of these key-shapes are featured in my *Coalport and Coalbrookdale Porcelains*, together with details of the standard styles of decoration and of the artists and gilders who embellished the wares.

The Coalport factory continued into the second half of the nineteenth century; indeed it still prospers today. The later history is given in Chapter 9.

DAVENPORT, *c.* 1793–1887

Messrs Davenport like the Coalport firms also produced a type of hybrid hard-paste porcelain, probably in the 1805–10 period, although we are not by any means certain when the production of porcelain was first added to that of earthenware at this Longport, Staffordshire factory. However, in general terms we can consider that from about 1810 the Davenport factory made a range of bone-china porcelains.

It is strange that this important firm, which produced glass as well as pottery and porcelain, should have marked so few of its early productions. I do not know of any marked teawares which can be dated before 1820, although such wares must surely have been made. Some very rare dessert-service components are known and these key-pieces enable us to identify unmarked pieces of the same form. Some few pieces bear the painted mark 'Longport', while other pieces bear the impressed mark DAVENPORT in curved form over an anchor device. The anchor occurs incorporated in several Davenport marks but you should not consider the anchor alone as sign of Davenport origin—it was also used at Coalport and at other factories. Some early Davenport porcelain marks are shown on the next page.

The printed mark shown at (C) was used from about 1815. Pieces bearing this mark can be of superb quality rivalling Spode, Swansea or any English manufacturer of the period, but alas these marked pieces are all too rare. Some especially graceful empire-style teawares were made in forms that seem unique to this factory. Do look out for these rare pieces such as the cup in Plate 84, or give yourself a treat and examine my reference collection!

DAVENPORT
LONGPORT

(A)

Impressed mark
c. 1805

(B)

Printed mark
c. 1810

(C)

Printed mark
c. 1815
in blue after
about 1850

From about 1825 the Davenport teaware and dessert-service forms tended to be influenced by the rococo-revival and many of the factory's basic shapes are very close to the Coalport forms of this period. I am also sure that much unmarked Davenport porcelain is to be found incorrectly labelled Rockingham. Attractive as the Davenport body is, it did present difficulties at times and one finds dinner wares especially, which failed to stand up to use, as the body developed wide cracks. This was soon overcome and the Davenport porcelains continued on a very high level. In the 1870s and 1880s some very colourful Japan patterns were produced in the Derby manner. The firm was turned into a limited liability company in 1881 but failed in 1887. The mark of the 1870–87 period is shown below. Pattern numbers were in simple progressive form without a prefix.

DAVENPORT
LONGPORT
STAFFORDSHRE

The standard book on all aspects of Davenport's many types of pottery and the porcelains is T. A. Lockett's *Davenport Pottery and Porcelain 1794–1887* (David & Charles, Newton Abbot, 1972), but typical examples are shown in my two large general books on British porcelain. The Davenport products offer great scope to the discriminating collector who wishes to search out unmarked examples and is not content to follow the masses in a search for marked pieces from the more fashionable factories.

DERBY, *c.* 1750 to the present day

In Chapter 5 we left our consideration of the Derby porcelain at the point when William Duesbury II had died, in 1797. The works were continued by Michael Kean seemingly with little or no change in the styles of decoration or in the general

Plate 84 An elegant Davenport porcelain cup of the early 1820s. Printed name and anchor mark. $2\frac{3}{4}$ inches high. *Geoffrey Godden, Chinaman*

high quality of the production. The body was compact with an almost waxy feel and the slightly whitened glaze has a warm mellow appearance. The porcelains are trimly potted and tastefully and well decorated. I prefer the simple white and gold designs such as the charming bowl in Plate 85.

In short Derby at this period set a very high standard and, apart from useful wares, the factory had practically monopolised the trade in decorative figures and groups. Before about 1805 the now standard mark (see p. 109) was neatly painted in a puce or blue enamel.

After about 1805 this same basic mark was painted in a red enamel and the quality of the painting of this mark became progressively worse, haphazard or hasty in the painting, as I have shown on p. 110. In the 1811–15 period the management of the factory had passed to Robert Bloor. Initially Bloor continued to respect the old high standards and continued to employ the old Crown Derby mark.

It is fashionable to decry the 'Bloor-Derby' porcelains and certainly he took the easy way by producing and selling, often by auction, a mass of gaily-painted 'Japan' pattern wares (Plate 86) some of which we must consider as 'seconds' or slightly faulty pieces. I prefer the earlier simple designs but these Japan patterns were inexpensive and rich looking and so met a vast middle-class market. These colourful Japan patterns are still in great demand today although their once inexpensive aspect is a thing of the past!

Plate 85 A superbly gilt Derby porcelain bowl of the 1795–1800 period. Puce mark (see p. 109). Diameter 6 inches. *Geoffrey Godden, Chinaman*

This decrying of Bloor-period Derby porcelain is somewhat overdone. Of course some pieces were made to a price or rather to a market but I can show you Bloor examples that any manufacturer of the period would have been happy to have made (see colour plate E). At the same time Bloor did certainly take measures to cut his considerable overheads. He reduced the painting staff, losing flower painters such as Thomas Steel to the Rockingham works. Other talented Derby ceramic artists went to the Coalport factory. While in the 1780s and 1790s the Derby factory had the high-class market almost entirely to itself, the position was quite different in the 1830s and 1840s with the competition from the great Staffordshire firms. In 1848, after various changes in management, the original Derby factory in Nottingham Road closed. A selection of Bloor-Derby marks are shown below.

Many helpful well-illustrated books have been published on the subject of Derby porcelains. You should try to locate a copy of John Haslem's classic *The Old Derby China Factory, the Workmen and their Productions* (George Bell & Sons, London, 1876). More recent works are listed on p. 275.

Plate 86 A Bloor-Derby tureen bearing one of the standard Derby 'Japan' patterns. Red mark (see p. 110), *c*. 1820. 6¾ inches high. *Geoffrey Godden, Chinaman*

KING STREET WORKS

The present Royal Crown Derby company is not directly related to the old works which we have been discussing. The new company was established in 1876. There was, however, a continuation, or offshoot, of the old factory, for on its closure a group of the former workmen set up a small works in King Street, Derby. At first these former employees were probably content to continue old-established and popular lines and to match earlier pieces, but they also produced biscuit figures and many novelties. In later years the great stand-by lay in the production of typical Derby 'Japan' patterns, pieces similar to those depicted in Plate 87, a page from one of the firm's illustrated catalogues. In 1935 the King Street works were taken over by the Royal Crown Derby Porcelain company, giving the relatively new firm a linkage with the original factory established by William Duesbury.

The King Street company traded under various names: 'Locker & Co. late Bloor' in the 1849–59 period, then as 'Stevenson, Sharp & Co.' in 1859–61, but the next partnership of Stevenson & Hancock is that normally associated with this small

No. 58.
Pastille.
Old Crown Derby Witches.

No. 53.
Tea, Saucer and Plate.
Old Crown Derby Witches.

No. 54.
Square Tray.
Old Crown Derby Witches.

No. 59.
Tea, Saucer and Plate.
Old Crown Derby Rose

No. 60. Octagonal Tray.
Old Crown Derby Rose

No. 55. Octagonal Tray
Old Crown Derby Witches.

No. 61.
Tea, Saucer and Plate.
Old Crown Derby Garden.

No. 56.
Watering Can.
Old Crown Derby Witches.

No. 57.
Cigarette Box.
Old Crown Derby Witches.

No. 62.
Tea, Saucer and Plate.
Old Crown Derby.

Plate 87 A page from the King Street Derby factory's pattern book showing typical re-issued Derby shapes and designs, *c.* 1910. *Author's Collection*

firm, and in 1861 the initials 'S' and 'H' were added one each side of a new version of the old crowned mark, only now the baton became (or looked like) crossed swords. This standard mark of the 1861–1935 period is shown below. Earlier name-marks of the previous partnerships were employed or the old, red, crowned crossed baton mark was copied.

GRAINGER-WORCESTER, *c.* 1801–1902

This firm's marks claimed the firm's establishment in 1801 but Thomas Grainger's experience in the porcelain trade goes further back. It would appear that Thomas Grainger senior was working at Worcester decorating Chamberlain or Caughley porcelain several years before 1801. This theory is based on several entries in the Chamberlain sale records, entries such as that of February 1794: 'Sold Thos Grainger, Worcester. Sundries damaged china. White thirds £1-1-0.' This purchase of inexpensive faulty white porcelain suggests strongly that Grainger was earning extra money by practising in his own time as a porcelain decorator. He was also paid money by Chamberlain for the 'entrance' of various painters. The Chamberlain records of the 1790s include various wages paid to Thomas Grainger but these probably relate to a young apprentice painter–Thomas's son.

In 1801 we find Thomas Grainger in partnership with the former Chamberlain landscape painter John Wood, establishing his own factory in St Martin's Street, Worcester. This factory should really be described as a decorating studio for I believe, like Chamberlain before him, Grainger at first decorated white blanks purchased from other manufacturers. Having thus established some sort of trade and built up retail outlets and connections he could branch out and go to the considerable expense of setting up his own factory to produce his own porcelains.

I believe that he had reached this stage by at least 1805 and that his early products were confined to useful wares, closely following in form and pattern the proven Chamberlain porcelains. Witness the tewares of pattern 209 in Plate 88. To many collectors these pieces are clearly of Chamberlain make but they would be wrong. Look closely at the knob shape, the dipping oval teapot opening and the way the cover sits down on it. These are early Grainger porcelains.

The early Grainger porcelains are seldom marked. Sometimes one finds painted name-marks such as 'Grainger-Wood & Co.', 'Grainger-Wood' or 'Grainger & Co.' or 'New China Works, Worcester', but these marks are rare and on teawares would only occur on the teapot and covered sugar-bowl, placed inside the covers following the Chamberlain habit.

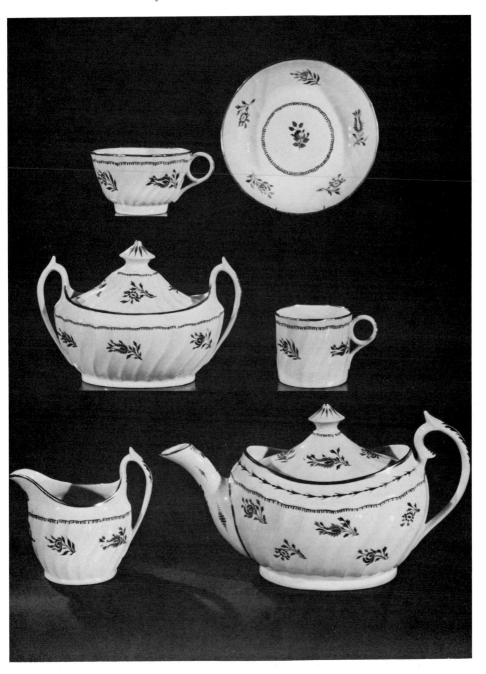

Plate 88 Representative pieces from an early Grainger-Worcester teaset. Pattern 209, *c.* 1810. Teapot 6¼ inches high. *Geoffrey Godden, Chinaman*

Between the years 1812 and 1839 the so-called 'New China Works' were under the control of Grainger, Lee & Co. In this period the wares became more richly decorated and the range of objects was greatly extended into the decorative field with large ornate vases and such pieces, also small animal models, rich baskets and the like. There was now a general tendency to copy some of the Minton porcelain shapes.

Thomas Grainger died in 1839, to be succeeded by his son George who amended the trading style to George Grainger (& Co), employing a variety of marks that incorporate the name in full, or more usually, related initials such as 'G.W.', 'G.G.W.', 'G.G. & Co' or 'G & Co'. Some of these Grainger marks are shown below.

1850–75

1860–80

1870–89

1889–1902

Apart from finely painted and gilt porcelains George Grainger also produced a durable ironstone-type body which he termed 'Semi-Porcelain' and this description or the initials 'S.P.' may be found incorporated in various Grainger marks of the 1848–60 period. He also produced some very good parian wares (p. 217), some of which were glazed and therefore look to the novice very like the standard bone-china body. Some of this glazed-parian was reticulated to form an all-over open-work design and other later pieces, made from about 1880, are very similar in general design and tone to the contemporary Royal Worcester pieces. In fact in 1889 this company took over the Grainger firm, although they continued under Royal Worcester management until 1902 when the Grainger works were finally closed. The Grainger marks were employed up to this closing date, so that we can regard the Grainger porcelains as having been produced for a little over a century, from 1801 to 1902. Thomas Grainger, who in the 1790s purchased damaged white 'thirds' from the Chamberlain works, established a factory that added considerable lustre to the history of Worcester ceramic art, a factory that produced a selection of porcelains that must have given the original buyer years of use and pleasure and today's collector considerable interest and delight.

Typical examples of Grainger porcelain are shown in my two large books but the main coverage is promised in a book being prepared by Henry Sandon under a title which should be self-explanatory but is not known at the time that I am writing these notes.

ROCKINGHAM, c. 1826–1842

The porcelain which we know as 'Rockingham' was made by the firm of Brameld & Co., working a quite small pottery on the estate of Earl Fitzwilliam (Marquis of

Rockingham), near Swinton in Yorkshire. The works had for a long period produced various types of pottery, the translucent porcelains being produced only in the last sixteen years of the factory's existence, between 1826 and 1842. Having made this point and having already stated that the pottery establishment was quite small, you can deduce that much of the unmarked porcelain attributed to this famous factory could not have been made there. I have stated elsewhere that if all the ceramics attributed to the Rockingham factory had been made there, the factory would have overflowed the not inconsiderable county of Yorkshire!

How do we then know what was, or what was not, made at this Yorkshire factory, managed in this period by Thomas George Frederick and John Wager Brameld trading as Brameld & Co.? Firstly, we have an assortment of pieces bearing one of several different marks, which are aptly described as 'Griffin marks', this device being taken from the armorial bearing or rather the crest of the Fitzwilliam family. Two of these marks are reproduced below; the pre-1831 versions were printed in red, the 1831–42 marks appearing in a puce colour. In addition to these marks we have a painted or gilt device comprising the letters 'cl' followed by a number. The significance of this is not known for certain but the initials are probably the abbreviation of 'class', as contemporary records include such entries as 'Rockingham tea pots, class 3'. These little initials can, however, be regarded as a helpful indication of Rockingham origin.

We also have built up a picture of the sequence of true Rockingham pattern numbers, so that we can safely regard any piece bearing a number outside these limits as *not* being of Brameld's manufacture. Rockingham porcelain dessert sets should bear numbers between about 410 and 850; teawares will have numbers within the brackets 407 and 1600, with some rather late (1840–42) fractional numbers $\frac{2}{1}$ to about $\frac{2}{150}$. Certainly, pieces bearing pattern-numbers greater than 2000 or above $\frac{2}{500}$ are not Rockingham.

Plate 89 A selection of marked Rockingham porcelain baskets painted with Sussex views, *c.* 1826–35.
Private Collection

The Rockingham porcelain is of the bone-china type, a little open or floury in
texture, with a glaze somewhat prone to fine crazing–an unhelpful statement as the
description covers so many English porcelains. A general description of the
Rockingham shapes and styles of decoration is also rather misleading. There is a
long-standing idea of Rockingham porcelains being rococo in form, painted with

green or other coloured grounds bearing charming little landscapes, but I can show you far more specimens of Alcock, Coalport, Minton or Ridgway porcelains that answer this description than I can find Rockingham wares of this type. The Bramelds at the Rockingham works naturally followed the current ceramic fashion; they did not necessarily introduce the style. Many specimens are quite modestly decorated with simple sprig designs or only with gold line-borders. Some of the most successful of the products were the undecorated biscuit (unglazed) porcelain figures.

Given the fact that porcelain was produced for a mere sixteen years, it is noteworthy that so many fine ornamental pieces were made and *relatively* few useful wares. This may well account for the bankruptcy in 1842, the fault lying in the neglect of the bread and butter pieces and the Bramelds aiming too high on the production of decorative items or over-costly wares. These ornamental porcelains, the delight of the collector today, include ornate vases and superb baskets–these are often enhanced with raised flowers in the Coalbrookdale-style and are painted with scenes or flowers (a good selection is shown in Plate 89)–inkstands, spill vases, letter or note racks and a host of other articles. Apart from the figures there are many fine animal models but the charming house or cottage pastille burners that are so often attributed to this factory do not seem to have been made there, in fact most are of Staffordshire origin.

Apart from the many unmarked pieces incorrectly ascribed to this factory by family tradition (or by dealer's enthusiasm!) I have to warn you that some reproductions or outright fakes occur with a representation of the Griffin-marks. These pieces, although well covered with decoration, are wooden-looking in regard to the painting, lacking the spontaneous touch of the originals, and the porcelain is lifeless and all too perfect.

Try to see a collection of true Rockingham porcelain such as that housed in the Rotherham museum. Several good historical accounts of the factory and the talented artists have been published in recent years: these are *The Rockingham Pottery* by A. A. Eaglestone and T. A. Lockett (revised edition published by David & Charles, Newton Abbot, 1973); *Rockingham Ornamental Porcelain* by D. G. Rice (Adam Publishing Co., London, 1965) and the same author's later book *The Illustrated Guide to Rockingham Pottery and Porcelain* (Barrie & Jenkins, London, 1971). The Sheffield City museum published in 1974 a most interesting little book by Alwyn and Angela Cox under the title *The Rockingham Works*. This includes much new information gleaned from original accounts and letters, indeed our new information on the 'cl' marks came from this slim soft-cover book.

WORCESTER, 1751 to the present day

We have in Chapter 5 discussed the early history of the first Worcester porcelain company, formed by Dr Wall and his colleagues in 1751 and we have taken the

Plate 90 A charmingly simple Flight period Worcester teabowl, dated 1795. *Geoffrey Godden, Chinaman*

story up to the Davis/Flight period, that is up to 1793.

We can now consider the later succession of partnerships up to the foundation of the Worcester Royal Porcelain company in 1862 (see Chapter 9). Let us first tabulate these partnerships and establish the dates for each change:

Flight & Barr	1793–1807
Barr, Flight & Barr	1807–1813
Flight, Barr & Barr	1813–1840
Chamberlain & Co.	1840–1852
Kerr & Binns (W. H. Kerr & Co.)	1852–1862
Royal Worcester Porcelain Co.	1862 to present day

Obviously between 1793 and the present time the styles changed greatly as they had done in the comparatively short period between 1751 and 1793. In the 1790s the production of the once standard blue and white wares had almost entirely ceased except for the traditional Royal or Queen Charlotte pattern.

The old reliance on Chinese-style designs had been left behind, and we find in the 1790s a simplicity in the designs. Teawares tended to have spiral fluting (a fashion not by any means confined to Worcester porcelains) and to be decorated with attractively simple sprig designs as on the up-turned tea-bowl in Plate 90, a typical specimen but interesting and unusual in that it is dated 1795. Dessert-services tended to be rather richer but still we find mainly elegant floral or leaf borders rather than overpowering heavy designs.

Plate 91 An elegant Flight, Barr & Barr Worcester crested plate, bearing the standard impressed initial mark, *c.* 1813–20. *Geoffrey Godden, Chinaman*

Dinner-services too were decorated with restraint, some admittedly bore rich Japan patterns but most had only a wide, coloured border, often of a pleasing pale colour, a border remarkable for its evenness of application and tone. Look at the Worcester soup-plate in Plate 91, from a service of the 1813–20 period. Some may question whether the owner's crest should appear in the centre or on the edge, or at all, but remember that such a service would have been a special order made to the customer's express requirements. Forget the crest if you wish; this porcelain plate is pure quality, the porcelain has a smooth unblemished surface, is of a pleasing, slightly creamy tint covered with a faultless translucent glaze. The gilding can hardly be much simpler and yet it sets off the shape and the porcelain itself to a remarkable degree. I am sure the owner derived much pleasure from his purchase and although it was only a modest order from the management's point of view it must have given them satisfaction too.

While the useful wares were tastefully restrained, the ornamental pieces–the vases, bulb-pots, spill vases, cabinet cups and saucers, inkstands and such objects– were very richly decorated. Scenic panels, historical figure subjects, shell and feather studies, also the floral compositions, were painted by a team of ceramic painters who worked in a painstaking meticulous style akin to miniature painting. In fact much of the work seems almost too good to enhance a vase because of its jewel-like quality. The main painted subject is set off against the finest quality gilding and superbly laid ground-colours.

I have spoken of ornamental wares but strangely the main Worcester factory in the 1800–40 period did not produce figure or animal models on any scale. Some very rare examples are recorded but in the main these decorative articles were left to the two other Worcester factories Chamberlain's and Grainger's, although from the 1850s to the present day the succeeding Royal Worcester company has specialised in fine figure models.

While describing the taste and quality of the Worcester porcelains of the 1800–20 period we can extend the discussion to cover the Flight, Barr & Barr porcelains of the 1820s and 1830s, although in the 1830s the decoration becomes somewhat heavier in style.

The Worcester porcelain body has even at this period a soapstone base, it is not a bone-china. It is compact or dense and so feels rather heavy but it is durable and strong in use and has a pleasing almost waxy feel. As a base for the decoration it can hardly be bettered. The body was, however, changed to bone-china probably in the mid or late 1830s.

Here is the key to the various Worcester name or initial marks with their periods of use.

FLIGHT	c. 1783–1792
F. & B., or Flight & Barr	c. 1793–1807
B.F.B., or Barr, Flight & Barr	c. 1807–1813
F.B.B., or Flight, Barr & Barr	c. 1813–1840

Thereafter we have Chamberlain & Co. (1840–52) to be followed by Kerr & Binns (1852–62) and then the 'Royal Worcester' company, see pp. 234–7.

The basic mark during the 'Kerr & Binns' or 'W. H. Kerr & Co.' period was circular in form marking, by the inclusion of four interwoven 'W's, the crescent mark and the '51' date, the now rather distant link with the Dr Wall company which had been formed in 1751 (p. 135). Other marks incorporated the name W. H. Kerr & Co., but the most novel mark was of shield shape. Not only did it give the initials 'K&B' and the place-name 'Worcester' but more importantly the last two numerals of the year such as 57 for 1857. Here we have the first effort consistently to record the year of production in a British ceramic mark. Furthermore, in the bottom left-hand corner of the shield device the artist was encouraged to place his initials, again an innovation. Sample Kerr & Binns marks are shown below.

Apart from the marks, the Kerr & Binns porcelains themselves stand apart from the other products of the 1852–62 period. The shapes were normally classically pure and simple, quite a change from the rather fussy Chamberlain & Co. productions.

Plate 92 A Kerr & Binns period Worcester shallow dish painted by Thomas Bott on a rich blue ground, dated 1857. Diameter 9½ inches. *Author's Collection*

The decoration was again elegant and fine, especially the tooled and chased gilding. Obviously very many styles of decoration were employed in this ten-year period but I will single one out for special mention. I refer to the superb quality porcelains made in imitation of the celebrated Limoges enamels, although many of the subjects are not antique. Rather it is the style that is emulated not the shape or subject, so that they are not mere copies of enamelled metal in a ceramic medium. The body was now a bone-china of the standard nineteenth-century type.

The style comprised the painting in a slightly tinted and slightly translucent white enamel of subjects laid over a rich deep-blue ground (see colour plate F). The handled shallow dish in Plate 92, from my own collection, illustrates the style and technique to perfection. The subject is ''Night' and this piece was painted by Thomas Bott who was, before his death at the age of forty-one in 1870, to build up a reputation for this type of ceramic painting. Bott also painted in full enamel colours and his work is normally initialled or signed in full. Thomas Bott senior should not be confused with his son Thomas John Bott (1854–1932), who painted in his father's style.

Messrs Kerr & Binns concentrated on the production of quality ornamental or cabinet pieces, although useful wares were also made, as were parian figures and groups. In all productions 'quality' seems to have been the watchword and when in 1862 W. H. Kerr wished to retire R. W. Binns was sufficiently encouraged by his previous success to form a new firm to continue in Worcester the production of fine porcelains. This was the Worcester Royal Porcelain Company commonly known throughout the world as 'Royal Worcester'–the story of which I must delay for the moment (see p. 234).

THE WELSH FACTORIES:
NANTGARW c. 1813 and c. 1817–1820;
SWANSEA c. 1814–early 1820s

We can consider the two Welsh porcelain factories together under one general heading as they were so closely connected.

In 1813 the Derby-trained ceramic artist William Billingsley joined with Samuel Walker in establishing a new porcelain factory at Nantgarw on the Glamorgan Canal which linked Cardiff to the Bristol Channel. These first experiments were unsuccessful or at least the percentage of failures in the firing made the production so expensive that the available funds were soon used up. The Government was appealed to for funds to enable this new Welsh industry to be established and the management of the Swansea Pottery factory was asked to report on the prospects.

Government funds were not forthcoming–a not surprising state of affairs–but happily Lewis Weston Dillwyn of the Swansea Pottery saw that if only production difficulties inherent in the very glassy paste could be overcome the project had great possibilities. Dillwyn therefore invited Billingsley and Walker to join him at Swansea to produce a commercially viable porcelain.

At Swansea the venture was a success; some superb porcelains were produced in the 1814–17 period. The great attributes are the very translucent bodies, the good glazes and the fine quality floral painting. I have written 'bodies' for there was no one Swansea body. Several very different bodies were employed and one must handle verified specimens in order to learn the characteristics of each. Some pieces have the appearance and feel of a true hard-paste very similar to the Paris porcelains of the same period. Many, but by no means all, of the Swansea shapes offer a good guide to their origin and for guidance on these forms you should consult the specialist books listed at the end of this section.

You must not place too much reliance on the 'Swansea' name-mark, especially the written version, for many fakes have been made. Sometimes the name occurs impressed into the porcelain occasionally with crossed tridents below. These

Plate 93 Two Swansea porcelain plates painted in London by independent decorators. Painted mark 'J Bradley & Co. 47 Pall Mall, London', *c.* 1820. *Messrs Christies*

impressed marks are more reliable than the overglaze-mark but until you have a good acquaintance with the Swansea (and Nantgarw) bodies, shapes and with the hand of the main painters you would be well advised to buy only from reputable sources and to arm yourself with a fully detailed receipt.

In December 1816 William Billingsley (and later Samuel Walker and William Weston Young) returned to Nantgarw to try again to produce fine porcelains on their own account. At Swansea Dillwyn's successors Bevington & Co. continued to decorate available blanks and they may also have made their own porcelains, so that the period of Swansea porcelain can be said to have continued into the early 1820s.

At Nantgarw between 1817 and 1820 Billingsley produced some fine delicate porcelains, some richly decorated. Other useful wares were of course somewhat sparsely painted with floral sprays or similar simple motifs for sale at competitive prices. It is believed that in or about 1820 William Billingsley and Walker left Nantgarw and were employed by John Rose of Coalport. This seems to be unproven or at least I do not know of any evidence to substantiate this belief, yet Billingsley under his assumed name of Beely was buried at Kemberton near Coalport on 19 January 1828.

After Billingsley had left Nantgarw, William Weston Young and the artist Thomas Pardoe remained for two years or so decorating the remaining stock of white porcelain and a final sale of the stock of porcelain moulds, etc, was advertised on 28 October 1822. John Rose of Coalport was reputedly the purchaser of much material from the Nantgarw and Swansea factories, and this is reflected in some later Coalport marks.

The Welsh porcelains had built up a high reputation with the many fine porcelain painters who were practising their craft in London early in the nineteenth century. The Welsh porcelains had captured a market previously enjoyed by John Rose of Coalport and a market also supplied by the importers of white French porcelains of fashionable new shapes. Many of the Welsh, Empire-style forms no doubt owe their origin to the London decorators who, I assume, sent novel or saleable French porcelains to Swansea or Nantgarw to be copied in the softer more pleasing Welsh porcelains. Much of the more ornately decorated specimens you will find referred to as 'London decorated'. This means precisely that: Swansea or Nantgarw blanks painted in London. The two Swansea plates in Plate 93 are of this class and they bear the mark 'J Bradley & Co., 47 Pall Mall, London'.

Some of these Welsh blanks, by the way, were decorated at the Chamberlain factory at Worcester (see the *Antique Collector*, April 1974, 'A Ceramics Enigma').

The Nantgarw porcelains sometimes bear the impressed mark NANTGARW/C.W. (the initials below standing for 'China-Works') but like Swansea a large proportion of pieces were completely unmarked. Reproductions occur of both the standard impressed marks and of the rarer painted name-mark.

The standard reference books are somewhat costly and difficult to locate but any serious collector of Welsh porcelain should consult the following: *The Pottery and Porcelain of Swansea and Nantgarw* by E. Morton Nance (B. T. Batsford, London, 1942); *Nantgarw Porcelain* by W. D. John (Ceramic Book Co., Newport, Mon., 1948, supplement 1956); and *Swansea Porcelain* by W. D. John (Ceramic Book Co., Newport, Mon., 1958). One could also consult W. D. John's more recent work: *William Billingsley 1758–1828* (Ceramic Book Co., Newport, Mon., 1968).

CHAPTER NINE

The later porcelains

We have already discussed some nineteenth-century porcelains and we can deal now with some other Victorian and later wares. 'Some', not 'all', for there were in the Victorian era hundreds of manufacturers, many of which were of short duration and very modest concerns, turning out inexpensive useful wares of a quite ordinary kind. We have few records of such makers and in general their products did not bear a mark.

Before we talk of the major later firms I must mention two typical classes which come within the term porcelain rather than pottery. Firstly, we have that body, 'parian', which spans practically the whole of the Victorian era, 1837–1901.

PARIAN

The parian body superseded the former white biscuit (p. 107) and in general is of a more creamy tint with a very slight glaze-like sheen. The body was introduced in the early 1840s by Messrs Copeland & Garrett, a partnership which succeeded the Spode firm in 1833. The body was originally termed 'Statuary Porcelain', underlining the intention to reproduce in miniature famous large-scale sculptures. In this aim the art-lottery called the 'Art Union of London' ably assisted and became the first patron. A contemporary account states that when the editor of the *Art Union* magazine visited the Copeland & Garrett factory at Stoke:

> we there witnessed the first efforts to secure popularity for the new art of porcelain sculpture. Two statuettes had been produced in it, one a graceful female bust, and the other 'the shepherd boy' after Wyatt, but they had not sold. The public did not show any sign of being prepared to acknowledge the real worthiness of the novelty; and it is by no means improbable that the process would have proceeded no further, had it not been our good fortune to urge upon Mr Garrett the wisdom of perseverance...a meeting was arranged by us between several sculptors...and Mr T. Battam, the artist of the works. The two honorary secretaries of the Art Union of London were also present. After a careful examination of the new material an opinion was pronounced decidedly in its favour...A commission from the Art Union of London followed, and this new art of parian sculpture was rescued from a peril that might have proved fatal in the first infancy of its career.

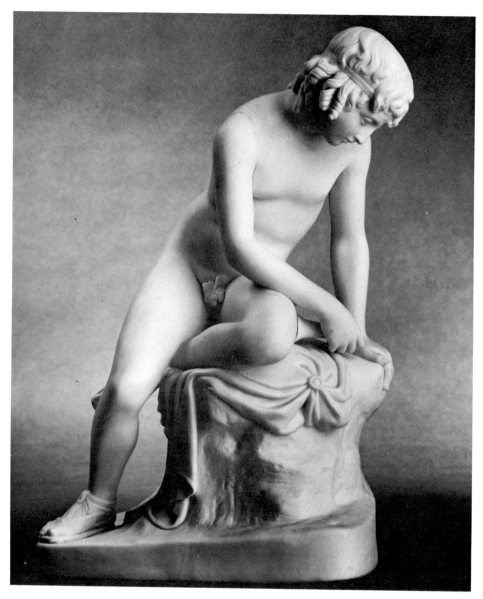

Plate 94 A marked Copeland & Garrett parian figure of Narcissus, after John Gibson's original, 1847. 12¼ inches high. *Author's Collection*

The first *Art Union* commission was for fifty copies of John Gibson's sculpture 'The Narcissus'. The total cost was a mere hundred and fifty pounds and the copies were available early in 1846. I have an early marked Copeland & Garrett example (Plate 94), showing fine workmanship and care in the finishing, but some later, post-1847 Copeland examples are not quite up to the standard of the first series.

When I speak of finish, you must remember that this or any other figure or group is assembled from many separately moulded components, each affixed with 'slip' or in this case diluted parian. The joints or seams have to be carefully smoothed after assembly and parts of the design sharpened with special tools, or sections have to be undercut, or additional small pieces, flowers, etc, added. All this is done by the person called a 'repairer'. He too has to ensure that the pieces are assembled in a natural-looking manner so that the figure has 'life' and does not look 'wooden'.

From the mid-1840s the leading firms, particularly Messrs Copeland, Minton, Wedgwood and the Worcester firms produced some very fine quality and most attractive parian figures, busts and groups. These are still relatively inexpensive and well worth seeking out but I must warn you that by no means all Victorian parian measures up to the best. Much, especially that produced by the smaller firms, was of a quite ordinary nature made down to a price and with little or no regard to originality or quality. At its best parian is very, very good; at its worst it can be very, very bad–these latter examples can be left well alone.

Apart from parian figures and groups most Victorian manufacturers produced in this versatile body a host of semi-ornamental useful objects–especially a multitude of relief-moulded jugs. Again the early ones can be extremely fine, particularly those bearing the name-marks of the leading firms but by the 1860s the quality and design had greatly degenerated as the smaller concerns sought to cut costs and to market cheap novelties. These last remarks apply equally to the hundreds of small objects made in parian: butter-dishes, trinket-dishes, ring-stands, etc.

Not all parian was left undecorated, the body could be tinted throughout or the surface only could be coloured in the normal manner and in some cases the leading manufacturers added some slight gilt enrichments to figures or groups. Firms such as Copeland, Minton and Royal Worcester also combined the matt, parian figures with glazed and decorated porcelain to produce imposing and often elegant centre-pieces (Plate 21), clockcases and similar articles.

The standard specialist book on parian is *The Illustrated Guide to Victorian Parian China* by C. & D. Shinn (Barrie & Jenkins, London, 1971). You could also refer to Chapter 7 of my *Victorian Porcelain'* (Herbert Jenkins, London, 1961).

While parian may be regarded as an inexpensive body for mass-production, from moulds, of figures, groups, busts and a host of useful articles, the body when coloured also did service as the ground for the most painstaking and individual method of decoration, the technique known as pâte-sur-pâte.

PÂTE-SUR-PÂTE

As the name (paste on paste or body on body) will suggest, this technique is of French origin. Indeed experiments were carried out at the French National Sèvres factory in the early 1860s in an effort to copy a Chinese technique. The result was, however, far different from the Oriental prototype but the experiment was to lead to the adaptation of quite beautiful effects by a process wholly ceramic, in that the

Plate 95 A Minton vase decorated in the pâte-sur-pâte technique by M. L. Solon, *c.* 1895. 8½ inches high. *Messrs Sotheby's, Belgravia*

design is built up of the body itself. The effect therefore does not depend on added enamel colours.

The result can be likened to a ceramic cameo. Tinted parian normally served as the ground either as a complete vase or other object or as a panel let into a plate. On to this coloured ground was slowly built up in white slip, layer by layer, a figure or other design, the details of which would be sharpened up or otherwise added to, or carved, to accentuate the applied relief-design. When complete this opaque mass was fired in the normal manner. The white parts became vitrified and semi-translucent so that in the thinner parts the darker ground showed through, resulting in a pleasing graduation of tint and the appearance of a finished cameo-like design (see colour plate G). Until the piece was fired all parts of the design were equally opaque–the skill of the artist being put to the test on vitrification–after which it was too late to correct any error in the depth of slip and colour.

The leading exponent of this painstaking process in England was Marc Louis Solon (1835–1913) who had been trained at the Sèvres factory and who, on coming to England in 1870, was employed by Messrs Minton at Stoke-on-Trent. Here he built up a richly deserved reputation for his masterpieces in the pâte-sur-pâte technique. These unique compositions comprised (or prominently included) tall, willowy, rather classical female figures in flimsy drapery. This style, seen on the vase in Plate 95, gradually gave way to children and cupids, somewhat better suited to small objects and to plates bearing small pâte-sur-pâte panels. Some rare pieces include the use of some tinted slip, rather than the normal white. So popular did Solon's work become, and so slow was the process, that he was asked to train apprentices in the same technique to help meet the market for these wares. Many of the apprentice pieces comprise floral compositions but some of the pupils progressed to figure work and while most collectors seek only pieces from Solon's master hands some of the apprentice pieces are extremely pleasing and sometimes quite inexpensive–compared to Solon's work. One of my 'specials' happens to be such an apprentice piece: the 1881 vase by Lawrence Birks in Plate 96. I try not to be too carried away by the fact that it was a bargain on my honeymoon, for surely it serves to typify the charm and quality of Minton's pâte-sur-pâte.

Solon's pupils at Mintons were Alboine Birks, Lawrence Birks, H. Hollins, T. Mellor, A. Morgan, F. Rhead, T. H. Rice, H. Sanders and C. Toft. Their work was sometimes initialled and rarely signed in full. Of these Solon trainees the two Birks brothers are generally accepted as the most talented. Alboine Birks (b. 1861) worked at Mintons from 1876 to his retirement in 1937 being mainly employed on pâte-sur-pâte work. He in turn trained Richard Bradbury who continued the tradition until he was called up in the Second World War. Although painted designs emulating to some degree the general effect have since been produced–as have been some moulded essays in the same manner–it seems unlikely that individual hand-worked pâte-sur-pâte can ever again be produced, for the cost of such pieces would, in time and money, be quite prohibitive.

Not all pâte-sur-pâte is Minton. Apart from the fact that several Continental

Plate 96 A Minton vase with pâte-sur-pâte panel by Lawrence Birks, one of Solon's apprentices. Year mark for 1881. 12½ inches high. *Author's Collection*

firms produced very good examples, British manufacturers did not leave Mintons to enjoy the market entirely without competition. Several firms produced good work in this field. The Royal Worcester and Grainger-Worcester essays in this style can be most attractive although they were generally restricted to floral compositions, excluding figure subjects. Messrs Moore Brothers of Longton and Brownfield & Sons of Cobridge also produced pâte-sur-pâte in the 1880s.

In terms of quantity Messrs George Jones of the Crescent Pottery at Stoke were the leading manufacturers of pâte-sur-pâte, and signed work by 'F. Schenk' often appears in the London sale rooms. However, in comparison with the Minton or Worcester examples these George Jones pieces are but poor relations and most of the Schenk designs seem repetitive as opposed to the one-off designs from Solon's hand. Nevertheless, the George Jones wares are often passed off as Minton and you would do well to note the characteristic forms and designs as illustrated in Plate 328 of my *Illustrated Encyclopaedia of British Pottery and Porcelain* and in Plates 433–4 of my *British Porcelain, an illustrated guide*. Chapter 8 of my *Victorian Porcelain* gives a good general account of English pâte-sur-pâte decoration, including a description of the process quoted from Solon's own 1901 account.

Now to my short account of the products of some of the leading late Victorian porcelain manufacturers. My selection is in alphabetical order.

BROWN-WESTHEAD & MOORE, 1862–1904

I have already mentioned the success of John Ridgway at Cauldon Place, Hanley, and how he was appointed Potter to Queen Victoria (p. 183). However, in 1856 the old trading style of John Ridgway & Co. gave way to Messrs Ridgway, Bates & Co., to be followed, on John's retirement in 1859 by Messrs Bates, Brown-Westhead & Moore and then from 1862 by Messrs Brown-Westhead, Moore & Co., a firm that continued until 1904.

In these forty-two years the Cauldon Place factory produced an amazing range of fine and decorative porcelain (also most types of earthenware) and although they continued to hold the Royal Warrant, their products are not generally known to present-day collectors as so little of their porcelain bears a trade-mark. In this respect the later partners followed John Ridgway's reluctance to use a name-mark.

Brown-Westhead, Moore & Co. exhibited at most of the international exhibitions of the period, winning well deserved praise. Of their display at the 1878 Paris Exhibition, George Augustus Sala wrote:

> Messrs Brown-Westhead, Moore & Co. of Cauldon Place, exhibit decorative porcelain and pottery of a high order in great variety, including elegantly designed vases, well modelled representations of animals, colossal candelabra and brackets of much originality of form, many of these productions being distinguished by great boldness and breadth of design...several of the dessert

Plate 97 A good quality Brown-Westhead, Moore & Co. plate of a basic shape registered in February 1870. Diameter 9¼ inches. *Geoffrey Godden, Chinaman*

services are decorated with designs from La Fontaine's fables, hunting subjects, and the like and many of the vases are painted with figures and heads of animals.

The partnership enjoyed the services of many talented artists, including Antonin Boullemier (from Sèvres and Mintons), T. J. Bott, G. Landgraff and E. Sieffert, but quite apart from these finely decorated porcelains the normal run of shapes are (to my eyes) extremely pleasing and display fine potting and finish. Take for example the standard plate shape, the basic form of which was registered on 1 February 1870 (Plate 97). Teawares often had attractively moulded rope-like feet.

In 1905 the firm was retitled Cauldon Ltd, which continued to 1920 when the title was slightly amended to Cauldon Potteries Ltd, and as such continued to 1962 when a further change to Cauldon Bristol Potteries Ltd, marked a further change in fortune.

COPELAND, 1847–1970

As related on p. 180 the famous Spode firm gave way in 1833 to the Copeland & Garrett partnership and within this 1833–47 period the traditional Spode regard to quality was continued and the new statutory porcelain or parian body was introduced (see p. 217). On the retirement of Thomas Garrett in 1847 W. T. Copeland (Alderman and Lord Mayor of London) continued the famous Spode works at Stoke under his own name. This title was slightly amended to 'W. T. Copeland & Sons' in 1867 to mark the entry of his four sons into the business. The Copeland title remained in use until 1970 when the new style 'Spode Ltd' was adopted to illustrate the continuous link with the Spode works and tradition.

From the late 1840s onwards Copelands were Mintons' great rivals, each of these nearby Stoke factories producing *tour de force* after *tour de force* in the hope of gaining the major medals at the host of international exhibitions of the period. While I happen to prefer the Minton porcelains it must be acknowledged that the Copeland wares are of superb quality. The flower painting is especially noteworthy and while Copelands were not as preoccupied as Herbert Minton was in the production of sumptuous Sèvres-style porcelains, the reasonably priced, high quality Copeland parian wares could not be matched by any other manufacturer. Parian apart, the plate of 1895 in Plate 98 is a typical and notable Copeland product. The delicate figure-painting is by this firm's famous artist Samuel Alcock and it is unusual in that it depicts contemporary dress, rather than the Watteau-type costume so fashionable on Victorian ceramics. Also noteworthy is the ground of beautiful bone-china uncluttered by covering ground-colours. The quality of the gilt border is also noteworthy and typical.

The Copeland marks are refreshingly simple, each including the name. Some of the later wares also incorporate impressed date marks indicating the month and year of manufacture such as S/79 for September 1879. A selection of standard Copeland marks is given below.

COPELAND

from *c.* 1851

from *c.* 1875

SPODE
COPELANDS CHINA
ENGLAND

Copelands
Jewelled Porcelain

from *c.* 1891

Plate 98 A Copeland plate painted by Samuel Alcock with 'Court Costume 1895'. *Author's Collection*

DOULTON (BURSLEM), 1877–present day

While Doultons of Lambeth had been a household name in the manufacture of stonewares from the first half of the nineteenth century, the company entered the field of fine porcelain at a comparatively late date, in the 1880s. However, these Doulton porcelains very soon made up for their late arrival and they soon established a very high international reputation–enjoyed to this day.

In 1877 the Doulton company entered into a partnership with Messrs Pinder,

Plate 99 A Doulton porcelain plate, the rose studies signed by Edward Raby, 1906. *Author's Collection*

Bourne & Co. of Nile Street, Burslem in the Staffordshire Potteries. For some five years good earthenware was produced until, in 1882, Doulton took over the old firm and under the new name 'Doulton & Co.' the production of Doulton fine bone-china was added to the existing range. A number of very talented artists were employed including Percy Curnock (1885–1919); David Dewsbury, the orchid painter (1889–1919); Edward Raby, the Worcester flower painter (1892–1919); and George White, the figure painter (1885–1912). We can see in the Raby painted plate (Plate 99) something of the light natural air that pervades some of the Doulton ceramic painting. This plate is of the early-1900s and is none the worse for that! Indeed, I have written elsewhere that, allowing for the taste of the time, the Doulton porcelains are among the most noteworthy of the 1890–1910 period.

Apart from finely painted and very richly gilt porcelain decorated in the conventional manner, Doulton's Burslem factory also produced some excellent glaze-effect wares and in more modern times a series of colourful figures and groups that have found international favour. In 1960 a fine new inexpensive tableware body was introduced under the trade-name 'English Translucent China'. This has been most successfully embellished with simple clean-looking modern designs and my own 'high-day and holiday' dinner and tea service is of this recent Doulton body.

Some of the basic Doulton porcelain printed marks are reproduced below but anyone who is interested in the Doulton story and the wide range of the company's products should read Desmond Eyles's *Royal Doulton 1815–1965* (Hutchinson, London, 1965), now unfortunately out of print.

MINTON, *c.* 1793–present day

When Mintons recommenced the manufacture of fine bone-china in 1816, completely new and rich shapes were introduced. Magnificent dessert and tea services were produced, many of which were decorated with rich ground-colours, ornate gilding and extremely well-painted panels. These pre-1850 Minton porcelains are often incorrectly ascribed to other factories, as a trade-mark was very seldom employed. Now, however, collectors can, by reference to my book *Minton Pottery and Porcelain of the First Period 1793–1850* (Herbert Jenkins, London, 1968), discover the basic and characteristic Minton shapes and styles of decoration. Collectors will also learn from this book (and from the factory records quoted therein) that Mintons produced a superb range of floral-encrusted porcelain of the so-called Coalbrookdale type, also some charming Derby-type figures and groups—pieces that are quite unrivalled for quality.

Progressing to the post-1850 period we find Herbert Minton rivalling Copelands in the production of tasteful well-finished parian figures and groups, and while I am impatient to discuss the porcelains, we must not forget that Mintons led the world in the production of 'majolica' and in many other types of earthenware.

I have mentioned the excellence of this company's pâte-sur-pâte (p. 219). To a large degree this high reputation was due to the employment of Léon Arnoux as

Art Director. Arnoux was a practising potter in his native France before joining Minton's Stoke factory in 1848. He was subsequently to win many international awards and it was stated that Arnoux 'will always be remembered…as among the most talented and accomplished Frenchmen who ever honoured our shores and aided us in the development of our art industries'.

Apart from the technical improvements introduced by Arnoux in new bodies, colours and the like, we can on a broader front attribute to him the Minton pre-eminence in the copies of the rich Sèvres porcelains (see colour plate H)–shapes and styles of decoration which for decorative articles were universally acclaimed and certainly they suited the richer styles of Victorian furnishing.

The presence of Léon Arnoux at Mintons certainly also attracted there many talented Continental artists and designers, who had left their own countries in the times of unrest to practise their art in this country. The French language must have been almost as common as English within the Minton factory! Not all Minton's artists were, however, of foreign extraction, for there were many talented English painters such as Thomas Allen, Thomas Kirkby, Richard Pilsbury or Jesse Smith, who could hold their own against all comers.

Nevertheless, it was the wealth of already internationally known Continental artists at Mintons that set the seal on this factory's success for quality porcelains. While the Continental factories were in decline the bright star of Minton was rising to fill the void. The work of Antonin Boullemier, a Sèvres-trained figure-painter deserves special mention for the charm of his composition and for the delicacy of his style. I have experienced great difficulty in selecting just one specimen to show the style and quality of Victorian Minton–for hundreds of pieces are able contenders for the honour but the plate shown in Plate 100, from a magnificent dessert-service, serves to illustrate several points.

Apart from the quite obvious overall quality of this plate, what especially strikes you? Of course, the wonderful even and mellow, almost liquid turquoise ground-colour. Many factories tried to emulate this Sèvres colour but none I think with the success achieved by Mintons (although it did on occasions fail when applied too thickly, resulting in a rather opaque colour and with some crazing or cracking away of the enamel). Note the quality of the gilding and especially the main borders around the rim and the panel. This is applied by the process known as 'acid gilding', a process introduced by Mintons in 1863 and later taken up by all the leading porcelain manufacturers. The pleasing contrast between the matt (or dull) and the burnished bright gold (and I do mean gold, not a cheap substitute) is achieved by the use of acid, hence the name. The parts to be left matt are recessed or eaten away by the use of acid (the rest of the plate being protected by an acid-resisting compound) so that when the gold is applied to the plate, after it has been washed and cleaned, some lies on the surface and is subsequently burnished while some is in the recessed parts and escapes the action of the burnisher. The effect, as you can see, well repays all the trouble involved in the various processes.

The figure subject panel, painted in monochrome (in shades of one colour), is also

Plate 100 A superb quality turquoise ground Minton plate with acid-gold borders. Printed and impressed marks, 1873. *Geoffrey Godden, Chinaman*

noteworthy for the free, light style of painting in the French manner. If one turns this plate over one notices the light weight, owing to the thin, workmanlike potting. One notices also the translucency of the pure English bone-china with its friendly, almost warm glaze.

On the reverse we find two basic types of factory mark. Those that are impressed and consequently were added during the manufacturing process and those that are added overglaze, while, or after, the piece was decorated. The later Minton marks are most helpful and well worth study. First, we find on this example the impressed name MINTONS (the 'S' was added from *c.* 1873, the singular version MINTON appearing between 1862 and 1873). We also have three small cyphers or letters denoting the potter, the month and year of manufacture; there is an arrow-like device signifying 1874–the year of manufacture. The impressed Minton year cyphers were employed from 1842 onwards and they are almost indispensable in determining the date of any example. The key to this system is given in my *Victorian Porcelain* and in my *Handbook of British Pottery and Porcelain Marks* (Barrie & Jenkins, London, 1968).

The overglaze marks comprise the standard globe-mark, with the crown, which was added in 1873 and the plural form of. the name MINTONS. This basic mark continued in use up to 1912 when laurel leaves were added each side of the globe. Previously to that, in 1891, the word 'England' had been added, giving way to the wording 'Made in England' in about 1902. (The basic Minton marks are shown below.) We also find the painted pattern number 'G.1595'. Pattern numbers can be a great help, not only for dating an object but also as a guide to the make, and I will explain their purpose further on p. 257. Here it is necessary only to state that Minton's 'G' series started in 1868 and that some fifteen hundred such designs had been introduced by 1874. Each stock pattern has a separate number but this relates only to the main design–for example each piece in this dessert set bears the same pattern number, yet each of the hand-painted panels is different. As a general rule pattern numbers appear only on table-wares not on vases and such ornamental pieces painted with individual designs.

This one plate has served to make several points but the story of Minton porcelain is a long and complex one–for it started in the eighteenth century and still continues. There is room here only to refer you to printed accounts where you can, if you so choose, look up details for yourself or feast your eyes on the illustrations of typical specimens. First, you have my *Minton Pottery & Porcelain* book, an account continued in Chapter 5 of my general book *Victorian Porcelain*. Other illustrations appear in my *British Porcelain, an illustrated guide* and in a further book I am preparing under the tentative title *Victorian Pottery and Porcelain, an illustrated guide*.

PRINTED MINTON PORCELAIN MARKS

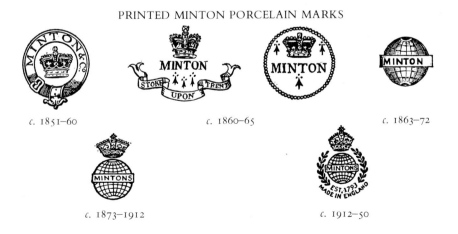

c. 1851–60   c. 1860–65   c. 1863–72

c. 1873–1912   c. 1912–50

ROYAL CROWN DERBY, 1876–present day

I have placed this entry for Derby porcelains under 'Royal Crown Derby' to underline the point that this company originally had no direct link with the earlier porcelain manufactories in this city.

The new company, originally titled the Derby Crown Porcelain Co. Ltd, was established in 1876 by Edward Phillips who had been one of the partners in the Royal Worcester Company. The new factory was in Osmaston Road and at first earthenware as well as bone-china was produced. The 'Royal Crown Derby' period dates from January 1890 when the company was officially appointed manufacturers of porcelain to Queen Victoria and the description 'Royal Crown Derby' was added to the trade-mark.

Printed mark,
c. 1876–89

Basic post-1890 mark.
The words 'made in England'
were added from c. 1921.

To a large degree colourful 'Japan'-patterns with their red, blue and gold area embellished the new wares in the manner of the earlier Derby porcelains and these traditional designs are still produced to this day, finding favour not only in England but in various overseas markets. Apart from these traditional designs the new Derby company produced a number of ornamental forms including figures and richly decorated vases and services.

The Royal Crown Derby flower-painters were supreme, and the signed work of A. Gregory, C. Gresley, William Mosley, James Rouse and Désiré Leroy, is well worth your study.

The piece I have selected to show you is a plate decorated by Leroy (Plate 101). This French artist worked for Mintons until about 1890, after which his signed work graces some superb Royal Crown Derby porcelain up to the time of his death in 1908. His compositions tend to reflect his training at the Sèvres factory, often comprising exotic birds in landscapes. This plate is painted in a typical pale mellow palette and for quality of painting can hardly be bettered. Some of Leroy's work is in the style of the Limoges-enamels, with white or slightly tinted enamels painted over a rich dark-blue ground. Désiré Leroy was also a gilder and he added the gilt embellishments to pieces he had painted. This plate bears, apart from the standard factory mark, the Royal Arms device and the year cypher for 1893. The key to this Derby date marking is given in my *Victorian Porcelain*.

In April 1935 the Royal Crown Derby company purchased the small King Street works which had been established in 1848 by some of the former Derby

Plate 101 A Royal Crown Derby plate painted in a characteristic delicate manner by Désiré Leroy, 1893. *Author's Collection.*

workpeople and so at this date the new company acquired an association with the original Derby factory which had been established by William Duesbury in the middle of the eighteenth century. As I have pointed out, the company still continues to add lustre to the very considerable reputation of Derby in the field of ceramics.

For further details of the later Derby porcelains there is *Royal Crown Derby China* by F. Brayshaw Gilhespy and D. M. Budd (Charles Skilton Ltd, London, 1964) or *Royal Crown Derby* by John Twitchett & Betty Bailey (Barrie & Jenkins Ltd, London, 1976).

ROYAL WORCESTER

I have already described (p. 212) how Messrs Kerr & Binns so successfully bridged the ten-year period between the winding-up of Chamberlain & Co. in 1852 and the formation of the Worcester Royal Porcelain company in 1862.

At first, in the 1860s, R. W. Binns was mainly content to consolidate the position gained in the previous period. Limoges-style enamelled porcelains continued to win high praise and many fine dessert-services were made and tastefully decorated in various styles. Great emphasis was placed on the production of figures not only in unglazed parian but in glazed and decorated finishes, some in the so-called Raphaelesque-style. Many later issues were expensively embellished with various tinted-gold effects.

Magnificent vases and other ornamental pieces were painted with figure-subjects by Thomas Bott, James and Thomas Callowhill, Charles Palmere or Josiah Rushton—the heads by Rushton can be quite delightful. The talented flower-painters included David Bates, George Hundley, James Sherriff and William Taylor but at this pre-1880 period the artists very seldom signed their work. Many pieces were painted with birds; grasses and heather studies seem to have been a Royal Worcester speciality.

The 1870s saw the production of really magnificent porcelains in the Japanese style, vases enriched with simple raised gold designs in different tints. Quality oozes from these pieces (see Plates 555–6 in my *British Porcelain, an illustrated guide*), but you will have to keep a sharp look-out for them as they are now very rare. Many of these Japanese-style Royal Worcester porcelains were modelled by James Hadley (1837–1903), who was, in my judgement, the finest ceramic modeller of the nineteenth century. After 1875 he worked as a free-lance designer but all his work seems to have been for the Royal Worcester company. In 1896 he established his own factory at Worcester where quality porcelains were produced under the trade-name 'Hadley-ware' but soon after Hadley's death in December 1903, the Hadley Works were taken over by the main company, which has continued to market Hadley-shapes to this day.

James Hadley modelled for the Royal Worcester company a charming series of children or young persons dressed in Kate Greenaway-style clothes. Not only were the figures and groups purely ornamental; some also served as baskets, dessert centre-pieces, condiments, candlesticks and the like. They were deservedly very popular and were produced over many years. Nearly all examples bear Hadley's incised signature but you must appreciate that this appeared on the original master-model, from which the moulds were made and the later castings produced. The signature does not mean that Hadley so much as touched the moulded figure bearing his name, although of course it reflects his flair and original modelling skill.

The very many types of Royal Worcester porcelain and the hundreds of different designs make my choice of a special exhibit extremely difficult; I have so many superbly painted pieces, including the reticulated porcelains by George Owen, each of which warrants special mention, yet I keep coming back to admire the elegant figure in Plate 102.

This serene figure, one of a pair, stands over sixteen inches high; its line and rhythm marks it as a James Hadley model, although much of the grace is lost in a flat photographic reproduction. The warm ivory-like body is set off so well by the wonderfully coloured and gilt costume. It typifies not only Hadley's skill as a modeller but the Worcester company's mastery of these Japanese-style ceramics. This pair of figures was introduced at the 1873 Vienna Exhibition and my pair bears the decoration year numerals for 1874, placed under the standard factory mark.

Nearly all Royal Worcester porcelain is clearly marked with one or other of the basic marks as shown below.

c. 1862–75   c. 1876–91   from c. 1891

Up to 1890 year-marks were added below printed versions. At first we find the last two numerals of the year, for example 73 for 1873, but from 1867 this system gradually gave way to single capital letters starting with A in 1867 and progressing in sequence (omitting F, J, O and Q) until Z was reached in 1888. In 1889 the letter 'O' was belatedly used and in 1890 an italic lower-case letter 'a'. In 1891 the words 'Royal Worcester, England' were introduced and in each successive year one dot was added, until 24 dots appeared to denote 1915. Details of later year-marks are given in Henry Sandon's standard book mentioned on page 237.

I cannot possibly give details of all the twentieth-century Royal Worcester productions but I must briefly mention the intricately modelled bird and flower studies by the late Miss Dorothy Doughty, most of which were issued as strictly limited editions. As a result of the international success of these studies the company

Plate 102 A graceful Royal Worcester figure modelled in the Japanese style by James Hadley. Date mark for 1874. $16\frac{1}{2}$ inches high. *Geoffrey Godden, Chinaman*

has produced a number of superbly modelled masterpieces–equestrian statuettes, animals, figures, groups and even fish studies.

To gain some idea of the range and quality of Royal Worcester porcelains you really must visit the museum housed on the factory site at Worcester, or if you cannot manage this you can refer to the excellent book, *Royal Worcester Porcelain, from 1862 to the present day* by Henry Sandon, the curator (Barrie & Jenkins Ltd, London, 1973). Turning to earlier books, R. W. Binns's own account of the company under his management makes most interesting reading for the serious student of Victorian ceramics. This now scarce book is entitled *Worcester China, a record of the work of forty-five years 1852–1897* (Bernard Quaritch, London, 1897). My own *Victorian Porcelain* has a useful chapter on the Worcester wares.

LOCKE & CO.

In 1895 Edward Locke who had been trained by the Royal Worcester company established his own small works–helped by his not inconsiderable family of eleven.

His products are mainly in the Royal Worcester style but seemingly made for the lower end of the market. The enterprise was not of long duration and closed in 1904–after losing a legal battle over the right to use the word 'Worcester' to describe the ware, a sole right claimed by the management of the Royal Worcester Company. The two Locke & Co. printed marks are given below, the first being used in the 1895–1900 period, the second between 1900 and 1904.

I have been unable to cover all the later Victorian porcelain manufacturers, and I have hardly been able to touch on the present-century products. One book in particular provides some insight into the number of firms producing ceramics in the late nineteenth century. This most valuable source book is Llewellynn Jewitt's *The Ceramic Art of Great Britain*, first edition 1878, enlarged and revised edition, 1883. I have myself edited and re-illustrated a new version dealing only with the nineteenth-century pottery firms, under the title *Jewitt's Ceramic Art of Great Britain 1800–1900*, and this was published by Messrs Barrie & Jenkins, London, in 1972 but is now out of print. Most twentieth-century English porcelain will be found to bear a trade-mark and from this you should be able to trace basic information on the manufacturer by reference to my big mark book the *Encyclopaedia of British Pottery and Porcelain Marks*.

CHAPTER TEN

On forming a collection

When I started collecting, and I have no memory of having made any such decision, I just naturally began to purchase with my modest pocket-money broken specimens of attractive eighteenth-century porcelain as others of my age might have spent their allowance saving for a new bike or model-train. There were then, I think, two basic types of collector: the man or woman who purchased, as opportunity and purse permitted, anything that attracted his or her eye without any overall plan, and the more studious collector who tended to specialise in order to build up a worthwhile collection showing the whole range of his chosen subject and its development.

Both types of collecting can give a lifetime of pleasure, the second the additional bonus of adding to our general fund of knowledge.

There is, however, today a third class of collector: the investor. Those who start with no great love of the subject but buy only because they seek a hedge against ever-increasing inflation and the lowering of the value of money and savings. I am not singling out the pound sterling. Almost every form of modern currency seems to be suffering from the same loss of confidence, and far-seeing collectors of most nationalities seek articles of beauty and rarity in which to invest their paper currency.

In my previous books I have steered well clear of the investment angle and have refrained from discussing price, but in seeking to give guidance now, I would be doing you a disservice if I did not offer some words on this tantalising topic.

Porcelains and most 'collectable' articles have tended over the past years to increase in value at a faster rate than inflation has eroded the value of money and certainly, their 'performance' has been better than stocks and shares. A Minton pâte-sur-pâte vase by Solon (see p. 220), which I sold in the 1950s for £172, in June 1975 fetched at auction £1750! Yet nobody can guarantee that this state of affairs will continue. There are fashions in collecting as well as in everything else. Besides, diamonds, pictures, coins or porcelains do not pay any interest or dividend. Any financial profit results only from a long-term capital gain. Do not expect to enter the market as a novice, buying in the wrong places at the top of the market, and show a profit at the end of the year!

You can, however, enter the market with great success if you have taken certain precautions. If you have researched your subject and learnt more about your speciality than the average dealer. If you bide your time and buy with discretion. If you buy from the right sources and if you are not afraid to take advice–or even to seek it. If you leave others to follow fashion and follow your own taste, not that of others. If you form a collector's collection!

This last scrap of advice will probably take some explaining but it brings us back to what collecting should be about, whether we are talking about collecting purely for pleasure or purely for profit, and for any combination of the two. Surely there can be few or any collectors who have not over the past ten years or so seen their collection multiply greatly in value, although this was not the reason why they started. It is not so long ago, in 1966 to be precise, since I wrote a popular little book entitled *Antique China and Glass under £5*. How times change! You would be hard pressed to keep within that limit today and this must be why the publishers allowed this little book to go out of print after a brief but profitable life.

There are collectors who seek to amass a great bulk of objects, perhaps a thousand teapots, and there are those who endeavour to form a collector's collection of teapots. In this case each one will have been chosen for it purity of design, for its beauty of decoration, because it helped to tell the story of the evolution of the vessel and its development in England. The changing basic shapes, styles and sizes will be illustrated with good perfect pots. Such a collection of perhaps a hundred teapots will be far more valuable than those thousand pots gathered without thought or real interest in the subject.

I have singled out teapots to make this basic point but it can be paralleled in all collecting subjects. Not only in single objects, jugs, sugar basins, animal models, figures, miniature cups and saucers or thimbles, but also in the wares of one factory or region. Only a collector with more money than sense would buy every example of Chelsea, Worcester or New Hall that came his way. Such a mass of objects would lack personality. One must use discretion, filling in gaps to show the whole picture, weeding out inferior pieces as you find (or can afford) the better specimens.

The choice of what one collects often arises from a chance acquaintance: you are perhaps given a trinket, maybe a model cat in porcelain. Or you take a fancy to a cottage night-light holder in a shop window or museum. You read a magazine article or book or, more likely today, you see Arthur Negus lovingly caress a Chelsea shepherdess on television. The countless seeds of collecting are floating in the wind and they settle as fate decrees. Most find a very fertile place to grow and to give years of pleasure.

Of course, there are many limitations, those of the purse and of space being perhaps the greatest hurdles. A newly fledged young school-teacher should not start to collect yellow-ground Dr Wall period Worcester porcelains, nor if he lives in a bedsitter should he seek to collect exhibition *tours de force*. He can, however, derive just as much pleasure from collecting less expensive small objects and often the restriction of space can be a distinct advantage–if only because one is forced to be selective. Also, one must not select a class of object that is almost impossible to find.

The ideal might be to collect a line that with a little trouble you can find, say, thirty objects a year in your price range, so that from that number of 'sightings' you could pick out ten to add to your collection.

Having chosen an object or factory, how would you expect to start collecting? The main sources of supply are: (a) dealers and (b) auction sales.

There are, of course, many different types of dealer and of antique shop. Indeed, many establishments that boldly display the description 'antiques' appear not to stock a single item over fifty years old let alone a hundred, but we need not worry about this for 'age in itself is not a virtue', and you *can* find a shop that does stock the type of object you are seeking. You will have acquired local knowledge of likely shops in your own district and if you hunt further afield there are now helpful directories, such as *The British Antiques Yearbook* or the *Guide to the Antique Shops of Britain* which should be available at bookshops and each of these is sold by many antique dealers. Or you can study the advertisements in the various collectors' magazines such as *Collectors Guide* to seek out people who advertise items in which you are interested. Many of the leading dealers belong to the British Antique Dealers' Association Ltd, and a list of members may be obtained free on application to the Secretary of the Association at 20 Rutland Gate, London, SW7 IBD.

Do not be afraid of entering these or other grand-looking shops—many of my most exciting finds have come from such establishments. An item that is out of this world to you may be only an average specimen to a specialist and he will be glad to take a modest profit on cost and at the same time make a new customer. Dealers should always remember that it is in their own interest to foster new collectors. Many believe, as I do, that the best form of publicity is to give the collector a bargain. He or she will (hopefully!) always remember a kindness or a bargain and will return again and again to that dealer. At the other end of the scale do not forget the 'junk shops'. Great finds have been made in such places—and at jumble sales!

Probably the most important first step for any collector is to make friends with a knowledgeable dealer or collector, who is prepared to guide or advise the novice and to help him avoid the many traps that await the unwary or the over-confident. On your part you must remember that the dealer has to get his living from his chosen trade, so do not expect, as a right, free valuations, nor credit on articles that he could have sold ten times over. If you want to see the cream of his new stock, see that you pay at once and do not haggle when you both know the price is reasonable.

Purchase at auction can present problems. You have only to read the conditions of sale printed in the catalogue to learn that the auctioneer claims only to be an agent and that he disclaims (in most cases) responsibility for an incorrect description or for any faults. This is not to say that all lots are miscatalogued or that every article is sprayed over to hide the cracks. Most lots are genuine and perfect and reasonably described, depending on the knowledge of the auctioneer or his cataloguer, but you do not get the full guaranteed invoice that most dealers will give and you will not have an opportunity to change your mind. If you do buy at auction make sure that you *carefully* view the goods on the appointed view day and if you attend the sale in person make sure that you are not carried away into giving more than your predetermined limit and that you do not start bidding for lots which you have not examined just because they seem cheap– there is usually a good reason for this.

If you cannot attend the sale yourself, you may leave commissions with a porter (who will expect a tip if he is able to purchase the items), or direct with the auctioneer (who will not require extra payment as he cannot accept commission from the buyer and the seller), or alternatively you can discuss the sale with your dealer friend who may well be able to give you valuable advice and be prepared to act for you.

Although I have just written that an auctioneer should not accept commission from both the buyer and the seller, some firms–including Christies and Sothebys but not Phillips–now charge a 10 per cent buyer's premium. So that if you make a buying bid of £100 you will be required to pay £110. In some cases you will also be charged Value Added Tax at the current rate on your purchase.

When buying at auction do carefully view the goods offered and study the conditions of sale and other notices printed in the catalogue.

With certain classes of articles you may be able to employ other methods of purchase. You can place advertisements in specialist magazines publicising your requirements but such exercises are best left until you really know your subject and can distinguish the wheat from the chaff. Also, the resulting postal delivery (and often return) is not suited to delicate porcelain.

You may ask how one acquires this knowledge that will permit one to know the good from the bad. The trouble with such a question is who is to say that one thing is good, the other bad? Different people at different times have different standards. Some types of Victorian or Edwardian porcelain are today commanding very high prices and there are many serious collectors of such wares but some thirty years ago these objects would have been scorned. Our tastes change; time hides faults or helps to reveal assets. One must also bear in mind that as fashionable eighteenth-century porcelains become harder to find and more expensive to purchase so collectors will tend to seek other initially less fashionable and inexpensive wares. Certainly the nineteenth century produced a bewildering range of collectable items. I cannot claim all were good pots but then a collection does not have to comprise only perfectly conceived and produced items. Witness the great collections of pot-lids, of fairings, of mass-produced Staffordshire figures. Few of these can be termed good from a potter's or artist's point of view–but what pleasure they have given collectors and what service and satisfaction they gave to the original purchasers of these humble wares.

To appreciate a good form you probably need some experience. It may help to have had some training in the craft of potting, to have coaxed a shapeless lump of clay into a graceful, balanced shape on the potter's wheel. One can also divide the bad from the good by viewing a large museum collection such as that housed in the Victoria and Albert museum–or at least you can tell which pieces or types you admire and which you dislike.

If one cannot be taught what is good and what is bad, at least one can learn to appreciate quality. To appreciate quality and varying styles or types of porcelain one can make good use of not only museums but also the auction galleries. Here, particularly in the London 'Rooms', one can see and handle, on the advertised view days before the sale, a large quantity of very varied objects. These are not always displayed to advantage and they are often extremely dirty but they are available and this is the important thing.

I may well be prejudiced as a dealer but I cannot but think that the most helpful source of learning is a dealer's shop–not any dealer but a specialist in the subject of your choice. In such an establishment you would expect to find a select group of articles which not only can you handle at leisure but the dealer should be able to discuss the pieces intelligently and give valuable guidance should you wish for it. In my shop in Worthing I have tried to combine the best features of a museum with those of a shop. There is a permanent reference section where callers can examine typical or documentary dated or marked examples of English eighteenth-century porcelains. These reference pieces–some of which are featured in this book–are not for sale, but we also aim to have available to purchase a good range of collectable articles, from rare early porcelains to individual modern items by promising and talented craftsmen.

I hope always to be able to stock a selection of very modestly priced pieces for the new collector or for those with modest means, and in order to help the novice I am not afraid to have some interesting or rare pieces that have suffered honest damage. It is all very well to stock only perfect articles priced in hundreds of pounds but most collectors would surely welcome the chance to buy an attractive piece at a tenth of the price and overlook the chip or crack that will explain the low asking price. Perhaps one of my most exciting buys was the purchase of a group of Worcester porcelains from the Trustees of the famous Dyson Perrins collection at Worcester. Here, relegated to a storeroom, was a mini-collection of duplicate or otherwise surplus items not available to the thousands of persons who visit this splendid collection each year. Now collectors or other museums have the opportunity to own these neglected pieces. At the same time the Trustees obtained a useful sum with which they could purchase new articles not as yet represented in the collection. One wonders how many curators, museum committees or trustees have stored away such duplicates which will never be shown to the public?

There are admittedly differing views on the sale of surplus museum specimens but even such seemingly unimportant pieces as odd cups can, once freed from their storage cupboards, give instruction and joy to the novice collector. Let me quote briefly from my 1966 book *Antique China and Glass under £5*:

> ...There is probably no better way to know thoroughly the various English (or Continental) porcelain factories and their characteristics than to gather together a representative collection of cups. Once you can tell the difference between a Bow blue and white cup and a Lowestoft one, or between a Bristol hard-paste cup and

a Plymouth, then your ground work is sound and can be enlarged upon. All would-be collectors of eighteenth-century English ceramics should form a collection of typical cups: many costly mistakes could be avoided if they did so...

No matter how modest your collection, you should compile a catalogue, preferably in a loose-leaf book allowing one double-sided page to each item. Here you should describe each article giving the main sizes and a drawing of any factory mark and a note of any unusual feature. Give also details of the source of the purchase with the date and the cost. From time to time as you come across similar specimens in museums or illustrated in books or collectors' magazines, you should add this cross-reference information to the relevant page in your catalogue. You could also add information on the prices similar pieces have fetched at auction, if you are able to follow closely the London sale rooms.

You will then have a check-list of your collection, its sources and cost and in these troubled times such a basic record could be most useful. While I am being morbid it is worth mentioning that such a written record should be backed by photographs, or group photographs of several pieces if the cost of individual photographs worries you. These photographs and the catalogue (or a copy of it) should be kept separately from the collection so that if you do suffer a serious fire you do not lose both the collection and the supporting records. Of course, if your collection grows to be a valuable one you will need to take out separate insurance cover and not depend on the cover given in a normal householder's comprehensive policy. There will also be a greater need to have an up-to-date valuation carried out by a specialist.

I have just mentioned books and collectors' magazines: today you can easily spend a small fortune on reference books, for they are both numerous and costly and they will inevitably become even more expensive as the cost of raw materials and production increases. Yet to get the full benefit of collecting and to keep yourself up to date with recent discoveries you must have (or have access to) some of the more reliable sources of information. The specialist collector of one factory's products should have all relevant books on his shelves, and this is not excessively expensive, but the general collector has a bewildering assortment of volumes available.

If you were to ask me to choose for you just six general books on English porcelain I would list the following which are arranged in date order:

(1) *A History and Description of English Porcelain* by William Burton (Cassell & Co., London, 1902)

(2) *Old English Porcelain* by W. B. Honey (Faber, London, 1948; revised edition 1977)

(3) *English Blue and White Porcelain* by Dr Bernard Watney (Faber, London, 1963, revised edition, 1973)

(4) *British Porcelain 1745–1850*, edited by R. J. Charleston (E. Benn, London, 1965)

(5) *British Pottery and Porcelain for Pleasure and Investment* by Henry Sandon (J. Gifford, London, 1969)

(6) *British Porcelain, an illustrated guide* by Geoffrey Godden (Barrie & Jenkins, London, 1974)

I should make a few comments on these books. The first, written by a practical potter and ceramic chemist, William Burton, is now quite scarce, having been published as a limited edition of 1200 in 1902. It is, however, well worth searching for. You will find here much sound common sense, a very good ground-work. Admittedly some facts on the eighteenth-century factories are now out-dated but the good points outnumber the bad and Burton helpfully included information on the leading modern (*c.* 1900) manufacturers and their current productions.

In choosing W. B. Honey's *Old English Porcelain* I am permitting myself a little nostalgia, for I was brought up on 'Honey', as this volume is affectionately termed, and furthermore I had the good fortune to know and to be advised by this great authority when I was but a novice schoolboy collector. His writings reflect his own personal taste so that some wares are rather hastily dismissed, but you should still have this classic on your shelves–and refer to it often. We now have the benefit of a new and revised edition published in July 1977.

You may have been surprised that I included Dr Watney's specialist book on blue and white porcelain in my list of general books. This is because his book gives such a good and detailed history of all English eighteenth-century porcelain factories and because it discusses at length the differing bodies and other characteristics. Even if you do not happen to share my love of underglaze-blue decoration, do treat yourself to this book.

English Porcelain 1745–1850, edited by R. J. Charleston, Keeper of the Department of Ceramics, Victoria and Albert Museum, is made up of chapters written by specialist contributors. It gives a sound coverage of all the major eighteenth-century factories but the section on the nineteenth-century wares is rather inadequate.

Henry Sandon's book *British Pottery and Porcelain for Pleasure and Investment* is an inexpensive but reliable general book covering a wide field of English ceramics and including many interestingly fresh illustrations.

My own *British Porcelain* is richly illustrated with over 550 plates, giving teeth to its sub-title. Many of these illustrations show characteristic shapes or other features and support the concise text. The coverage ranges from Bow, Chelsea and 'Girl in the Swing' productions to late nineteenth- and early twentieth-century porcelains such as Royal Worcester. The trouble with so many books on the earlier wares is that they completely disregard the Victorian and later products. To fill this gap I published in 1961 my pioneer work *Victorian Porcelain*.

I have naturally had to confine my choice to those titles published before 1978 and if you read these pages in later years there may well by then be excellent new books available. Other, mainly specialist books are listed in the sections dealing with the different factories or types of decoration. If you want to identify a factory mark then you would turn to my *Encyclopaedia of British Pottery and Porcelain Marks*.

A fuller general list is given in the bibliography but in general terms one can leave the mass of inexpensive all-embracing books that stock bookshop shelves. An author who seeks to cover all European or the world's porcelain factories in a hundred pages can hardly be expected to add much to our fund of knowledge. It is far better to save up and buy a worthwhile book. A notable exception to this rule is *The Observer's Book of Pottery and Porcelain* by Mary & Geoffrey Payton (Frederick Warne & Co. Ltd, London, 1973), wonderful value at £1·10p.

Of course, British readers have access to a wealth of books, old classics as well as the newer works, through the public libraries. Obviously some libraries hold larger stocks than others or have different specialities but each can draw on the stock of others and your local library staff should be able to obtain for you any reference book you may desire. You may have to consult some early, rare or expensive volumes within the library, rather than be permitted to read them at home, but this is an understandable condition designed to conserve the book for the benefit of all. It is a small price to pay for the privilege of reading the hundreds of available books.

Many of the articles to be found in the collectors' magazines are of the greatest importance. They often publicise new discoveries or cover subjects not found in standard books. They can reflect the specialist knowledge of collectors, museum curators or others who may not wish to write a full-length book on their subject. You should make it your business to read all the main magazines that may be expected to carry articles relating to your subject or to include advertisements of dealers (or others) of a like interest. Most town or city libraries will stock these magazines but the monthly outlay is not all that great and you should try to buy at least one yourself. Perhaps you could come to some arrangement with collector friends by which you each subscribe to one and circulate them all among yourselves.

The main British monthly magazines that are likely to often include articles on porcelains are: *The Antique Collector* (Chestergate House, Vauxhall Bridge Road, London, SW1V 1HF); *Collectors Guide* (City Magazines Ltd, 1–3 Wine Office Court, Fleet Street, London, EC4A 3AL); *The Connoisseur* (Chestergate House, Vauxhall Bridge Road, London, SW1V 1HF).

Of the weeklies *Art and Antiques Weekly* sometimes includes interesting articles relating to ceramics, mainly the later types, and *Country Life* also publishes helpful articles which may prove of interest. New discoveries are often first published in the learned papers contained in the *Transactions of the English Ceramic Circle*. Details are available from Messrs W. and J. Mackay Ltd, Lordswood, Chatham, Kent.

Mention of the English Ceramic Circle prompts me to mention clubs. There are many local and regional collectors' clubs which hold meetings or discussions with expert speakers or arrange outings to museums. Your local library or the museum curator should be able to give you details of any in your locality. Some, such as the very active Northern Ceramic Society, publish an informative 'Newsletter' and even a journal, free to members. Even if you do not live in the north these society publications are well worth the subscription. As I write the Hon. Membership Secretary and Treasurer is Anthony Thomas, Bramdean, Jacksons Lane, Hazel Grove, Cheshire.

Other very useful sources of information are provided by courses, seminars or the like. There is the Keele College Summer School in Staffordshire. Also the Morley

College weekend seminar held annually in London, normally in November. You can obtain details by writing to the Morley College Ceramic Circle, Morley College, 61 Westminster Bridge Road, London, SE1.

I run a series of study meetings at Worthing, ranging from beginners' weekends to others that deal in depth with troublesome subjects such as the porcelains of the 1790–1820 period–the New Hall wares and the many firms that produced similar wares, Chamberlain and Grainger-Worcester, Miles Mason porcelains, etc. I regard these study weekends as being my most successful venture, for not only do we have specialist speakers but we are also able to have available to see *and to handle* a good representative display of the pieces we are discussing. I also encourage collectors to bring along problem pieces to discuss and, of course, they can ask questions of the panel and so air points that they may not fully understand or pose questions on subjects not covered in the reference books. I started these 'study weekends' to help the private collector but as it turned out many dealers and representatives from leading auction houses have joined our gatherings. All, I think, have spent a most enjoyable, interesting and profitable weekend. You can obtain details from Geoffrey Godden, Chinaman, at 17–19 Crescent Road, Worthing, Sussex.

There are, I know, many aspects of collecting which I have not touched on, and some of these will be discussed in the next chapter. Then we can roam over several points that have not fitted into the main story.

CHAPTER ELEVEN

Some helpful hints

I have now covered at least the basic facts about the various types of porcelain bodies, about the manufacturing processes and the ways in which the completed forms are embellished. I have also given an outline history of major British porcelain factories from the 1740s to the present century and in the last chapter I have offered some advice on forming your own collection.

This is just a beginning. We can (or should) never stop learning and one of the best ways to learn about any one type, or class, of ceramic is to write a magazine article or 'paper' on the subject. Such an article need not be intended for publication, although if it is, you may well hear from other interested collectors who can add to your own knowledge. However, the main object of the exercise or 'project' is to research the subject–not merely to *précis* other people's published views but to go back to fundamentals, to recheck all known, or supposed, facts. This can be great fun and is most rewarding and thought-provoking.

DAMAGED PIECES

We can now turn to some outstanding points. I shall start with damaged pieces. You will probably find that about half the available specimens of old porcelains have suffered some damage over the years, indeed in some shops nearly all the pieces seem damaged. Some say that one should reject all faulty examples no matter how minor the injury. This is good advice–if your purse is long and if you are collecting purely as an investment. If, however, you aim to be a true collector you will find this bad advice. I shudder to think of the interesting documentary pieces I would have missed had I been interested only in mint specimens.

When I started collecting in my very early teens I begged from my father damaged pieces that he was throwing out because they were (then) unwanted. I acquired a triangle-marked Chelsea crayfish salt in this way and very many other interesting objects which served at very little cost to familiarise me with the different pastes and potting characteristics of these wares. I do not know how I could have gained this vital groundwork, had it not been for these badly damaged examples. I certainly could not have afforded to buy perfect pieces even at the then ruling low prices, and there were few other opportunities for an eager schoolboy to handle antique porcelains. Perhaps this is why I am so keen today to have available for interested would-be collectors a selection of pieces that they can not only see but also handle–my reference collection.

Of course, there are degrees of damage. A large discoloured crack across the face of a plate or dish is not to be recommended but I see little to complain about in minor cracks or small edge chips, especially in useful wares made for everyday use. Such damage I call 'honourable' or 'honest' and I marvel that so much has remained free of such faults for some two hundred years. How long can we expect our present-day teapot to remain mint?

For my money I prefer examples that are not ashamed to show their little blemishes to those painted-up articles that have become the curse of sale rooms, antique fairs and some dealers' stocks in recent years. Such pieces are all too often sold as perfect, or at least the repairs are not explained and one acquires a badly damaged article at a fancy price–having paid unwittingly for the restorer's art or craft–together with a liberal spray of new paint. This practice is one of the main reasons why you must ask for a detailed invoice or receipt when buying and, if no damage is pointed out to you, see that the article is described on the invoice as perfect or as being in unrestored state. If such statements are not forthcoming you can draw your own conclusion!

The restorer can do a very useful job and I have nothing against a modest amount of respraying when you are aware that such work has been carried out. To my mind it is much better to buy damaged pieces in their unrestored state, being fully aware of all the faults, and then if you so wish have the repairs carried out yourself. If you cannot trace a good china-restorer in the yellow pages of your telephone directory or in a collectors' magazine, your dealer friend can no doubt put you in touch with one, or you can turn yourself into a do-it-yourself repairer. If you come along to one of our 'study meetings' for beginners you will probably find available a selection of modestly priced damaged pieces to use as study pieces or to have repaired if you wish.

BAKING CRACKS

It is correct to distinguish between damage inflicted in use and the faults that can occur during manufacture. We must always remember that the eighteenth-century potters were pioneers, working under great difficulties with materials that were not absolutely pure or constant, and that the temperature of the kiln could not be controlled as the heat in modern kilns can, with their oil or electricity-firing. Small wonder that some old pieces show tears, open cracks, or other firing or baking faults. A baking crack is in effect a contraction of the body and the crack will be slightly open at the edge with perhaps the glaze having flowed slightly into the opening. Such characteristic features are almost standard on some early porcelains, such as Chelsea, and it is nearly but not quite, true to say that a Chelsea piece without a baking fault or without a ground-flat foot should be rejected as a fake.

SECONDS

It is often forgotten that many pieces of now antique pottery and porcelain were sold at a low price as 'seconds' or even as 'thirds'. In recent times we may call these 'export rejects' and the reject shops which sell nothing but slightly faulty wares do a roaring trade. This is no new idea; at any period a manufacturer is loath to smash up articles that can be sold to redress some, or all, of his costs.

If today's manufacturers produce faulty wares with all their up-to-date equipment and refined raw materials it is small wonder that we find so much eighteenth-century porcelain that is a little short of perfection. Perhaps the article was slightly over-fired so that the underglaze-blue has somewhat blurred or run with the glaze, or perhaps a handle has slightly warped out of true. To a hard-up housewife such minor defects were almost welcomed if the price of her porcelain was that much reduced. My lord in his stately home might equally have welcomed the reduction when buying crockery for the kitchen or for the staff.

FAIRS

When discussing repaired pieces just now I mentioned antique fairs. These come in all sizes, the father of them all in two senses is the Grosvenor House Fair held in the great room of that famous Park Lane hotel facing Hyde Park. Here you will find a splendid gathering of superb goods tastefully set out on elegant stands and presented by knowledgeable dealers. You may not find a great bargain but you will have little or no cause otherwise to fault your purchase.

At the other extreme you have a multitude of small local fairs or antique markets, where you may well have a lucky purchase but where you would be well advised to have your wits about you. In between these extremes you have some very worthwhile and well organised fairs with knowledgeable and reputable exhibitors. I have in mind particularly the Chelsea Fair, the Kensington, the Solihull and the Guildford Fairs. At all of these I have made very good purchases, but it does help if you can join the queue quite early on the opening day. With the Grosvenor House Fair you will need to have an official invitation to the opening but in the case of other fairs it would seem that you need only purchase on the day a modestly priced ticket. Speaking of openings do note that in most cases the official 'opening' may be some hours after the public are admitted. If you turn up at the advertised opening at, say, two or three in the afternoon you will probably find all the bargains have been purchased by the rush of buyers who were there when the doors opened at eleven.

The advantage of fairs to the collector lies in the fact that he can see under one roof at one time a gathering of stocks from a wide range of dealers and often from different parts of the country. In many cases the dealers will have saved special pieces to grace their stands and while you may have to pay a premium for the privilege of seeing such a large gathering, it is often well worth the extra cost. If you should wonder why the price may be inflated you can reflect on the cost of the stand and the extra overheads and advertising.

Plate 103 A unique Lowestoft porcelain tankard of the 1790 period, purchased at an antique fair for
£11! 4½ inches high. *Author's Collection*

Speaking of advertising, many organisers make great play of the fact that each
exhibit has been vetted by the expert committee but as this committee seems, in
most cases, to be made up of the exhibitors themselves, you should still insist on a
detailed invoice. I am not suggesting that they are dishonest, only that they may not
have specialist knowledge. I could tell you many stories about strange happenings in
fairs but I will restrict myself to an experience that happened several years ago when
these provincial antique fairs were in their infancy. It was the usual crowded

opening with a mad rush of dealers and others trying to cover every stand in the minimum of time, and I found myself pushing past a fellow dealer who had just picked up a tankard. Seeing me he kindly said, 'Isn't this your cup of tea?' It certainly was! A fine unique English Lowestoft crested and initialled tankard in mint state (Plate 103). In rather a dream I purchased this for eleven pounds. It turned out later that the selling dealer had previously shown this to a leading expert who pronounced it a fake–no doubt because of its unique nature and superb state which made it almost 'too good to be true'! Having been told that it was not 'right', this dealer proceeded to offer it cheaply on his stand–to my joy!

It is perhaps human nature to try to palm off one's mistakes on others but you can also reflect on the advantages of really knowing your subject so that you can reap the rewards offered by the less specialist dealers.

REIGNS

You may hear references to various periods or reigns when the age of porcelain is being discussed. Here is a brief list of periods from 1700 onwards and you will see that the description 'Georgian' is a very loose one ranging from 1714 to 1830.

William III	1691–1702
Queen Anne	1702–1714
George I	1714–1727
George II	1727–1760
George III	1760–1820
George IV	1820–1830
William IV	1830–1837
Queen Victoria (hence Victorian)	1837–1901
Edward VII	1901–1910
George V	1910–1936
Edward VIII	1936
George VI	1936–1952
Queen Elizabeth II	1952–

The term Regency is usually considered to embrace the 1800–1820 period.

AMATEUR DECORATION

I have mentioned the independent professional decorators who, working in London and at other centres, embellished blank or white pottery or porcelain. Even today there are many commercial firms who decorate, by contract or for their own subsequent sale, blank wares made by other firms.

However, by no means all these 'outside decorated' wares were professionally painted, for it was fashionable in the nineteenth century for amateurs to paint on pottery or porcelain. One of my earliest magazine articles dealt with such Victorian attempts at china-painting (see *Country Life*, 2 October 1958) but the fashion or craze goes back further than the Victorian era. From the early 1800s the Coalport firm supplied thousands of blanks to amateur and professional painters and the records of the Chamberlain company at Worcester show that it too supplied not only white porcelains but also complete sets of ceramic colours and also on occasions the company's artists gave lessons in china-painting. One entry in June 1806 shows these expenses charged to a Prince Bariatinsky at Cheltenham:

A complete set of colours	£1/ 1/0d
Pencils, oil, knives, etc	8/0d
A batch of bronzes	10/0d
Regilding a plate and three candlesticks	19/0d
Eight lessons in painting	£6/16/6d
Expenses to Cheltenham	£5/16/0d

Sometimes such amateur home decoration bore gilding and this was fired and burnished at the factory as numerous charges show, but as a general rule this amateur work did not include gilding and the colours tended to be rather muddy and the painting rather wooden or laboured. Notwithstanding all these faults the painters tended to sign their work fully and often a date was added. For this reason alone the amateur painting can be of great interest.

LIMITED EDITIONS

Within recent years various manufacturers have produced pieces in 'limited editions' of say five hundred examples. Many of these pieces bear explanatory marks and in some cases each item is numbered, for example 'Number 100 of a limited edition of three hundred'.

Such pieces cater for the collector or investor who seeks built-in rarity but while there are merits in some of the finer productions, such as the Royal Worcester figures or groups, I can see little merit in mass-produced commemorative plates and the like. You can all too easily glut the market even with a limited edition of two hundred–if only one hundred persons wish to own that particular item.

Limited editions will always have their devotees, and by all means join them if you wish, but do judge the piece on its quality and design, not on the fact that only five hundred were made.

Most antique objects exist in very small numbers. They are very much rarer than these modern limited issues and in many instances only one or two examples are known or at least can be expected to come on to the market.

UNIQUE PIECES

I, and other dealers, are often shown porcelains which the owner fondly claims to be unique or 'nearly unique'. (Do note that there are no degrees of uniqueness, an article is either unique or it is not!) In most cases this claim is nonsense for ceramic articles were originally made in commercial quantities. Printed designs were always mass-produced: if you were only making one you would not go to the considerable expense of having copper-plates engraved. Moulded articles will likewise have been mass-produced and articles bearing pattern numbers will be stock designs.

OTHER FALLACIES

I could fill this book with fallacies, ranging from the fond belief that because the cracked saucer belonged to one's grandmother it must be valuable to the idea that Americans are queuing up to pay hundreds of dollars for a stained and rightly discarded willow pattern plate or lidless teapot. Owners bent on selling their unwanted knick-knacks tend to make unwarranted claims as to its age, playing family arithmetic to make an Edwardian teaset Queen Anne (who reigned before the secret of making porcelain was discovered in Britain) in the belief that age in itself is a virtue!

Family arithmetic runs something like this: 'Oh but it *must* be two hundred years old because it belonged to my grandfather and he died aged ninety and my mother lived to be seventy and I'm over fifty, so you see, it is really well over two hundred years old.' There is an overlap of generations–the seventy-year-old mother was not born as grandad passed on at ninety! It is also rather unlikely that dear grandad purchased the dinner service on his first birthday! If your grandfather should be rash enough to buy a copy of this book, that will not make it an antique!

FOREIGN WARES

In the nineteenth century and particularly in the present century porcelains of foreign manufacture were being imported into England, indeed the great mass of cheap porcelains such as were sold at the popular resorts were of French or German make or sometimes of Japanese origin. Most of these wares will not bear a factory mark but from 1891 onwards they should display their country of origin. If you find the fuller description, 'Made in Germany', the object can be dated after about 1910.

These foreign porcelains will be of a hard-paste with a glittery glaze and often embellished with cheap thin watery 'liquid gold' that does not need burnishing but which tends to rub off quite easily when it is regularly dusted or washed.

WASHING

It is surprising how wonderful porcelain and ceramic real gilding can become once it has been cleared of the grime that accumulates over the years. But once clean you should submit your porcelains to a minimum of washing and take elementary precautions–the water should be warm rather than hot. Use a plastic bowl rather than a metal or stone sink, and if you can cap your taps with those rubber nozzles so much the better. Do not use abrasives such as Vim. Do not use bleach if the article has any gilding. Do dry the object well with a soft, not a harsh cloth. Watch out for damages for the water may melt the glue and the object may come apart.

I find a shaving brush an ideal tool for washing china, it is soft but the long hairs will get in all the crevices. It is almost indispensable when you are washing floral encrusted porcelains and you can dry these intricate pieces with a hair-dryer.

FILING SYSTEM

You will, as you read books or magazines, come across interesting facts or references that you may need for further research. Also you will come across interesting pieces in museums or private collections. All this information should be carefully filed away where you can find it again at short notice. You need a filing system.

The easiest method is to write, or type, your notes on separate sheets of paper and to place these in a lever-arch file under the initial letter of the subject–so that for example this little note would be filed under 'F' for Filing System perhaps with a cross reference at 'R' for Research.

The essential point is to note the source of the information. I have a list of all my reference books, each title having its own initial-prefix and number. This number is pencilled inside the relevant book and in extracting a useful quotation or fact I have only to write at the head of each note the book number and the page. For example, G.72 p. 254 readily identifies for me this book and its page.

You can build up your filing system as your reading and other studies dictate, and in time you will have a most useful mini-library at your finger-tips.

CENTURY DATING

You will find many references in books, magazine articles and such-like to the eighteenth or the nineteenth century and many people do not seem at all clear as to the meaning of these designations. Indeed, they can be incorrectly used. The eighteenth century does *not* include dates in the 1800s. If we speak or write of the seventeenth century we mean the period from 1600 to 1699 and the eighteenth century relates to the period from 1700 to 1799. The nineteenth century relates to the period 1800 to 1899, while the twentieth century commenced in 1900.

CIRCA

Whilst we are discussing dates, I should point out that we use the word '*circa*' to mean 'about', so that when we say '*circa* 1780' it is an approximate, rather than an exact dating. You will often find a date prefixed with the initial '*c*'. It is used as the abbreviation of *circa* and again indicates an approximate date.

Plate 104 A pair of Continental hard-paste figures showing an overglaze gold anchor mark and a late type of pierced vent-hole, *c.* 1900+. 2¾ inches high. *Geoffrey Godden, Reference Collection*

FAKES

By now you will know how to distinguish most blatant fakes. You will know that most English porcelains are of the soft-paste variety and that fakes of Chelsea, Bow, Derby or Worcester porcelains are nearly always of a cold, glittery, hard-paste body.

You will know that the easiest part of the faker's craft is to reproduce the mark of the original and that in the cheaper mass-produced fakes the mark is prominently placed. Look at the little pair of hard-paste present-century Continental figures of cupids with goats in Plate 104–quite attractive in their way when one considers that the factory price was the equivalent of a few pence, but look at that outsize gold anchor mark on the reversed group! Note also that little blow-hole and keep well away from supposedly eighteenth-century English figures or groups displaying this feature.

Brash fakes of this type should not fool even novice collectors but some early Samson reproductions are of very good quality and being themselves now 'antique' they have acquired a certain respectability and pedigree, although they are still hard-paste. The best Samson reproductions can also be most decorative. At one

Plate 105 A Booths' earthenware bowl in the Chelsea or Worcester style, *c.* 1910. Diameter 8½ inches. *Godden of Worthing Ltd*

study meeting I had put out on a table just such a French copy of a Chelsea figure–as an example of what not to buy–only to find a group of ladies going into raptures over it. To them it was the most desirable of objects and from a decorative point of view they were quite right.

Not all fakes are hard-paste. Some are even of an earthenware body and are therefore opaque. The copies of Worcester porcelain made by Booths of Tunstall still fool some people. Plate 105 shows a typical bowl and the copies of standard Worcester blue and white objects are quite good and when marked they bear this device.

Even Chelsea porcelain was copied in earthenware on the Continent and only recently I received a series of letters from a most excited American who thought he had discovered a key-piece that was to upset all previous writings on the Chelsea factory, for his piece was dated 1740! He went into great detail in describing this piece but neglected to state that it was pottery not porcelain! The blatant mark should have given warning, for apart from the large size, that mark was just too good to be true. It comprised not only the anchor device but the word 'Chelsea'

and the date 1740! Do note that the word 'Chelsea' does not occur on genuine anchor-marked specimens. Indeed the place-name will not occur in painted form at all, except on later non-Chelsea wares where the name is used only to distinguish the pattern which the manufacturer may fancy has a Chelsea flavour.

I have in previous books pointed out that the Swansea and Nantgarw marks were widely copied, also some fake Derby and Rockingham marks are to be found but the great mass of post-1800 marks are above suspicion, for it only pays the faker to use his mis-spent skill on commercially valuable, highly collectable wares. However, as certain classes of later, even present-century wares command high prices the faker has turned his attention to such articles. Sometimes he merely changes the mark, replacing a minor name with the mark of a fashionable manufacturer. When such works first come on the market they are often passed as genuine because the collectors are not expecting reproductions, but as the faker puts more and more specimens on the market–normally by way of the auction sales–so the experts are alerted by the sudden flood of new unrecorded types.

The Wedgwood Portland-vase trade-mark has been added to certain types of the fashionable 'Fairyland Lustre' wares–a genuine example of which is shown in Plate 106. I am not a lawyer but as this Wedgwood mark is a registered trade-mark the faker must be running a risk, quite apart from the protection offered by the Trade's Description and the Misrepresentation of Goods Acts. Again you will see the advantages of dealing with a reputable firm where knowledge will be backed by a guarantee.

PATTERN NAMES

Many marks incorporate or feature only the name of a particular pattern, for example Willow, Rose, Abbey, Pekin or Asiatic Pheasants. These names in themselves do not give any indication of the maker nor were they intended to. These and many other standard designs were mass-produced by several firms, large and small.

Perhaps the only reason in making this point is to try to stem the flood of letters I receive from owners wishing to know the age and make of their plate bearing only the name of the pattern. I'm sorry, it can't be done!

PATTERN NUMBERS

Painted pattern numbers are to be found on a large range of British porcelains from about 1790 onwards and while few, if any, *numbers* are unique to any one factory, they can be a positive method of identification when the factory pattern books are available and in the other instances they can very often be of great help in tracing the manufacturer or in dating an object.

The purpose of a pattern number was basically to enable the retailer and the customer to identify or re-order a given pattern; it also enabled the manufacturers

Plate 106 A Wedgwood 'Fairyland-lustre' porcelain circular plaque, *c.* 1920. Diameter 13¼ inches.
Godden of Worthing Ltd

to price, invoice and identify their wares. Each factory had a set of pattern books in
which the numbered designs were drawn in colour. The various painters copied the
master designs from the pattern books and painted the appropriate pattern number
under the article. As a general rule pattern numbers are found only on English
porcelains and then mainly on useful wares–teasets, dessert and dinner services (and
parts thereof) rather than on ornamental objects such as vases, although these when
decorated with a stock design could also be numbered.

   The patterns were numbered consecutively as new designs were introduced. This
was straightforward until an unwieldy number such as 999 was reached; in some
cases the numbering was then restarted at 1 placed under the numeral 2/ showing
that the number was from the second series. Such a number I have described as a
fractional pattern number.

   In some other instances the new series of patterns was distinguished by a letter prefix, so that pattern 999 might be followed by A1. Some other factories continued their numbering consecutively so that their patterns climbed into several thousands. Therefore there are three possible pattern numbering systems–the fractional, the prefixed and the consecutive; once the number 999 or 1000 had been reached the various factories used one of these three alternatives.

A study of factory pattern books, accounts and other records or the pieces themselves enables the system followed by each major factory to be classified and in some cases the date of introduction of various patterns to be gauged. Basic information on the systems used by the main porcelain factories of the 1780–1840 period is given below but, of course, I cannot give you details of the numbering systems employed by the host of small nineteenth-century firms.

Barr, or Barr, Flight & Barr, Worcester (also *Flight*, and *Flight, Barr & Barr Porcelains*) *c.* 1783–1840.
No pattern numbers used, although gilders' or painters' numbers may occur but these numbers are low and do not exceed 30.

Caughley (or '*Salopian*') *Porcelain, c.* 1775–1799
No pattern numbers used, although gilders' numbers may occur in gold on the inside of the foot-rim; these numbers are low, not exceeding 28.

Chamberlain-Worcester, c. 1786–1852
Progressive pattern numbers but system not started until *c.* 1790. Pattern No. 100 reached by 1797; 400 by 1807; 610 by 1812; 790 by 1817; 1000 by 1822. The numbers then climb to 1752, restart at 2000 and proceed to 2624, recommence at 3000 and continue to 3099, then 4000 to 4099 and 5000 to 5019.

Coalport–the John Rose Company (and successors), *c.* 1797–present day
Porcelains made prior to *c.* 1805 do not bear a pattern number. Numbers 1 to 999 used to *c.* 1824. Early numbers are very rarely found. After pattern 999 a *fractional* system was introduced: 2/1, 2/2, 2/3 etc, to 2/999. Pattern 2/783 bears the date 'April 27th 1832'.
New system 3/1, 3/2, 3/3, etc, to 3/999 used *c.* 1833–38.
New system 4/1, 4/2, 4/3, etc, to 4/1000 used *c.* 1839–43.
New system 5/1, 5/2, 5/3, etc, to 5/1000 used *c.* 1844–50.
Fractional numbers 6/1 etc, 7/1 and 8/1 and so on were also employed, but later on in the nineteenth century progressive numbers were employed and continued into the present century. These later wares with progressive numbers will bear a self-explanatory printed trade-mark and are consequently unlikely to be mistaken for the wares of other factories.

Coalport–Messrs Anstice, Horton & Rose *c.* 1800–1814
Progressive numbers: 1 to at least 1419.

Copeland & Garrett, c. 1833–1847
Progressive numbers following on from Spode's system. Pattern number (approximate) 4700 introduced in 1833.
Pattern number (approximate) 7260 reached by mid-1847. *Progressive* numbers continued by successors Messrs W. T. Copeland until *c.* 1852 when number 9999 had been reached. A new series with the letter D prefix was then started.

Davenport, c. 1793–1887
Progressive numbers. One thousand designs had been issued by about 1855 and before the closure in 1887 the number had exceeded four thousand.

Derby, c. 1750–1848
Derby porcelains produced prior to *c.* 1780 do not bear a pattern number. Subsequently, between *c.* 1780 and 1810 *progressive* numbers were employed. These normally occur painted below the painted crown, crossed batons and 'D' mark (see p. 109). Derby porcelains of the 1810–48 period seldom bear a pattern number; small numbers near the rims of plates, etc, are the painters' or gilders' personal identification marks. Derby-*type* porcelains of the 1790–1815 period bearing *only* a pattern number are likely to be of Pinxton manufacture.

Grainger, Worcester (Grainger Wood *c.* 1801–1812; Grainger Lee & Co. *c.* 1812–1839; G. Grainger & Co. *c.* 1839–1902), *c.* 1801–1902
Progressive numbers 1 to 2019, *c.* 1801–1839. *New* progressive numbers 1 to 2000 *with the addition of a small cross c.* 1839–1845. After *c.* 1845 fractional numbers were employed 2/123 etc. Later the prefix G was used.

Minton, c. 1797–present day
Progressive numbers to *c.* 1850, then *letter prefixes* employed. Early porcelains of the *c.* 1797–1805 period bear only a pattern number, prefixed 'N' or 'No.', such early numbers being in the 1–120 range. From about 1805 to 1816 the pattern numbers were painted below the Sèvres-like crossed 'S' (or 'L') mark.
These numbers progress from 15 to about 948. Messrs Mintons did not produce porcelain between the years 1816 and 1824. After 1824 *progressive* numbers normally occur, painted in a small (about $\frac{1}{8}$ inch in height) neat manner and such porcelains very rarely bear a factory mark. Minton patterns in the 1300–4200 range were issued in the 1830s, patterns 4200–7500 between 1840 and 1845. In November 1850 the letter prefix A was used and all subsequent Minton pattern numbers bear a letter prefix, including A, B, C, D, E, G, H, M, NP, O, P, PA, S and X.

Nantgarw, c. 1813–1814 and 1817–1822
Nantgarw porcelains do not normally bear a pattern number. When one occurs it is *progressive*, non-fractional and without prefix.

New Hall, c. 1781–1835
(Hard-paste porcelain during the 1781–1812 period)
Progressive pattern numbers were sometimes but not always prefixed 'N' or 'No.',
often painted in a rather free, hasty style, the numbers being some ¼-inch high. Here
is a typical example:

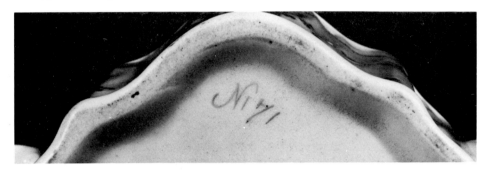

New Hall pattern numbers up to about 940 occur on pre-1812 hard-paste
porcelain. The series seems to have been re-started at 1040 for the fine, white, bone-
china body which was introduced *c.* 1812. Although much post-1812 New Hall
porcelain bears the printed mark of the words NEW HALL within a double circle, a
great number of pieces (especially with hand-painted patterns) were unmarked and
are not generally classified as New Hall. Porcelains of the 1812–35 period bearing a
pattern number (painted in bold style with numerals ¼-inch high) in the 1040–2200
range are possibly New Hall. It should be noted that the pattern number was
painted only on the larger New Hall teawares, not on cups and saucers. Several
other firms or potters produced New Hall-type simple floral designs. These (unnamed) porcelains also bear simple progressive numbers and really the often quoted
New Hall 'N' or 'No.' prefixed numbers are of little help unless you can check that
the number does in fact match the relevant New Hall design. In this respect David
Holgate's book *New Hall and its Imitators* is of the utmost assistance.

Pinxton, c. 1796–1813
Progressive pattern numbers not exceeding 600. Derby-type porcelains bearing *only*
a pattern number are probably Pinxton. Some pattern numbers were prefixed 'P'
but in most cases just the pattern number was applied. Typical Pinxton forms are
shown in my *Illustrated Encyclopaedia of British Pottery and Porcelain* but we must
remember that very many pieces do not bear a pattern number.

Ridgway (various partnerships), *c.* 1802–1855 +
Progressive numbers on dessert and dinner wares, normally painted in neat, rather
largish numerals about ¼-inch high *without* 'N' or 'No.' prefix. Early teawares have
progressive numbers followed before a thousand was reached by *fractional* numbers
expressed under '2/', i.e. 2/1, 2/2, etc. The interesting point here is that the numbers

climb above one thousand and proceed to 2/9999, continuing 5/1, 5/2, etc, so that a teaset bearing the pattern number 2/2351 cannot be Coalport, for example, for the Coalport pattern numbers stopped at 2/999 and then continued 3/1, 3/2, etc. Ridgway *ornamental* objects, vases, etc, bear numbers expressed in fractional form 4/1, 4/2, etc. For further information on Ridgway wares see my *Illustrated Guide to Ridgway Porcelains* (Barrie & Jenkins, 1972).

Rockingham or *Swinton Porcelains*, c. 1825–1842

Progressive numbers employed on useful wares to about number 1563; subsequently some few fractional numbers were used. The existing pattern books show numbers 2/17 to 2/78. Some extra patterns may have been issued but any pattern numbers above 2/200 do not relate to Rockingham porcelains. Yet hardly a London sale catalogue is issued without porcelains bearing pattern numbers such as 2/3800, 3/4023 and 4/278 being attributed to the Rockingham factory. Ornamental objects, vases and such objects do not bear pattern numbers. Many examples of Rockingham porcelain bear painted or gilt 'class' numbers preceded by the initials 'cl' or 'c'; these are not really pattern numbers but are a most useful guide to the identification of Rockingham wares.

Spode, c. 1743–1833

Progressive numbers were used on porcelains and earthenwares, normally without the prefix 'N' or 'No.' The numbers on early (c. 1796–1810) unmarked porcelains are usually painted in bold neat numerals. After c. 1810 the pattern number follows the written name 'Spode' unless one of the several printed marks occur on a piece, but early examples bear only the pattern number. Good details of Spode pattern numbers are given in Leonard Whiter's *Spode*. The sequence of Spode numbers was continued by the successors Messrs Copeland & Garrett (1833–47) and then by Copelands.

Swansea Porcelain, c. 1814–1822

Progressive pattern numbers, probably not exceeding 600. Most Swansea porcelain, in fact, does not show a pattern number. Swansea-*type* porcelains bearing higher numbers are of Coalport or other manufacture.

MAKER'S MARKS

The maker's marks to be found on so many examples of British ceramics can be of the greatest help to collectors, but they can also be most misleading. Indeed, if you were to set out to reproduce a valuable article the easiest part of the exercise is to fake the mark. However, most marks are above suspicion, particularly the nineteenth and present-century trademarks (but see p. 257).

Ceramic marks were applied in three basic ways:

(1) They were incised (cut into the body) or impressed into the unfired clay during

the first manufacturing process. It will be apparent that such marks cannot be added later by a faker although they can be employed by anyone setting out to make an outright fake. Indeed the standard impressed 'Wedgwood' name-mark has been employed with slight variations by other firms hoping to pass their own products as those of the famous firm, but here I am straying from our subject, porcelain, into the field of pottery.

(2) Marks can be applied *under the glaze* in a painted or a printed form. These were applied early in the manufacturing process before the piece was glazed, and again these are not often faked–except when there was a definite attempt to palm something off on the unsuspecting collector. Some Continental hard-paste reproductions of costly Worcester porcelain will for example bear the underglaze-blue square-mark of the original.

(3) Most marks, however, were added *over* the glaze as the decorating process was drawing to a close and most marks were printed to save time as hundreds or thousands of pieces would bear the same standard factory mark.

These three classes represent only the very basic methods. To the incised and impressed types we could add the seal-marks (impressed from a metal or fired clay seal) or the relief-moulded marks where the device stands up above the surface. All these marks which were added before the object was fired we could call 'clay marks'.

All these marks, however they were applied, could include one or more identifying points. The most helpful is, of course, the full name-mark, for example, 'R. W. Martin & Bros, London & Southall' but most marks incorporate initials only. Single initials such as 'B' or 'M' are not all that helpful as they fit many potters, but three or more initials together can normally be linked to a definite person or firm, especially when a town is added to the initials. Often one of the towns making up the Staffordshire Potteries was shown by its initial, so that the mark 'H & C' with 'B' underneath can correctly be related to Messrs Heath & Greatbatch of Burslem. The main Staffordshire Pottery towns were Burslem, Cobridge, Fenton, Hanley, Longton and Tunstall; luckily each has a different initial.

Some marks have only a trade-name or a device such as an anchor or crown. These are, of course, unhelpful to the novice but in most cases each mark can be identified and dated by reference to modern standard mark books such as my *Encyclopaedia of British Pottery and Porcelain Marks*, but do not expect one of the inexpensive handbooks to answer all your queries.

The following general guides will help in determining the period of many objects.

Marks incorporating the Royal Arms are of nineteenth- or twentieth-century date.

Marks incorporating the name of the pattern are subsequent to 1810 and often much later.

The word 'Limited' or the standard abbreviations denote a date after 1861.

The words 'Trade Mark' indicate a date subsequent to the Act of 1862.

The word 'Royal' in a firm's title or trade name indicates a late date.

The word 'England' denotes a date after 1891.

The words 'Made in England' evidence a twentieth-century date, normally one after 1910.

The words 'Bone China' or 'English Bone China' also indicate a twentieth-century date.

It is also best to disregard any date incorporated in a printed mark–these so often relate to the real, or claimed, date of the firm's establishment or of the period when the design was introduced.

However, many of the large firms employed semi-secret forms of dating their wares. Most pieces produced by Mintons from the 1840s, by Wedgwood from 1860, by the Royal Worcester Company from the 1860s and by the Royal Crown Derby Company from 1882, bear such devices, the keys to which are given in my large encyclopaedia of marks.

In some instances month and year numbers were impressed into the plates or dishes as they were made. Such potting marks usually take the form: J·01 or 1·01, for January 1901. Markings impressed into thin porcelain can be more easily seen if the piece is held against a strong light.

RETAILER'S MARKS

Some wares bear not only the maker's mark but also that of the ordering retailer or shipper, showing the district or country for which such pieces were made. A large quantity of porcelain from about 1810 onwards may bear only the name of the retailer, be it a large London firm such as Goodes or Mortlocks or a more humble retailer in a country town selling perhaps local view wares to trippers. No book can list all such retailers but the periods of the more important London firms are given in my encyclopaedia of marks.

VARIOUS MARKINGS

Many pieces you will come across bear several types of marks. Let us look at the reverse side of the Minton plate in Plate 107. First, you may just see at 'A' the rather indistinctly impressed name mark MINTONS with the plate-marker's personal tally mark, and at 'B' the quartered square device which is the year cypher for 1881. Next at 'C' you have the diamond shape design registration device (here applied upside down) which will indicate (by reference to the Table given on p. 269) the day, the month and the year that the shape, in this case the pierced border motif, was first registered. This system of marking was commenced in 1842 and continued until 1883, after which the registrations were numbered in sequence (see Table on p. 270). All these marks were applied before the plate was fired–they are the clay marks.

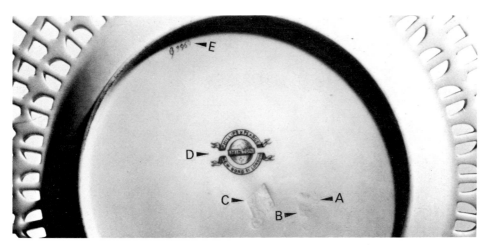

Plate 107 Reverse of a Minton porcelain plate showing the various factory marks as detailed in the text. *Author's Collection*

Turning to the overglaze markings applied after or during the decorating processes, we have at 'D' the standard printed Minton globe-mark surrounded by the London retailer's name and address. In this an old engraving of the mark has been used, for the firm added 'S' to their name-mark in 1872, nine years before this plate was potted. Lastly at 'E' we find the hand-painted pattern number, with the prefix 'G'. This series ran from 1868 to *c.* 1900 and this number was introduced in 1879.

From this one plate we can therefore tell which factory produced it, the year and also the fact that the pierced border was a registered design. We further can learn the name of the retailer who would have stocked this piece or service and sold it to the first user. The pattern number also enables us to check with factory records and in some cases to trace the artist and the original cost of the article. Indeed, the back of a plate can often be more interesting than the front!

Unluckily not all pieces are as completely marked as this and often we have no mark at all.

UNMARKED WARES

An unmarked piece is not necessarily early. It may be so, but more likely the piece was made by a person or firm without a well-known name. In general the products of a large established company will bear a clear trade-mark advertising the origin of the piece, for in part the buyer is expected to prefer goods produced by a nationally known firm, and the purchaser is often happy to pay extra for the guarantee of quality, but Bill Jones working in a Burslem backstreet pot-bank can hardly be expected to have wasted precious seconds marking his wares, if his name was unknown outside his home town.

Plate 108 A charmingly simple modern porcelain bowl bearing the personal seal-mark of David Leach, 1974. Diameter 5 ins. *Geoffrey Godden, Chinaman*

A CLOSING NOTE

Do remember to follow your own taste, but always to respect quality and try to buy the best you can reasonably afford. Such well chosen subjects will give you the greatest pleasure and reward.

One last little snippet of advice: I have, in the main, been discussing old or antique porcelains, but remember these were once new and that they were purchased by the housewife or loving husband for use and for pleasure. You too can follow this example and keep a weather-eye open for pleasing examples of contemporary porcelain. These need not be costly limited issues which can run into three figures. Some of the modern English studio potters now produce some delightful individual porcelains and my last illustration (Plate 108) demonstrates the appeal of a present-day production. These articles can be far superior to some of the avidly collected earlier factory-produced porcelains.

I hope you have enjoyed this book and that you have gained some help from my experiences. I trust too that you will enjoy some 'good hunting' and, having been bitten by the collecting bug, will 'live happily ever after'.

Have fun!

Appendix

TABLE OF REGISTRATION-MARKS 1842–1883

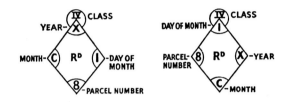

Above are the two patterns of Design Registration-Marks that were in current use between the years 1842 and 1883.

The left-hand diamond was used during the years 1842 to 1867. A change was made in 1868, when the right-hand diamond was adopted.

INDEX TO YEAR- AND MONTH-LETTERS

Showing the date of the first registration not necessarily the date of manufacture.

YEARS

1842–67		1868–83	
Year = Letter at Top		*Year = Letter at Right*	
A = 1845	N = 1864	A = 1871	L = 1882
B = 1858	O = 1862	C = 1870	P = 1877
C = 1844	P = 1851	D = 1878	S = 1875
D = 1852	Q = 1866	E = 1881	U = 1874
E = 1855	R = 1861	F = 1873	V = 1876
F = 1847	S = 1849	H = 1869	W = (1–6 March)
G = 1863	T = 1867	I = 1872	1878
H = 1843	U = 1848	J = 1880	X̄ = 1868
I = 1846	V = 1850	K = 1883	Y = 1879
J = 1854	W = 1865		
K = 1857	X = 1842		
L = 1856	Y = 1853		
M = 1859	Z = 1860		

MONTHS (BOTH PERIODS)

A = December	I = July
B = October	K = November (and December
C or O = January	1860)
D = September	M = June
E = May	R = August (and 1-19
G = February	September 1857)
H = April	W = March

REGISTRATION-NUMBERS

A simple progressive system of design-registration came into being in January 1884, to replace the old diamond-shaped device (see p. 269). Such official numbers are normally prefixed 'R^d N^o'. The period of registration can be gauged by reference to the following Table.

DESIGN-REGISTRATION NUMBERS FOUND ON WARES FROM 1884

(These numbers are normally prefixed by 'R^d N^o', and were registered between 1 January and 31 December of the year stated.)

Numbers	Year	Numbers	Year
1 − 19753	1884	291241 − 311657	1897
19754 − 40479	1885	311658 − 331706	1898
40480 − 64519	1886	331707 − 351201	1899
64520 − 90482	1887	351202 − 368153	1900
90483 − 116647	1888	368154 − 385087	1901
116648 − 141263	1889	385088 − 402912	1902
141273 − 163762	1890	402913 − 424016	1903
163767 − 185712	1891	424017 − 447547	1904
185713 − 205239	1892	447548 − 471485	1905
205240 − 224719	1893	471486 − 493486	1906
224720 − 246974	1894	493487 − 518414	1907
246975 − 268391	1895	518415 − 534962	1908
268392 − 291240	1896		

Bibliography

MARK BOOKS

Handbook of Pottery and Porcelain Marks by J. Cushion and W. B. Honey (Faber, London, 1956).

Pocket Book of British Ceramic Marks by J. P. Cushion (Faber, London, 1959, third revised edition, 1976).

Encyclopaedia of British Pottery and Porcelain Marks by G. A. Godden (Herbert Jenkins (Barrie & Jenkins), London, 1964).

Marks and Monograms... by W. Chaffers. British section of latest 15th edition revised by G. A. Godden (William Reeves, London, 1965).

Handbook of British Pottery and Porcelain Marks by G. A. Godden (Herbert Jenkins (Barrie & Jenkins), London, 1968).

GENERAL STANDARD REFERENCE BOOKS

The Ceramic Art of Great Britain by L. Jewitt (Virtue & Co., London, 1878, revised edition 1883). A revised and reillustrated edition covering only the period from 1800 onwards was published by Barrie & Jenkins Ltd, in 1972.

Analysed Specimens of English Porcelain by H. Eccles and B. Rackham (Victoria & Albert Museum, London, 1922).

English Pottery and Porcelain by W. B. Honey (A & C Black, London, 1933. 5th edition 1962).

Old English Porcelain by W. B. Honey (Faber, London, 1928; revised 1977).

English Porcelain and Bone China 1743–1850 by B & T Hughes (Lutterworth Press, London, 1955).

The Concise Encyclopaedia of English Pottery and Porcelain by R. G. Haggar and W. Mankowitz (A. Deutsch, London, 1957).

Victorian Pottery and Porcelain by G. B. Hughes (Country Life, London, 1959).

Victorian Porcelain by G. A. Godden (Herbert Jenkins, London, 1961).

English Porcelain Figures of the 18th Century by A. Lane (Faber, London, 1961).

British Porcelain 1745–1850, edited by R. J. Charleston (E. Benn, London, 1965).

English Ceramics by S. W. Fisher (Ward Lock, London, 1966).

An Illustrated Encyclopaedia of British Pottery and Porcelain by G. A. Godden (Herbert Jenkins (Barrie & Jenkins), London, 1966).

English Pottery and Porcelain by G. Wills (Guinness Signatures, London, 1968).

Investing in Pottery and Porcelain by H. Morley-Fletcher (Barrie & Rockliff, London, 1968).

British Pottery and Porcelain for Pleasure and Investment by H. Sandon (J. Gifford, London, 1969).

The Observer's Book of Pottery and Porcelain by M. & G. Payton (Frederick Warne & Co., London, 1973).

Fine Porcelain and Pottery by S. W. Fisher (Octopus Books, London, 1974).

An Illustrated Dictionary of Ceramics by G. Savage and H. Newman (Thames & Hudson, London, 1974).

British Porcelain, an Illustrated Guide by G. A. Godden (Barrie & Jenkins, London, 1974).

Pottery and Porcelain Tablewares by J. P. Cushion (Studio Vista, London, 1977).

English Ceramics, 1580–1830, edited by R. J. Charleston & D. Towner (Sotheby Parke Bernet, London, 1977).

SPECIALIST BOOKS ON INDIVIDUAL FACTORIES OR TYPES

BOW
British Museum Catalogue of the 1959 Bow Exhibition by Hugh Tait.

BLUE AND WHITE
English Blue and White Porcelain of the 18th Century by S. W. Fisher (B. T. Batsford, London, 1947).

English Blue and White Porcelain of the 18th Century by B. Watney (Faber, London, 1963, revised edition 1973).

BRISTOL
Champions Bristol Porcelain by F. Severne Mackenna (F. Lewis, Leigh-on-Sea, 1947).

CAUGHLEY
Caughley and Worcester Porcelains 1775–1800 by G. A. Godden (Herbert Jenkins, London, 1969).

Caughley Porcelains—A Bi-Centenary Exhibition. Exhibition catalogue by M. Messenger (Shrewsbury Art Gallery, 1972).

CHELSEA
Chelsea Porcelain. The Triangle and Raised Anchor Wares by F. Severne Mackenna (F. Lewis, Leigh-on-Sea, 1948).

Chelsea Porcelain. The Red Anchor Wares by F. Severne Mackenna (F. Lewis, Leigh-on-Sea, 1951).

Chelsea Porcelain. The Gold Anchor Period by F. Severne Mackenna (F. Lewis, Leigh-on-Sea, 1952).

COALPORT

Coalport and Coalbrookdale Porcelains by G. Godden (Herbert Jenkins, London, 1970).

DAVENPORT

Davenport Pottery and Porcelain 1794–1887 by T. A. Lockett (David & Charles, Newton Abbot, 1972).

DERBY

The Old Derby China Factory by J. Haslem (G. Bell & Sons, London, 1876).
Crown Derby Porcelain by F. B. Gilhespy (F. Lewis, Leigh-on-Sea, 1951).
Derby Porcelain by F. B. Gilhespy (Spring Books, London, 1961).
Derby Porcelain by F. A. Barrett and A. L. Thorpe (Faber, London, 1971).
Royal Crown Derby by J. Twitchett and B. Bailey (Barrie & Jenkins, London, 1976).

LIVERPOOL

English Blue and White Porcelain of the 18th Century by B. Watney (Faber, London, 1963, revised edition 1973).
The Illustrated Guide to Liverpool Herculaneum Pottery by A. Smith (Barrie & Jenkins, London, 1970).

LONGTON HALL

Longton Hall Porcelain by B. Watney (Faber, London, 1957).

LOWESTOFT

The Illustrated Guide to Lowestoft Porcelain by G. Godden (Herbert Jenkins, London, 1969).

MASON

The Masons of Lane Delph by R. G. Haggar (Lund Humphries, London, 1952).
The Illustrated Guide to Mason's Patent Ironstone China by G. Godden (Barrie & Jenkins, London, 1971).
See also 'Miles Mason' by R. G. Haggar in *Transactions of the English Ceramic Circle* (vol. 8, part 2, 1972).
Mason Porcelain and Ironstone 1796–1853 by R. G. Haggar and E. Adams (Faber, London, 1977).

MINTON

Victorian Porcelain by G. Godden (Herbert Jenkins, London, 1961).
Minton Porcelain of the First Period by G. Godden (Herbert Jenkins, London, 1968).

NANTGARW

The Pottery and Porcelain of Swansea and Nantgarw by E. M. Nance (Batsford, London, 1942).

Nantgarw Porcelain by W. D. John (Ceramic Book Co., Newport, Mon., 1948. Supplement 1956).

NEW HALL

New Hall Porcelain by G. E. Stringer (Art Trade Press, London, 1949).

New Hall and its Imitators by D. Holgate (Faber, London, 1971).

PARIAN

Victorian Porcelain by G. Godden (Herbert Jenkins, London, 1961).

The Illustrated Guide to Victorian Parian China by C. and D. Shinn (Barrie & Jenkins, London, 1971).

PINXTON

The Pinxton China Factory by C. L. Exley (Mr and Mrs Coke-Steel, Stutton-on-the-Hill, 1963).

PLYMOUTH

Cookworthy's Plymouth and Bristol Porcelain by F. S. Mackenna (F. Lewis, Leigh-on-Sea, 1947).

English Blue and White Porcelain... by B. Watney (Faber, London, 1963, revised edition 1973).

ROCKINGHAM

The Rockingham Pottery by A. A. Eaglestone and T. A. Lockett (Rotherham Library and Museum, Rotherham, 1964). Revised edition 1973, published by Messrs David & Charles, Newton Abbot).

Ornamental Rockingham Porcelains by D. G. Rice (Adam Publishing Co., London, 1965).

The Illustrated Guide to Rockingham Porcelain by D. G. Rice (Barrie & Jenkins, London, 1971).

The Rockingham Works by Alwyn & Angela Cox (Sheffield City Museum, 1974).

SPODE

Spode and his Successors by A. Hayden (Cassell & Co., London, 1924).

Spode: A history of the family, factory and wares from 1733 to 1833 by L. Whiter (Barrie & Jenkins, London, 1970).

SWANSEA

The Pottery and Porcelain of Swansea and Nantgarw by E. M. Nance (Batsford, London, 1942).

Swansea Porcelain by W. D. John (Ceramic Book Co., Newport, Mon., 1957).

WORCESTER

A Century of Potting in the City of Worcester by R. W. Binns (B. Quaritch, London, 1865, second edition 1877).

Worcester China, 1852–1897 by R. W. Binns (B. Quaritch, London, 1897).

Coloured Worcester Porcelain of the First Period by H. Rissik Marshall (Ceramic Book Co., Newport, Mon., 1954).

Worcester Porcelain by F. A. Barrett (Faber, London, 1963, revised edition 1966).

The Illustrated Guide to Worcester Porcelain by H. Sandon (Herbert Jenkins, London, 1969).

Royal Worcester Porcelain by H. Sandon (Barrie & Jenkins, London, 1973).

TRANSACTIONS

Apart from these standard reference books the *Transactions of the English Ceramic Circle* contain some highly interesting papers. These *Transactions* are published by Messrs W. & J. Mackay Ltd, Lordswood, Chatham, Kent.

The Newsletters and Journal of the Northern Ceramic Society are also most informative (Secretary, Diana Darlington, 5 Lynton Court, Lynton Lane, Alderley Edge, Cheshire). These and other societies organise interesting lectures and exhibitions and they should be supported.

TAPE-RECORDED TALKS

Apart from standard reference books, many of which are rather out of date, the collector now has available a series of tape-recorded talks specially prepared by Geoffrey Godden. Each cassette runs for approximately eighty minutes and is supported by an illustrated supplement where some seventy or more typical or key pieces are depicted (mainly in group poses). These numbered objects are discussed in the recorded talks, which contain a wealth of up-to-date information.

The initial series of cassettes feature Miles Mason, Chamberlain-Worcester, Caughley, Lowestoft and Dr Wall Worcester wares, but more subjects are due to be added to the range. Details are available from Geoffrey Godden, 17–19 Crescent Road, Worthing, Sussex.

SEMINARS

In recent years several organisations have arranged courses, study weekends or seminars, these can be most instructive and interesting as leading authorities are available to share their knowledge and to be questioned. Information on these events can be obtained from the following and other like courses may be advertised in collector's magazines

The Secretary, Morley College Ceramic Circle,
Morley College, 61 Westminster Bridge Road,
London S.E.1.

Re Keele University Course in Staffordshire contact
T. A. Locknett, 6 Tideswell Road, Hazel Grove,
Stockport, SK7 6JG.

The Secretary, The Antique Collectors' Club
Clopton, Woodbridge, Suffolk

Geoffrey Godden–Chinaman,
17–19 Crescent Road, Worthing, Sussex

COLLECTORS' MAGAZINES

The main magazines which may be expected to include articles of interest to collectors of English porcelains include:

Antique Collector, Chestergate House,
Vauxhall Bridge Road, London, S.W.1.

Antique Finder, Antique Finder Ltd,
Baron Publishing, 5 Church Street,
Woodbridge, Suffolk

Art and Antiques Weekly
Independent Magazines (Publishing) Ltd
181 Queen Victoria Street,
London EC4V 4DD

Collectors Guide, City Magazines Ltd,
1–3 Wine Office Court, Fleet Street,
London, EC4A 3AL

The Connoisseur, Chestergate House,
Vauxhall Bridge Road, London, S.W.1.

The Antique Dealer and Collectors Guide,
see *Collectors Guide*

Index

Italic figures indicate Plate Numbers